A SOCIOLOGY OF THE SOVIET UNION

A Sociology of
the Soviet Union

Gary Littlejohn

MACMILLAN PRESS
LONDON

First published 1984 by
THE MACMILLAN PRESS LTD
London and Basingstoke
Companies and representatives throughout the world

ISBN 0 333 29426 2 (hard cover)
ISBN 0 333 29427 0 (paper cover)

Typeset in Great Britain by
Illustrated Arts

Printed in Hong Kong

Contents

viii   *Contents*

Acknowledgements

My first thanks must go to Hillel Ticktin, who supervised the thesis on which this book is based. I should also like to thank Stephen Feuchtwang, Barry Hindess, Paul Hirst, Professor Marie Lavigne and Professor Pierre Lavigne, all of whom read parts of my thesis and whose comments improved it. None of them is responsible for the remaining deficiencies, or for the views expressed here.

G.L.

Introduction

This book aims to provide an overview of the Soviet Union, and to evaluate a fairly wide range of material with a view to making a theoretical contribution to the sociology of the Soviet Union. It is hoped to throw new light on the empirical evidence discussed, but it cannot claim to be a definitive analysis. The large number of lengthy works on quite specific aspects of Soviet history and social structure should make it clear that it is beyond the capacity of any one person to provide a definitive account of such a vast, complex and controversial society. Consequently, while covering quite a broad range of issues, I have tried to do so in a spirit of contributing to a continuing debate, rather than of settling those issues.

The topics examined were chosen to help analyse the extent and forms of class relations in the Soviet Union. Yet the factors influencing the class structure stem from the major institutional features of the Soviet Union: the economy; politics and the state; the welfare system and forms of consumption; and the occupational structure with its associated wage differentials and consequent effects on the distribution of income. Hence any discussion of the Soviet class structure has to take these features seriously. These features are of considerable interest in their own right, quite apart from their relevance to the class structure, and it is hoped the respective chapters can stand on their own to some extent for readers particularly interested in these topics. However, taken together these topics do enable one to address the terms in which the Soviet Union judges itself, and seeks to present itself to the rest of the world: whether class relations are being superseded, whether mass democracy is being promoted, and whether centralised economic planning is the basis of such developments.

These are questions with profound political and social implications. For those who have not yet made up their minds (and perhaps even for those who have but wish to review the evidence) the question of the differences and similarities between capitalist and socialist societies offers a way into thinking about a huge range of issues which can scarcely be avoided by any sentient adult. Such issues necessarily involve giving some account of Marxist theory, even if it is only to describe it as the ruling ideology in the Soviet Union. At the beginning of this book, however, classical Marxist theory is also seriously considered as a means of analysing the social structure itself. To explain why there is such an explicit concern with theory it is probably useful to indicate in broad terms the thrust of the argument.

The theoretical approach adopted to the analysis of the Soviet class structure is based on a critique of the classical Marxist approach to class, as well as of common sociological approaches to class, particularly the Weberian conception of class. These issues are the concern of Chapter 1, which outlines an alternative approach to class structure based on a conception of relations of production which differs from the classical Marxist approach, particularly in avoiding any reliance on the labour theory of value for defining relations of production and hence for demarcating class boundaries. This approach is introduced in the first chapter because it largely defines the choice of problems dealt with in the rest of the book.

Chapter 2 provides an outline of developments in Soviet agriculture from the Revolution to the end of the 1920s. By criticising common conceptions of such developments, it argues that the strategy of socialist transformation adopted with the policy of forced collectivisation from late 1929 was economically unnecessary and politically disastrous. The purpose of this chapter is to throw the contemporary class structure of the Soviet Union into historical relief, by indicating the historical context out of which many contemporary features of the Soviet Union developed. It is hoped that this will indicate that many features of the contemporary social structure are historically specific, rather than being necessary features of a state socialist society.

The 1920s were a period when the future development of the Soviet Union was still an open question, and when new attempts to construct a socialist society in an underdeveloped economy were being made. These attempts took place in a context of extremely important debates about economic development, industrialisation, rural class structure, democracy, culture, the relation between party and state, and international relations. Even today, many debates about the nature of the Soviet Union, whether conducted inside or outside the country, revolve around implicit or explicit analyses of the 1920s. Furthermore, many of the contemporary features of Soviet society were constructed at that time or developed soon afterwards in response to problems which occurred in the 1920s. Finally, it is widely acknowledged that the experience and debates of this period continue to be relevant for developing societies. Rather than concentrating on the political history of the time, or on the economic debates themselves, which in their content and sophistication were not rivalled in the West until at least the 1960s, a chronological account of the 1920s is given. There is a particular emphasis on agriculture, where the main problems of the period were encountered. This account of the historical context in which the main issues arose should make it easier to understand the issues themselves.

Following from this, the analysis of relations of production in the 1960s and 1970s is begun in Chapter 3, where the relations between different kinds of economic agents, particularly collective economic agents (economic units) are examined, using the approach developed in Chapter 1 to analyse the relations of production as relations between economic agents which affect their relative economic capacities. It is argued that, because such capacities are always subject to change through processes of struggle and negotiation, an important but hitherto rather neglected aspect of the relations of production concerns the policies of economic agents. Consequently, the manner in which agents at various levels in the economy calculate both their own internal state and the course of action which they adopt with respect to other agents is subjected to detailed scrutiny in this chapter.

Chapter 4 analyses the legal and political conditions of the relations of production, since in the Soviet Union such economic relations are operative primarily between state agencies, or collective agencies whose relations to the state agencies are legally and politically regulated by the state. Consequently, the issue of the 'withering away of the state' with the decline of private property is considered, as well as various common Western conceptions of Soviet politics. Related to this, the analysis of politics in terms of a series of 'arenas of struggle' is proposed, and in the light of this approach the capacities of the main central party and state agencies to regulate the economy (and hence to determine the relations of production by implementing effective economic plans) is reviewed. The conclusion from this review is that there are serious limits on the capacity of such central party and state agents to co-ordinate the division of labour, so that theories of an all-powerful totalitarian party or elite dominating Soviet politics and the economy are misguided. Nevertheless, it is argued that there is sufficient central control of the state agencies for one to be able to say that various state agencies do not pursue completely autonomous objectives. In other words, political relations between state agencies are not such as to preclude socialist planning of the overall economy.

Chapter 5 examines welfare and social policy as a means of assessing the importance of non-wage forms of income, and concludes that the overall effect of such forms of public expenditure is probably, as intended, to equalise incomes. This chapter also provides a historical account of the development of various aspects of the Soviet welfare state and analyses its contemporary difficulties and successes, thereby providing further insight into the workings of Soviet politics.

The issue of income equalisation is taken up again in Chapter 6, where the occupational structure and wage differentials are examined, prior to an overall assessment of the distribution of income, which concludes that a policy of income equalisation has been pursued fairly successfully over the past twenty-five years or so. Such a policy may now be running into difficulties of various kinds, but in so far as it has been successfully pursued it has meant that the connection between the distribution of income and the access of agents to the means of production has been partially undermined. Hence class relations have been seriously weakened in the Soviet Union, and it is concluded that they are non-existent within the state sector of the economy. However, this does not mean that there is no class structure in the Soviet Union, since collective farm members are still in a different class position from state employees. There may also be capitalist relations in the so-called 'parallel economy', but their extent must be severely limited by the official prohibitions on such activities, which means that, if resources are diverted from official purposes, this is largely done on an individual 'self-employed' basis. It is also argued that the 'intelligentsia' cannot be considered as a single stratum separated from the state-employed 'working class' or the collective farm members. Consequently, the official theory of the Soviet class structure must be considered to be seriously deficient.

The kind of approach just outlined differs from many sociological works on the Soviet Union. It deals with issues frequently considered the rightful domain of 'other' social sciences. This trend in sociology towards what seems like 'intellectual imperialism' has often caused resentment in other social science departments, but it is difficult to avoid if one is trying to deal with a society as a whole. A frequent response to this charge of imperialism is to concentrate on particular aspects of the social structure, where useful empirical work can be done. In the case of the Soviet Union, however, a great deal of such work has already been done, and at times one has to take stock, as this book tries to do. Yet this attempt at an overview avoids a comparative analysis of 'Soviet-type and Western' societies as a means of reaching its conclusions. It also tries to avoid providing merely an institutional description, even though this is necessary at times as a prelude to analysis. Both approaches, the 'comparative method' or institutional description, run the risk of underestimating the role of theory in reaching conclusions. Rather than expecting the conclusions to simply emerge from the evidence, as if the 'facts speak for themselves', the search for evidence has been informed by existing theory and has been used to criticise and develop the existing body of theory on the Soviet Union. It is for this reason that, for example, quite general problems in the analysis of class structure are raised in Chapter 1, or quite common conceptions of Soviet politics are criticised in Chapter 4. The re-evaluation of existing approaches seems to be both possible and necessary at

1
The Class Structure: Stratification or Relations of Production?

Introduction

The purpose of this chapter is to indicate what kind of approach is being used to analyse the Soviet Union in this book. This is necessary because of the continuing prevalence in sociology of analyses of class structures which fail to define sufficiently clearly the basis of the categorisation of classes. In other words, it will be argued that the prevailing modes of analysis of what is often called 'social inequality' or 'social stratification' fail to provide sufficiently clear theoretical grounds for distinguishing different classes, or for analysing class relations.

This is not to say that there is ready to hand a clear mode of analysis which is easy to use and which suffers from no problems, but rather that the prevailing approaches scarcely even attempt to analyse the determinants of class relations. The only exception is provided by analyses in the Marxist tradition, which at least attempt to theorise the determinants of class relations, using some conception of 'relations of production'. However, while such approaches have the merit of at least posing the problem of the determinants of class relations, it is not clear how far they have satisfactorily resolved the issues which they raise.

To illustrate the problems with prevailing sociological analyses of stratification in relation to the Soviet Union, it is worth briefly looking at the debate on 'industrial society'. During the 1960s it became fashionable in sociology to argue that capitalist and socialist societies were converging towards a common type of 'industrial society' whose main institutional features were determined by the 'logic of industrialism'. In other words, it was argued that certain 'core features' providing the conditions of industrial production would induce a reorganisation of the rest of the society so that such societies would become increasingly similar. This kind of economic determinism became very influential with the easing of East–West international tension at that time, and produced an 'industry' of its own in terms of publications.

A well-known article by Goldthorpe criticising such approaches appeared in the mid-1960s. This article, 'Social Stratification in Industrial Society', argues that the kind of stratification found in the Soviet Union is quite distinct from that in Western industrial societies.[1] Western societies are characterised by market stratification, which is, so to speak, an unconscious or unintended effect of the workings of the market. The Soviet Union is characterised by political stratification, which is in effect a deliberate outcome of the centralised control of society by the party and/or state. While these different kinds of stratification might produce similar results in terms of their outward appearance, the causes of these similarities are fundamentally different in the two kinds of industrial society. In Goldthorpe's terms, while such patterns of stratification may be 'phenotypically' similar, stratification in the Soviet Union is 'genotypically' distinct from that in the West. This article was a welcome break from what was at the time conventional wisdom in sociology, but there are problems with Goldthorpe's analysis.[2] There is no real attempt by Goldthorpe to specify the kinds of social relations between the strata which are produced by these different stratifying mechanisms, the market and the political structure. Consequently there is no real basis for empirical analysis based on conclusions drawn from this distinction, since the nature of the different kinds of strata is opaque. To put it another way, the different ways in which the market and the political structure generate strata are not analysed in a way that shows why the resulting strata really are different, even though they might appear similar. This causes real problems for any research into this issue, because attempts to develop ways to measure the underlying differences are frustrated. Any attempt to measure these differences must use indices which are related to the mechanisms or processes producing the stratification, and to the effects of these mechanisms or processes on the strata themselves.

Stratification: Theory and Evidence

This difficulty is shared by many approaches to stratification which, like that of Goldthorpe, are influenced by the work of Max Weber. The general problem of such approaches is that the absence of a clear theorisation of the social relations operative between different strata has meant that the stratification system has usually been treated as qualitatively homogeneous (strata or classes having more or less of some quality, attribute or possession). Where the stratification hierarchy has not been treated as qualitatively homogeneous, as in certain 'multidimensional' approaches, the strata or classes have been conceived as defined by the concatenation of various dimensions, like status and power, which are themselves poorly theorised, and whose interaction in structuring the strata is also unclear. Thus the avoidance of treating stratification as entailing a homogeneous hierarchy is achieved after a fashion, but the benefits are dubious. However, this has still resulted in theoretically arbitrary dividing-lines being drawn between the strata (or class positions), leading to an approach which fails to evaluate the theoretical basis on which evidence of different kinds is collected.

Evidence of social phenomena does not simply drop like ripe fruit. The process of data collection is also a process of construction, since evidence has to be classified and sorted even as it is collected, and this process inevitably implies using concepts. Sociologists quite often fail to recognise the theoretical nature of even the most mundane empirical work, and hence they treat the process of gathering evidence as in some sense separate from (and usually prior to) the process of theory construction. Such a separation is literally impossible, but if the criteria for classifying or sorting evidence are not clear, one runs the risk of implicitly or explicitly ignoring the theoretical nature of 'gathering' evidence. This will probably lead to adverse effects in terms of the analysis of that evidence.

Where one is using already existing sources, as is usually the case in the Soviet Union, the evidence must be used on the basis of both a theoretical evaluation of its conceptual basis, and where necessary what might be termed a technical critique of the process by which the empirical results were compiled. Clearly, the more details recorded about the process of collecting, sorting and performing the original calculations on the material, the better, since they are then more amenable to reworking in terms of the critique. This means that even where a decision is made to use certain indices of stratification or the class structure, their pertinence to the analysis being conducted will vary. The relative merits of the various sources is thus a worthy matter for discussion in each case. A technically competent piece of empirical work may well be irrelevant to the concerns of the analysis, but often the researcher is in a position of being able to use empirical material compiled by others whose theoretical concerns were different from those of the researcher. The data may nevertheless be in a form that renders them open to reworking, i.e. to recalculation which transforms them into indices, albeit imperfect ones, of the theoretically specified mechanisms in which the researcher is interested.[3]

Weberian Stratification

The danger with stratification theories influenced by Weber is that this critical appraisal of evidence will be neglected. This is because such theories themselves face serious difficulties in specifying what are the mechanisms which generate strata. The best way to show this is to examine the work of Max Weber himself. Yet one cannot do this very easily without examining the intellectual origins of his work, since it is very influenced by classical political economy, and contains a response to Marx's critique of the concept of class used by political economy. So it is here that one must begin.

The concept of class was being used by the Physiocrats, if not by earlier economists, and was related to their theory of the distribution of income. The concept was based on the classification of the population of, say, eighteenth-century France, into distinct groups, each with their own source of income. What made the groups distinct in such analyses was their possession of an asset which gave them that income or revenue. Usually, there were three such assets in classical political economy – land, labour and capital – with entrepreneurial or managerial skill sometimes forming a fourth asset. The basis on which these 'factors of production' constituted assets for the classes which owned them was not posed as a problem by these economists (including those whom Marx called 'vulgar'). That is, the social conditions, which both made these 'factors of production' generate revenues and enabled the factors (and hence their revenues) to be appropriated by certain categories of economic agents called classes, were not considered problematic. Consequently, as we shall see, there was no theoretical basis for saying there should only be three classes, and not more: as has just been indicated, sometimes a fourth factor (or asset) was admitted, which implied a distinction between profit (entrepreneurial skill) and interest (capital) as forms of revenue. The analysis of the way in which these factors generated revenue went little further than an acknowledgement that such revenues were generated in production and/or exchange. The theory was more concerned with the amount of income distributed to each class and with features affecting the flow of revenue than with the analysis of the determinants of such revenues.

This concern with what Marx called 'relations of distribution' was the main target of Marx's critique of such theories of class. It is precisely the kind of problem generated by the 'revenues' approach to class which Marx is criticising in his famous unfinished chapter on class at the end of *Capital*.[4] The chapter on classes comes in a section entitled 'Revenues and their Sources', and follows a chapter on 'Distribution Relations and Production Relations', in which he says:

> Let us moreover consider the so-called distribution relations themselves. The wage presupposes wage-labour, and profit – capital. These definite forms of distribution thus presuppose definite social characteristics of production conditions, and definite social relations of production agents. The specific distribution relations are thus merely the expression of the specific historical production relations.[5]

After demonstrating this with respect to profit (of enterprise), interest, and capitalist ground rent, Marx continues:

> The so-called distribution relations, then, correspond to and
> arise from historically determined specific social forms of the
> process of production and the mutual relations entered into
> by men [*sic*] in the reproduction process of human life. The
> historical character of these distribution relations is the
> historical character of the production relations, of which
> they express merely one aspect. Capitalist distribution
> differs from those forms of distribution which arise from
> other modes of production, and every form of distribution
> disappears with the specific form of production from which it
> is derived and to which it corresponds.[6]

Thus, when in the chapter on classes Marx criticises the conception of classes as constituted by the identity of revenues and
sources of revenue, it is already clear to the reader that he considers that the sources of revenue are determined by the relations of production, which are social conditions (and consequently subject to historical change). It is also implicit that
the analysis of revenues (for example, of their amount and the
forms of their distribution) should not be completely identified
with the analysis of the sources of revenue, i.e. with the analysis
of the social conditions which constitute them as revenues.
However, distribution relations are one aspect of production
relations, so the analysis of the forms of distribution of income is
a part of the analysis of production relations, and hence of the
class structure.

To reiterate, the 'revenues' approach, which treats class relations solely in terms of relations of distribution, without analysing the social conditions of their existence, forms the object of
the critique developed by Marx in the unfinished chapter on
class. If one has no theoretical basis for saying that these groups
(and not others) possess these assets (and not others) as their
source of income, and that the possession of these assets is what
constitutes these groups as classes, then there is no defence
against adding other groups to the class structure. A class then
becomes any group constituted by the possession of a socially
distinct source of income. In criticising this position which
treats revenue as determining class, Marx says:

However, from this standpoint, physicians and officials for example would also constitute two classes, for they belong to two distinct social groups, the members of each of these groups receiving their revenue from one and the same source. The same would also be true of the infinite fragment-ation of interest and rank into which the division of social labour splits labourers as well as capitalists and landlords.[7]

In other words, although classical political economy divided society up into three great classes (the 'holy trinity' of land-owners, labourers and capitalists, whose sources of revenue – land, labour and capital – are as naturally homogeneous as beetroot, music and lawyers' fees), it did so on a basis which allowed for the elaboration of 'an infinite fragmentation of interest and rank' since it lacked an adequate analysis of the division of labour. It thus opened the way for the analysis of the class structure in terms of an inadequately theorised concept of stratification, i.e. in terms of a geological metaphor of strata which did not distinguish strata in terms of some theory of the social relations operative between the members of the different strata. This latter approach requires a principle of stratifica-tion, i.e. a quantitative measure which enables one stratum to be placed higher or lower than another on what is implicitly a qualitatively homogeneous scale. Initially this principle of stratification was the amount of income.

As Marx's analysis indicates (contrary to those who treat the unfinished chapter on classes simply as evidence of the diffi-culties of Marx's own position), the tendency to add to the number of classes, and to analyse them simply in terms of the distribution of income, these tendencies result from an in-adequate theorisation of the division of labour. An adequate analysis of the division of labour would enable one to sustain a defensible categorisation of economic agents into classes. This categorisation would be defensible on the grounds of the social relations which the theory stated were in operation between the different economic agents.

It is now much easier to understand the work of Max Weber, which provides an illuminating and influential example of the sociological elaboration of the 'revenues' approach to class. Thus the continuing, if unacknowledged, influence of classical political economy on the sociological analysis of class derives from Weber. He defines a class as any group of persons occupying the same class position (so the most pertinent kind of economic agent is the human individual). The concept of class position for Weber refers to:

> the typical probability that a given state of (a) provision of goods (b) external conditions of life and (c) subjective satisfaction or frustration will be possessed by an individual or a group. These probabilities define class position in so far as they are dependent on the kind and extent of control or lack of it which the individual has over goods and services and existing possibilities of their exploitation for the attainment of income and receipts within a given economic order.[8]

A little later Weber writes:

> The concepts class and class position as such only designate the fact of identity or similarity in the typical situation in which a given individual and many others find their interests defined. In principle control over different combinations of consumer's goods, means of production, investments, and capital funds constitute class positions which are different for each variation and combination.[9]

Ignoring the subjective aspect (satisfaction or frustration) of this definition of class, which is related to his conception of economic action, it is clear from the definition of class in terms of control of goods and services and their exploitation for incomes and receipts that Weber is using a 'revenues' conception of class. The result is that class positions are different for each variation and combination of assets, thus producing an 'infinite fragmentation of interest and rank', or, in other words, a highly differentiated stratification hierarchy in terms of class position. Precisely because there is no theorisation of what constitutes an asset, or possession of an asset, there is no clear basis for demarcating class positions from one another. Consequently any lines drawn between the strata are necessarily arbitrary.

A skill can be an asset, and a high level of skill constitutes for

Weber a 'monopolistic asset' commanding a monopolistic position, which enables him to treat the working class as a series of different class positions because of its 'qualitative differentiation', i.e. the variety of skills within it. This basic definition of class position (in terms of 'chance in the market' as determined by the acquisition of assets) is later added to by Weber: as well as 'acquisition' class, Weber also introduces the concepts of 'property' class and 'social' class. A property class is one where the class position of its members is primarily determined by the differentiation of property holdings. This produces two difficulties for Weber's theory. First, it indirectly subverts the distinction between 'class' and 'status group', the latter being defined in terms of 'social honour'. For example, slaves change from being a negatively privileged status group to a negatively privileged property class. This is inconsistent with the original definition of class which refers to actors in the market. Slaves are not actors in the market. Second, it creates problems as to the definition of an acquisition class. Weber's concept of property is not theoretically elaborated – it is simply an enumeration of such things as human beings, land, mining property, fixed equipment, ships or money. Consequently it is difficult to distinguish it from the assets which determine the chance in the market of an acquisition class. For example, ship-owners appear as both a property and an acquisition class, and many of those listed as members of acquisition classes might under the above listing of property be considered as members of property classes – namely, industrial and agricultural entrepreneurs, bankers and financiers. The concept of a 'social' class also has its problems: it is actually a *plurality* of class positions between which an interchange of individuals on a personal basis or in the course of generations is readily possible or typically observable. In other words, a 'social' class refers to a unity of various different class positions on the basis of what would nowadays be conventionally termed 'social interaction' or else on the basis of 'social mobility'. An example of a 'social' class is the working class as a whole. This is ironic in view of Weber's criticism of Marx:

> The unfinished concluding section of Karl Marx's *Kapital* was evidently intended to deal with the problem of class

unity of the proletariat, which he held existed in spite of the high degree of qualitative differentiation.[10]

It should be clear that this is a misunderstanding by Weber, but Weber's use of the concepts of 'property' class and 'social' class clearly represents an attempt to have one's cake and eat it. Weber is able (at considerable theoretical cost) both to maintain a highly differentiated view of the class structure, and to refer to what to him plausibly appear as important lines of demarcation within the stratification hierarchy.

The other interesting aspect of Weber's theory is, of course, the distinction which he makes between class stratification and stratification in terms of other phenomena which affect 'the distribution of power' – namely, 'status groups' and 'parties'. This is the major development which sociology has added to the class analysis of classical political economy – the supposed generalisation of stratification to other non-economic aspects of social relations. In the case of Weber this is related to his attempt to develop the microeconomic theory of transactions in the market into a general theory of social action. Each of these two other aspects of the distribution of power requires a principle of stratification analogous to the amount of income in the class hierarchy. In other words, they each require a quality or attribute or dimension (call it what you will) which the strata possess or do not possess to some degree. The theoretical basis for the two stratification principles introduced by Weber is even more opaque than that for level of income. The two principles are *prestige* and *political power*, and the latter is implicitly distinguished from the more generalised conception of power to which all three aspects of stratification are thought to refer. At least the level of income is measurable by a socially determinate means in a market economy: namely, money. The concepts of prestige and political power used by both Weber and the many later studies using a 'three-dimensional' (and sometimes 'multidimensional') approach to stratification require subjective judgement, either by the researcher, a panel of judges, or those being investigated, as to the distribution of prestige and political power. This produces the most banal kinds of research, such as correlations of the degree of 'status consistency' between the rankings on each dimension or international comparisons of prestige hierarchy rankings. It is not the process of ranking according to some quantitative index that is the problem with such research, or the use of the word 'stratification' (which is also used by some Marxists, usually in the phrase 'class stratification'), but the failure of such approaches to theorise adequately the determinants of the stratification with which they are concerned.[11]

Marx's Theory of Classes under Capitalism

Since Marx's critique of classical political economy raised the problem (not yet resolved in conventional sociological theory) of the determinants of the class structure, it is appropriate to examine his own position. As is clear from his critique, the determinants of class are to be found for Marx in the analysis of the relations of production, which, in showing the relations between various economic agents, amounts to an analysis of the division of labour. Because most of *Capital* is concerned with capitalist relations of production, Marxists frequently tend to argue that the whole of *Capital* is about class analysis, but this is of little help in deciding which are the most salient features of the relations of production for class analysis. Fortunately Marx gives some indication in the critique discussed above which appears at the end of volume 3: the reproduction schemas in volume 2,[12] which indicate how the capitalist mode of production as a whole reproduces itself, are of considerable importance, since in reproducing itself capitalism reproduces its class structure. To situate the discussion of the reproduction schemas, one must first discuss the labour theory of value and the reproduction of the individual capitalist enterprise (which appear in volume 1[13] and already constitute a partial analysis of capitalist relations of production).

While there is some dispute among Marxists about whether the 'law of value' only applies to the production of commodities, even those who limit it to commodity production usually see it as related to a more general law of the distribution of labour-time among different production processes.[14] If the latter, more general law is also referred to as 'the law of value', then the law of value expresses the proportion of the total labour-time available to a society (within a given time period, say a year) which is devoted to a particular production process. Each of the products of that production process thus embodies a value which is a fraction of the proportional labour-time devoted to that production process. In other words, if one thousand products are produced in a year, then each product embodies one-thousandth of the value of that production process. If two thousand products are produced, then the value of each product is halved. Thus the value of each product is inversely proportional to the productivity of the production process associated with it. The value of a product thus refers to the amount of labour-time (as a proportion of the total socially available labour-time) which is necessary to produce it: the value of a product is the embodiment of the socially necessary labour-time required to produce it, and the socially necessary amount of labour-time depends on the productivity of the particular production process and its economic relation to other production processes. In the case of commodity production, according to Marx, where the fact that commodities are exchanged has an effect on the social distribution of labour-time between different production processes, the absolute amount of labour-time embodied in a product is not measured. Only the *relative* amount of labour-time is measured, and this occurs in the process of commodity exchange where the relative amount of labour-time is expressed by the ratios in which the commodities exchange for each other. If one pound of sugar regularly exchanges for ten pounds of potatoes, then for Marx this is because these physical quantities of the products each take the same amount of socially necessary labour-time to produce. Whether that labour-time is one hour or five days cannot be directly measured by this exchange ratio of one to ten, which only indicates the relative value of the products. This 'exchange value', as Marx calls it, forms the basis for the price of commodities, once money becomes an integral part of commodity exchange. According to Marx, this occurs on the basis of one commodity becoming a socially acceptable measure in terms of which all the other exchange ratios are established.

Commodity exchange, then, for Marx, establishes a series of social relations between economic agents (including monetary relations) which allow the distribution of labour-time among different production processes to develop considerably, involving profound changes in the division of labour. In cases where this leads to the development of capitalist production, which depends crucially on commodity exchange (and particularly on the social appearance of labour-power as a commodity), the economic reproduction of each capitalist enterprise (with its associated production processes) depends on commodity exchanges. Marx thus begins analysing capitalist relations of production by the analysis of the reproduction of the capitalist enterprise in terms of the value embodied in each of its elements and the value created by that enterprise. Schematically, these elements are designated in the following diagram:

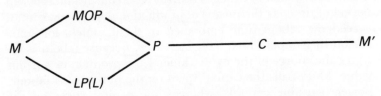

As is well known, in this schema M represents a sum of money sufficiently large (with the right social conditions) to be used as capital, i.e. to be used to purchase means of production, MOP, and labour-power, LP, which are necessary for capitalist production. Labour-power is the capacity to labour (a capacity entailing both physical and intellectual capacities), and it is this capacity or ability which is purchased by the capitalist. However, as with any production process, capitalist production requires the combination of labour, L, the activity of work, with the means of production. It is the amount of time spent in labour, the socially necessary labour-time, which determines the new value of the product of each production process. However, the total value of the product also includes the value of the means of production (which are themselves products embodying labour-time) transferred to the product over a period of time. The product, P, is treated as a commodity, C, and is sold for money, M', the superscript indicating that this is usually more than the original sum of money.

In other words, Marx is arguing that commodity relations, conceptualised in terms of the theory of value, establish certain relations between the elements of the capitalist production process which enable it to reproduce itself economically. The value of the product, a commodity, is determined by the value transferred to it by the means of production and by the value of the labour-time spent on producing it. For the value of the product to be greater than the outlay spent on producing it, Marx argues that the value of the labour expended on it must be higher than the value of the labour-power which was bought by the capitalist for the period of the production process. This is possible precisely because labour-power (a capacity) is not the same as labour (an activity), and the very conceptualisation of value (as a proportion of the total socially available labour-time) means that only labour can create value. The value of the means of production which is transferred to the products over a period of time, as the means of production depreciate, cannot exceed the labour-time embodied in them, unless for some reason their replacement cost increases. Because labour is for Marx the source of the extra value of the product, or surplus value, Marx calls the capital spent on the purchase of labour-power 'variable capital', whereas the capital spent on the purchase of the means of production is called 'constant capital'. The variable capital varies in amount between the beginning and end of the production process, because it is the source of the surplus value which appears as profit when the commodity is sold.

To sum up Marx's analysis of the reproduction of the individual capitalist enterprise, then, it can be said that it presupposes a certain social distribution of the means of production such that certain economic agents, capitalists, possess them, while others, agents, wage-labourers, do not, and must therefore sell their labour-power to reproduce themselves economically. Starting from this differential access to the means of production, the analysis indicates how a process of production of commodities by means of commodities can reproduce that social distribution of the means of production, with capitalists able to purchase them and wage-labourers unable to purchase them. It thus provides a partial analysis of how the class structure is reproduced.

As Marx recognises in volume 2, an analysis of how capitalist enterprises reproduce themselves cannot be a full account of how a capitalist economy reproduces itself. An analysis of the distribution of labour-time (value analysis) is necessarily partial if it is not related to an analysis of the physical distribution of the product: an analysis in terms of 'use-value', as Marx calls it. The concept of 'use-value' refers to the physical properties of the product (as understood by science at a particular time) and to the demand or 'need' for the product: if a product is not wanted, it has no use-value, so it is a waste of labour-time to produce it, and hence has no value either, according to Marx. The main aspect of the use-value of products with which Marx is concerned in the reproduction schemas of volume 2 is whether the products are means of production or means of consumption. As is already evident from the analysis in volume 1, the class relations between different categories of economic agent are concerned with their relation to the means of production (crudely, possession or non-possession of the means of production), so an analysis of the distribution of the product which is conducted in terms of a distinction between means of production and means of consumption is likely to elucidate the process of the social distribution of the means of production, and consequently aid the analysis of the class structure.

Since Marx is dealing with a wholly capitalist economy, all production processes are capitalist and hence reproduce themselves by commodity exchange. In this sense, they are economically independent of one another in that the continuing economic activity of each enterprise depends on the success of its commodity operations. A capitalist enterprise producing means of consumption will purchase its means of production from one or more capitalist enterprises producing means of production. A capitalist enterprise producing means of production will be staffed by personnel who purchase their means of consumption from a variety of capitalist enterprises. Marx thus sees the interdependence of the production of means of production (Department I) and production of means of consumption (Department II) as an important aspect of the division of labour. The reproduction schemas of volume 2 of *Capital* are concerned with how the different classes of economic agents (capitalists and wage-labourers) in the two Departments derive their revenues from their differential access to the means of production. Capitalist and wage-labourers in Department I buy their means of consumption from Department II, as do capitalists and wage-workers in Department II. However, only capitalists buy the means of production from Department I, and this is true whether they themselves are Department I or Department II capitalists. In other words, only other capitalist enterprises are customers for Department I products, whereas both wage-labourers and capitalists are customers for Department II products. Indeed, it is the social character of the demand for the product, rather than its physical properties, which determines whether it counts as a Department I or Department II product. Coal or electricity, for example, can be both means of production and means of consumption.

Since each capitalist enterprise is attempting to make a profit, and, if successful, is in Marx's view reproducing itself according to the value diagram reproduced earlier, what the reproduction schemas must do is indicate how this is possible for a whole economy composed of capitalist enterprises. This means that the amount of labour-time devoted to producing Department I products must be such as to satisfy, broadly speaking, the requirements of Department II for means of production (consisting mainly of raw materials, ancillary materials and instruments of production). Similarly, Department II must be able, broadly, to satisfy the demand for its products from capitalists and wage-labourers in both Departments. In explaining the reproduction of the capitalist economy, then, the reproduction schemas simultaneously explain several things:

(a) the proportional distribution of labour-time between different production processes, which must enable individual enterprises to make a profit;

(b) the physical distribution of the product, so that the economy is physically capable of continuing with production;

(c) the social distribution of the means of production, which is effected through the physical distribution of the product by means of commodity exchange, at the same time as the means of consumption is distributed.

The social distribution of the means of production, however, is the main determinant in this process. It determines the form of the production process (the conditions under which labour is combined with the means of production), and consequently which agent disposes of the product. Hence it determines the kind of revenue (profit, wages) available to each class of economic agent and the relative amounts of these revenues. The social distribution of the means of production thus determines the social distribution of the means of consumption. In other words, the reproduction schemas, in explaining the relations of production, also explain the relations of distribution and the basic class structure of a capitalist economy. This is what might be called the 'hidden secret' of the reproduction schemas. As already mentioned, Marx refers to these schemas in volume 3 when mounting his critique of the view of class maintained by classical political economy, so it is only 'hidden' from those sociologists who tend not to read the apparently technical economic parts of Marx's work.

Problems with Marx's Analysis

Of course, the reproduction schemas are of considerable potential interest to economists from two points of view:

1. In the history of economic thought, they constitute a link between Quesnay's *Tableau Economique* and the development of both input–output analysis and the Soviet use of material balances.
2. The reproduction schemas, in indicating the complex conditions to be fulfilled, according to Marx, for the reproduction of the capitalist economy, also indicate that the potential 'problem areas' are numerous, and are thus also the starting-point of Marx's theory of capitalist crises. However, the reproduction schemas will not be appraised from those standpoints here. What is of concern here are the possible problems with this analysis, and the extent to which it can be used as a basis for class analysis.

It is evident that the labour theory of value is an important element in this analysis. In this sense, Lenin's well-known summary[15] of the Marxist position on classes is quite correct:

Classes are large groups of people differing from each other by the place they occupy in a historically determined system of social production, by their relation (in most cases fixed and formulated in law) to the means of production, by their role in the social organisation of labour, and, consequently, by the dimensions of the share of social wealth of which they dispose and the mode of acquiring it. Classes are groups of people one of which can appropriate the labour of another owing to the different places they occupy in a definite system of social economy.[16]

The problem which must be raised in the light of recent critiques of the labour theory of value[17] is its role in the analysis of class, and, if it is to be abandoned, the problem of possible alternative ways of analysing relations of production and class structure must also be discussed. No attempt will be made here to provide a detailed exposition of the recent critiques of the labour theory of value, or of criticisms of them.[18] Rather, a few comments will be made indicating the limitations of the concepts associated with the labour theory of value for the analysis of the division of labour.[19] This can most readily be done by examining various other aspects of the division of labour, since Marx's analysis of the division of labour is by no means exhausted by the reproduction schemas. There are clearly present in Marx's work three aspects of the division of labour, though he does not designate them by the following terminology:

(1) *The technical division of labour.* This refers to the form of organisation of the unit of production, here called the 'enterprise', for brevity. Marx refers to this as the 'division of labour in the factory', which refers to the way in which labour is combined with the means of production. This entails determinate forms of co-operation and supervision, and is related, among other things, to the technology being used.

(2) *The division of social production.* This refers to the division of production into socially distinct branches, such as steel, aviation or electronics. It could also be used to refer to the division between Department I and Department II, though certain parts of some branches of industry (such as coal, electricity or water production) could be considered to be in different Departments. Marx sometimes refers to this as the 'division of labour in society'.

(3) *The social division of labour.* This refers to the division

of economic locations such that the agents occupying them have differential access to the means of production. These agents need not be human individuals, for example a joint-stock company could occupy the position of capitalist. Marx's analysis of the relations of production is about precisely this – the social distribution of economic agents in relation to the social distribution of the means of production.

The distinctions which Marx makes by discussing these aspects of the division of labour constitute a significant advance over most economic and sociological discussions of the division of labour. Theorists from Smith to Durkheim have treated the division of labour as in effect emanating from individual differences in aptitude and hence skill. Thus they tend to treat all aspects of the division of labour as arising out of the division of labour in the factory (or on the hunt). While the other aspects of the division of labour may be described, the fact that they are treated simply as effects of an apparently primary (or even primordial) cause means that the articulation of these three aspects is poorly theorised. In Marx, on the contrary, there are various indications as to how to theorise their articulation. The division of social production, for example, clearly affects the technical division of labour. The development of a new branch of production, say microprocessors, may well affect the technical division of labour within enterprises in other branches of production. This has already happened recently with the introduction of rudimentary robots into car production, and is now affecting the technical division of labour in the enterprises of car-component manufacturers, as microprocessors are introduced to improve economy and reliability of performance.

However, some of the effects which Marx attributes to the technical division of labour and the division of social production create problems for his conception of the 'social division of labour' if it is defined in terms of the relation of economic agents to the means of production. For example, the increase in the scale of production, according to Marx, means that the scale of production becomes too great for one person to supervise. This is related in Marx's analysis to the virtual disappearance of the 'captain of industry' and the development of a category of managers. This is just one indication among several which show that Marx himself argues that various economic activities which he attributes to capital can become specialised and differentiated, rather than residing in a single agent.

Rather than the individual capitalist owning his own money capital and means of production (including his factory and land), who supervises the production process and sells the product, we discover a whole series of economic agents at various points in *Capital*. Each of these agents has its own source of revenue. With the increase in the scale of production, the capitalist may borrow money for investment from bank capital (interest), while the land may be in the possession of a landowner (capitalist ground rent). The supervision of the production process involves a management hierarchy drawing wages (Marx likens it to the ranks of an army), while commercial capital specialises in wholesale and retail selling (commercial profit) and employs clerks as well as manual workers for bookkeeping and warehousing purposes (again, drawing wages). The joint-stock company, as already mentioned, may replace the individual capitalist (interest of various kinds, including share dividends). While Marx attempts, with varying degrees of success, to reconcile the explanation of these sources of income with the labour theory of value, the concept of value does not really explain why such agents appear. Consequently, the differentiation of economic activities attributed to capital threatens to disrupt the conception of the 'social division of labour' because it is clear that the relation to the means of production is not the same for all agents whom Marx treats as capitalist. Whereas Marx can allow for specialisation among labourers as part of the development of the technical division of labour, the specialisation among capitalists raises the issue of the basis of capitalist possession of the means of production. The distinction between possessors and non-possessors of capital seems to be based on the labour theory of value, yet it is not easy to explain the incomes of some of the 'capitalist' agents in terms of the distribution of surplus-value. This can be briefly indicated by pointing to the problem of capitalist ground rent and the problem of the distinction between productive and unproductive labour.

Both kinds of differential rent (I and II) and absolute ground rent presuppose the formation of a general rate of profit under capitalism. They appear as a surplus profit over and above the general rate, and accrue as a source of revenue to the landowner (who may also be the capitalist). Rent thus accrues as an effect of technical (fertility or market location) determinants in the case of differential rent, or of political or legal determinants in the case of absolute rent. Furthermore the social development of a 'class' of landowners is also apparently a matter which cannot be explained in terms of the labour theory of value. Hence a variety of other determinants are introduced as affecting the division of labour without recourse to the labour theory of value. Yet they are thought necessary to explain the distribution of income. A similar point can be made with unproductive labourers such as managers and clerks in a manufacturing capitalist enterprise, and clerks and manual workers engaged in warehouse work in a commercial capitalist enterprise. These workers are not thought to produce surplus value, hence they are unproductive; yet they are necessary to the processes of capitalist production and commodity exchange. Here again agents are introduced as determining the distribution of surplus-value, yet they are explained in terms of either the technical division of labour or the social division of production.

In other words, the labour theory of value on its own does not enable one to decide where to demarcate the boundaries between classes. Do any of the agents just mentioned constitute classes in their own right or are they fractions of a larger class? On what basis does one decide? Clearly any such decision must be made on the basis of the social relations which the theory postulates as operative between the different categories of economic agent, but the problem here is that both the production (or non-production) of surplus-value and *other* determinants are introduced by Marx to explain the social relations operating between the various agents (the relations of production, and relations of distribution which are an aspect of production relations). The introduction of the other determinants is an implicit recognition of the inadequacy of the labour theory of value on its own for explaining class relations, yet the other determinants create difficulties for the labour theory of value, as the continuing debates on ground rent and unproductive labour bear witness. The introduction of determinants of the division of labour which are not derived from the labour theory of value also opens the door for other such determinants, for example what may be loosely referred to as 'ideological deter-minants'. It would, for instance, be possible to construct an argument that the economic activities of various religious bodies (maintaining priests and buildings, and so on) also affect the relations of distribution. If one treats all those who are not manual wage-labourers in the primary and secondary 'sectors' of the economy as unproductive, in an attempt to reconcile the diversity of economic agents with the theory of value, then one would find oneself arguing that the majority of the population were exploiters. Any attempt to widen the category of the exploited by introducing other agents into it would involve the recognition of the pertinence of some deter-minants of the division of labour, but not others. It is extremely difficult on the basis of the labour theory of value to see on what grounds the choice could be made to recognise only some of these determinants, particularly since it is clear that Marx's position allows for a constantly changing division of labour.

Implications for a Theory of Class

If the labour theory of value cannot explain why some agents should be counted as possessors of the means of production (with their income deriving from this possession thereby count-ing as surplus-value), and if other determinants of the division of labour are to be recognised for the purpose of demarcating class boundaries, then a variety of problems have to be faced. (Indeed, some of these problems have to be dealt with even if one does accept the labour theory of value, but wishes to allow for additional determinants of the class structure.) If a variety of determinants are to be admitted as relevant to the definition of classes, there is a danger of a collapse into the 'infinite fragmentation' position that I have criticised in Weber and the other 'revenues' theorists of class. This is because the 'inter-section' of a variety of determinants of the division of labour may well produce a whole series of demarcation lines between groups of economic agents. There is no need for all such cleavages to demarcate the same groups of agents. In other words, the effects of some determinants may be to cross-cut or else to sub-divide the groupings of agents generated by the effects of other determinants. One possible way round this problem is to treat some determinants as relevant for the purposes of class definition, and others as not relevant. This is what the labour theory of value in effect attempts to do. However, in my view it fails because, in realising that theoretical priority cannot be given to the physical act of labour and thus in emphasising the social conditions of labour, the labour theory of value 'allows back in' other determinants of the division of labour without a clear specification of their relevance. In so doing, it not only allows a differentiation of the labourers, but a differentiation of the non-labourers who possess the means of production – namely, the capitalists. The acceptance of the differentiation of capitalists threatens Marx's concept of effective possession of the means of production (whether this is defined as legal ownership or *de facto* control), since each of the different kinds of capitalist specified by Marx controls *some* of the conditions of production, and consequently secures a revenue. Yet none of these capitalists could be said to possess the means of production in the sense of controlling them to the exclusion of other kinds of capitalist. It is only in relation to the labourers that the capitalists might be said to collectively possess the means of production. Yet even this remark does not resolve the problem of the unproductive labourers whose work is a condition of the specialisation of the different kinds of capital. Can one say that unproductive labourers such as managers do not also control some of the conditions of production?

What is needed, then, are grounds for treating some determinants of the division of labour as relevant for the definition of classes, and others as not relevant. However, even if one succeeds in defending such grounds, the very admission of a variety of determinants of the division of labour still poses a problem for any theory of class. This problem is that there is no reason to suppose that different determinants (whether legal, political, technological or whatever) will be equivalent in their mode of operation or effect. Even if only some of the determinants affect the class structure, the other determinants are still operative. Hence, even in a classless society, the social organisation of production involves various different demarcations between economic agents. Why then does class matter?

Without denying the importance of other lines of demarcation between economic agents which are not usually considered as class boundaries (for example, gender or race), one can say that the class structure matters because an economic agent's location in relation to the means of production can be a significant condition of action of that agent. This may seem a rather bland justification for the study of class relations, compared with the claims made by both Marxist and Weberian sociology that the class structure forms the basis for identifying significant or potentially significant collective actors. Yet this argument has something in common with such claims, for to say that the relation to the means of production can be a significant condition of action of an economic agent is to imply that such an agent may potentially act with other agents who have the same or a similar relation to the means of production.

In the Weberian tradition, parties are organisations aiming to affect the policy of the rulers, and may be formed on various bases, including status groups or (less likely in Weber's view) class position. The sort of class most likely to act 'communally' in Weber's view was a social class, which was defined in terms of the social interaction among its members. The classical Marxist use of class to identify potentially significant collective actors rests on the claim that the economy either directly or 'in the last instance' determines the superstructure, so that politics is primarily a matter of class struggle. In my view this claim has been cogently criticised as reductionist,[20] but it is still possible to say that economic agents may be potentially engaged in struggle along class lines (in the enterprise and elsewhere over other conditions of production) without reducing politics to class action. The problem of reductionism is that it attempts to reduce one level (or domain or instance) which is supposed to have effects in its own right to another level. The logical problem is how to reconcile the claim that a level has effects of its own with the claim that it is determined from outside, from another level with which it is somehow structurally connected but not merged. This is the problem of 'relative autonomy' of a superstructure determined 'in the last instance' by the economy, the problem being crudely that either politics is wholly determined by the economy, in which case it is difficult to treat them as distinct levels, or else the effects of the economy

on the separate domain of politics are theoretically indeter-
minate, in which case the claim of 'determination in the last
instance' cannot be sustained.

Yet it is possible to argue that class structure is potentially
relevant to political struggle if politics is not treated as a structurally separate domain but as a *process* of struggle (including
negotiation) between socially defined agents. If some agents are
in a position to control the conditions of production, and hence
to permit access to the means of production by other agents on
conditions which they, rather than the other agents, largely
determine, then potentially the relation to the means of production could either become an issue over which struggle takes
place or a demarcation line along which agents engaged in
some other struggle form into contending forces. However,
although the class structure could be considered a basis for
identifying potential collective actors, whether political
struggle takes place along class lines is less important than the
way the relation to the means of production opens up or reduces
the capacity for action of the various economic agents. To put it
another way, the class structure matters not because political
struggle primarily or potentially takes place along class lines,
but because the relation to the means of production gives
greater freedom of action to some agents and restricts the
capacity for action of other agents in a fairly systematic way. If
this cannot be demonstrated, then the concept of class cannot
be considered an important tool for analysing forms of social
organisation, no matter what grounds one offers for drawing
class boundaries.

Why should the social organisation of production give rise to
fairly systematic variations in the capacities of economic agents
because of their relation to the means of production? As we have
seen, the classical Marxist answer has been because the relation
to the means of production determines the sources of revenue
and the associated levels of income and consumption. This
could perhaps be criticised on the grounds that production and
consumption are interrelated, so that there are no grounds for
giving priority to the relation to the means of *production* as the
defining characteristic of classes. It is certainly true that if one
abandons the labour theory of value, one cannot claim any
ontological privilege for the production process *per se*, and in

an economy with an advanced division of labour other economic activities increase in importance as conditions of production, and cannot be treated as passive effects of the production process. However, since production is a necessary part of any economy, and since other economic activities can be considered as conditions of production, the use of a concept of relation to the means of production as a tool for analysing the division of labour as a class structure does not preclude reference to other economic relations. Rather, it is a way of dealing with the interconnections of economic relationships, since treating them as *conditions* of production relates other economic activities to production (which must be a feature of any economy, so the concept of relation to the means of production has a general applicability) without giving production a privileged position as the main or ultimate cause of the structure of the economy.

To some extent Marx was approaching such a position in his discussions of the differentiation of capitalist activities, many of which (such as banking) are not directly associated with production but which do form important conditions of production. It is because for Marx they formed such important conditions of capitalist production that he was able to treat them as providing access to the means of production which was basically the same kind of access as that of the industrial capitalist; in other words, Marx argued in effect that control of such conditions as finance capital and commercial capital provided access on the various capitalists' 'own' terms, by and large, whereas the access of the labourers to the means of production was for Marx largely on the terms of the capitalists. The problem with Marx's position lay not in his treatment of the class structure in terms of relation to the means of production, but his attempt to specify possession and non-possession of the means of production in terms of the labour theory of value. The specialisation of capitalists meant that possession could no longer be adequately conceived in terms of the legal analogy of a single agent with complete rights of use and disposal of the possessed object, since the control of the social conditions of use and disposal of that possession gave other agents effective access to the benefits of that possession (the means of production). Consequently the distinction between a class of agents possessing the means of production and a class which did not possess them was threatened, and the idea of a single line of demarcation between the classes based on the labour theory of value ran into serious (and, in my view, fatal) difficulties. However, as already indicated, if one does not have a single line of demarcation between agents, and if one admits of a variety of determinants of the relation to the means of production (and hence a variety of agents whose relation to the means of production differs in important respects) then there is a danger of falling into an 'infinite fragmentation' position, or denying that class matters.

'Possession' of the Means of Production

Paradoxically, the solution to this is probably to concede that the traditional concept of possession or control of the means of production is problematic. If it is conceded that possession can never be totally exclusive to one agent, or even to a class of agents, because the capacity to use and dispose of a possession is always dependent on social conditions and hence on the relative capacities of other agents, then one is forced to specify what the relative capacities of the various agents are and to analyse how far these capacities determine and are determined by access to the means of production. In other words, since the social organisation of production always involves relations between economic agents (the relations of production), all economic agents have *some* access to the means of production, since they condition the access of those agents most directly concerned with production. Relations between economic agents become class relations when certain agents are able to establish a predominance over the conditions of access to the means of production: that is, when certain agents are able to establish a relatively exclusive control over the means and conditions of production. When this occurs, other agents are only able to gain access on terms which are significantly determined by the 'possessing' agents, and thus the capacity to act of these other agents is significantly restricted. If one argues that there are various agents with differential access to the means of production, then the only way to avoid falling into the 'infinite fragmentation' approach is to argue that the relations between some of those agents are such that collectively those agents effectively establish relatively exclusive access to the means of production: that is, other agents' access is largely determined by the relations between the first group of agents. Rather than legel ownership or control by a particular *kind* of agent being the criterion of class relations, it is relations between various somewhat different kinds of agent that establish their predominance as a class over the means of production, restricting the access of other economic agents. The result of this restriction is a reduced, and different kind of, capacity for action by the 'excluded' agents.

To put it another way, differential access to the means of production not only enables *all* agents to act *in* the division of labour, since it provides their conditions for action; differential access also enables *some* agents to act more effectively *on* the division of labour. That is, their relation to the means of production also enables some agents to co-ordinate the diverse economic activities of other agents, thus partially determining the conditions for their own actions. It is for this reason that the relation to the means of production can be considered a potentially important demarcation line between economic agents, because it can enhance the capacity of some agents to act upon their own conditions of existence, while restricting the capacities of others to do so.

Clearly one major aspect of the ability to secure one's own conditions of existence is the ability to alter the distribution of income in one's own favour, thereby gaining access to the resources necessary to 'secure' one's own conditions. Classes exist where a group of agents can use its access to the means of production to co-ordinate important aspects of the division of labour, and thereby more or less secure that group's own conditions of existence. It is the causal connection between access to the means of production, co-ordination of the division of labour and the 'securing' of a group's conditions of existence (with related consequences on the distribution of income) that gives the concept of class its analytical power.

If such a boundary demarcating systematic differences in the capacity for action of various economic agents can be shown to be a feature of the social organisation of production, then a class structure is a significant aspect of the social formation in question. This is not to deny that economic agents on different sides of this boundary are differentiated by other determinants which also affect their capacity for action; nor is it to deny that such other determinants may have important effects on the way an economy is organised. It is simply to affirm that the class structure is a theoretically significant feature of a social formation wherever relations of production generate a series of social locations, the conditions of which give the agents occupying them differential access to the means of production in a manner which systematically enhances or diminishes their capacity for action on the division of labour. Since the conditions of production are always changing in response to the struggles between agents, the enhancement or diminution of the capacity for action of agents can never be a static affair. Hence, when making such general remarks about the class structure, it is difficult to be more specific about the extent or forms of access which determine such differences in the various agents' capacity for action.

In the case of capitalist relations of production, the restrictions on the access to the means of production are effected through the 'control' by some agents of the conditions of commodity exchange. The accumulation or concentration of substantial amounts of money as capital enables the agents in a position to decide how that capital is to be used to become predominant in determining the social distribution of the means of production, and hence the distribution of income, while the capacity of other agents to determine such outcomes is seriously reduced. The maintenance of such systematic differences in the capacity for action must be in part an effect (even if unintended) of the policies of those agents with access to the means of production on favourable terms. Otherwise in circumstances where other agents were struggling to improve their access to the means of production there would be little to stop those other agents from eventually altering the conditions of production in their own favour, since the very fact of the division of labour means that all economic agents have some impact, however minimal, on the conditions of production. Consequently, both the maintenance and the transformation of relations to the means of production involve policy decisions on the part of various economic agents.

Class Relations and the Division of Labour under Socialism

In the case of state-socialist societies, one of the issues for analysis is the extent to which access to the means of production is open, i.e. the extent to which class relations have been abolished. Certainly this is the main criterion by which such societies judge themselves and justify their policies, and it forms one of the main issues for debate in commentaries on such societies. How would one decide whether or not there was fairly exclusive access to the means of production? In other words, what pattern of differential access to the means of production would prevent some agents from predominating in a fashion which seriously diminished the capacities of other agents? To claim that a situation arises where no set of agents predominates in determining the conditions of access comes close to claiming that the division of labour does not produce differential capacities in economic agents: in other words, that the division of labour does not produce important effects, and does not really matter. This would amount to saying that the conditions of action of economic agents either did not affect economic agents, or affected them all equally. In that case it would make no sense to talk of a division of labour. However, if a set of agents does predominate in determining the conditions of access to the means of production, this does not necessarily mean that they are able to determine access on terms which systematically favour themselves. The co-ordination of the diverse activities of various economic agents is almost bound to place the co-ordinating agents in a position where they predominate in determining the terms of access to the means of production, and hence the distribution of income. Yet such agents do not form a class if they are unable to use their predominant position to secure for themselves a disproportionate share in the distribution of income, or otherwise substantially enhance their capacity for action at the expense of other agents. In other words, a set of agents may predominate in determining access to the means of production in a way which prevents other agents from 'dictating the terms' of access, yet those predominant agents might themselves be unable to use their position to 'dictate their own terms'. In such a case, the predominant agents cannot be considered a class. The central planning agencies in state-socialist societies could in principle be considered as such a set of agents, provided it could be demonstrated empirically that they were only 'holding the ring', in the sense of following policies which prevented all agents, including themselves, from securing the disproportionate benefits which can result from privileged access to the means of production. This would imply that non-class societies would have a very egalitarian policy with respect to the distribution of income and that this policy was being fairly effectively pursued.

To sum up the discussion so far, then, it could be said that various determinants of the division of labour only produce relations of production which can be called 'class relations' when they generate conditions of access to the means of production which permit substantially greater scope for some economic agents to act in and on the division of labour, taking on functions of co-ordination of the diverse kinds of economic activity engaged in by various economic agents, and when the conditions for this predominant access to the means of production permit the predominant group of agents to secure for themselves substantial benefits, particularly in the form of diverting to themselves a disproportionate share of the total real income of the social formation in question. Consequently, while it is difficult to envisage a division of labour in which no agents have a predominant access to the means of production, in certain social formations the conditions under which some agents do predominate may be such that agents with a lesser capacity for action are still able to establish sufficient access to the means of production to prevent any agent or group of agents from using their predominance to affect substantially the distribution of income in their own favour. This would imply 'multiple' access to the means of production, i.e. a series of overlapping forms of access.

It follows from this argument that the concept of 'social ownership of the means of production' which has traditionally been used by classical Marxism to describe socialist or communist relations of production must be reconsidered. If any division of labour entails agents with different capacities, some of which are determined by their different relations to the means of production (differential access), then non-class relations of production cannot be conceived of as referring to the ownership or control of the means of production by society as a whole. That would be to deny that the division of labour does indeed differentiate between economic agents. Nor could the means of production be considered to be under the control of an agency which somehow represents society as a whole, since any such agency would necessarily be composed of sub-agents who could be considered to have privileged access to the means of production, particularly if a serious criticism could be mounted of the claim by that agency to represent the whole of an internally differentiated social formation. Hence any concept of social ownership of the means of production (that is, of classless relations of production) must take account of the very complexity of an advanced division of labour, which implies a multiplicity of relations between economic agents. That very multiplicity or complexity of relations may well provide the conditions in which agents who would otherwise be less powerful could gain sufficient access to the means of production to prevent the predominant agents from using their social location largely for their own benefit. Thus any concept of 'social ownership' or 'communal possession' cannot refer to a series of undifferentiated agents, each of which has access to the means of production on the same terms, but rather to a set of conditions where the form of access of one set of agents does not seriously preclude the access of other agents. This would imply a situation of continuous negotiation and struggle between agents to prevent unacceptable restrictions on their own capacity for action deriving from their differential relations to the means of production. Since the outcome of such a continuous struggle could not be guaranteed, classless relations of production cannot be conceived of as a 'point of stasis', a state of affairs which could be thought of as necessarily reproducing itself. Thus a classless society cannot be considered as the end-point of a process. In particular, it cannot be considered as the 'goal of history' and social formations cannot be assessed by 'measuring their distance' from such a goal. State-socialist societies are often considered as 'transitional social formations'. However, this is not because they are at a certain staging-point down the road of progress to an ideal state of affairs, but rather because it can presumably be demonstrated that class relations have been seriously weakened. Since the continuous process of struggle between agents means that there is no state of affairs in which the process of restoration of class relations cannot begin, it is probably better to avoid the phrase 'transitional social formation', or else to restrict its use to designating social formations where major transformations of the relations of production are taking place. The 'state of play' of the relations of production, with regard to whether these involve a class structure – and if so what the conditions and effects of this are – this 'state of play' can only be decided after a fairly detailed examination of various possible determinants of the division of labour.

Conclusion

The position to be adopted in this book, therefore, will be to concentrate on analysing relations of production and class structure without attempting to reconcile this analysis with the labour theory of value. Instead, the decisions as to the demarcation of different positions within the class structure will have to be made in the light of historically specific analyses of the division of labour in a particular society, the Soviet Union, without attempting an *a priori* delimitation of the determinants of the division of labour.

The analysis of the Soviet class structure, then, requires a theoretical specification of the causal mechanisms generating a variety of economic locations and of the possibly distinct mechanisms distributing agents to the different locations, as a basis for categorising agents into classes. It has been argued here that a concept of relations of production which admits of a variety of determinants of the division of labour would be the best way to approach this specification, and that this causal specification must be historically specific. However, as should be clear from the above discussion of the problems involved, only those determinants which affect the access of agents to the means of production, and consequently their capacity for action in and on the division of labour, can be considered as relevant for the analysis of class. On the basis of this theoretical specification of class relations, it is possible to appraise empirical indices of the class structure in terms of their pertinence to the theoretical concerns of the analysis. Consequently the relationship between the theoretical basis of the empirical material being used and the analysis being conducted must be kept under constant review. It is hoped that this book succeeds in doing so.

Notes

1. J. H. Goldthorpe, 'Social Stratification in Industrial Society', in R. Bendix and S. M. Lipset (eds), *Class, Status and Power*, 2nd edn, Routledge & Kegan Paul, London, 1967.
2. The article was criticised at some length in my unpublished dissertation for the Diploma in Soviet Studies, University of Glasgow, in 1968, entitled 'Education and Social Mobility in the USSR'. The criticism was that the claim that stratification in the Soviet Union was phenotypically similar to, but genotypically distinct from, stratification in the West was empirically misleading. The dissertation argued that Goldthorpe's reliance on S. M. Miller's article 'Comparative Social Mobility', *Current Sociology*, 1960, was somewhat misplaced, since Miller had inaccurately computed the rates of social mobility in the USSR on the basis of data provided by A. Inkeles and R. A. Bauer, *The Soviet Citizen*, Oxford University Press, 1959. Correct use by Miller of the data produced by Inkeles and Bauer, it was argued, would have shown that the Soviet Union had a different 'mobility profile' from that of the USA. This conclusion was further supported by the use of Miller's criteria in the analysis of the data for women supplied by Inkeles and Bauer. While this sort of criticism of Goldthorpe was correct as far as it went, it did not question the arbitrary nature of the categories used for constructing Miller's social mobility tables, nor did it question Goldthorpe's analysis of the difference between market stratification and political stratification. Goldthorpe's analysis was mainly relied upon in the dissertation as a means of criticising convergence theory.
3. This position is based on that of B. Hindess, *The Use of Official Statistics in Sociology*, Macmillan, London, 1973.
4. K. Marx, *Capital*, volume 3, Lawrence & Wishart, London, 1972.
5. Ibid, p. 882.
6. Ibid, p. 883.
7. Ibid.
8. M. Weber, *The Theory of Social and Economic Organisation*, The Free Press, New York, 1964, p. 424. I have used the term 'class position' instead of the translation 'class status' because the latter may be confused with Weber's concept of 'status'.
9. Ibid.
10. Ibid, p. 427.
11. The bland phrase 'social stratification' is symptomatic of this theoretical

vagueness, but it should be pointed out that substituting a phrase like 'social inequality' does little to help, unless backed by some theoretical support; on its own the phrase 'social inequality' merely avoids the assumption that forms of social differentiation coalesce into strata.

12. K. Marx, *Capital*, volume 2, Lawrence & Wishart, London, 1967.
13. K. Marx, *Capital*, volume 1, Lawrence & Wishart, London, 1970.
14. See G. Littlejohn, 'State, Plan and Market in the Transition to Socialism: The Legacy of Bukharin', *Economy and Society*, vol. 8, no. 2, May 1979, pp. 212–15, for a brief discussion of the views of Bukharin and Preobrazhensky on this issue.
15. V. I. Lenin, 'A Great Beginning', in *Collected Works*, vol. 29, Lawrence & Wishart, London, 1965, pp. 409–34.
16. Ibid, p. 421.
17. See I. Steedman, *Marx after Sraffa*, New Left Books, London, 1977; and A. Cutler, B. Hindess, P. Q. Hirst and A. Hussain, *Marx's 'Capital' and Capitalism Today*, vols 1 and 2, Routledge & Kegan Paul, London, 1977, 1978. These critiques are by no means the same. *Marx's 'Capital' and Capitalism Today*, for example, contains a critique of the Sraffan concept of the economy.
18. For example, L. Harris, 'The Science of the Economy', *Economy and Society*, vol. 7, no. 3, August 1978. It must be said, however, that Harris's article seems to be based on the supposition that one cannot both understand the labour theory of value and be critical of it. The debate is continued in *Economy and Society*, vol. 8, no. 3, August 1979.
19. Various somewhat different comments on the difficulties of using the concepts of the labour theory of value for analysing the division of labour have already been made in G. Littlejohn, 'Economic Calculation in the Soviet Union', *Economy and Society*, vol. 9, no. 4, November 1980.
20. See, for example, P. Hirst, 'Economic Classes and Politics', in A. Hunt (ed.), *Class and Class Structure*, Lawrence & Wishart, London, 1978, pp. 125–54; or B. Hindess, 'Classes and Politics in Marxist Theory', in G. Littlejohn, B. Smart, J. Wakeford and N. Yuval-Davies (eds), *Power and the State*, Croom Helm, London, 1978.

2
Hammer and Sickle: Problems of a Worker–Peasant Alliance

Introduction

While many of the contemporary institutional features of the Soviet Union were established in the 1930s, this chapter focuses on the period from 1917 to late 1929 in an attempt to show the historical reasons for the conjunction of industrialisation and forced collectivisation in the 1930s, a conjunction which has left such a deep imprint on the structure of Soviet society. There have in recent years been a number of analyses of the reasons for this conjunction which have attempted to break from the widely accepted view that there was a necessary connection between forced collectivisation and rapid industrialisation.[1] It will be argued here that a policy of voluntary collectivisation could and should have been pursued much more vigorously throughout the 1920s. Furthermore, it will be argued that the New Economic Policy (NEP) would have faced fewer problems if the conditions for such voluntary collectivisation had been secured. This would have provided more investment funds than were actually available in the late 1920s and early 1930s for rapid industrialisation, thus easing the implementation of the first Five Year Plan.

Although the analytical focus of the chapter is on the problems of a worker–peasant alliance, the discussion will concentrate on the peasant side of that alliance. This is because it was here that the most serious weaknesses in the implementation of state policy in support of such an alliance became evident. Thus the intention is not to deal with all the economic or political aspects of the period, but rather to examine the aspects most closely associated with the origins of the crisis which developed in the NEP at the end of the 1920s. This crisis of the years 1928 and 1929 was largely the result of the manner in which agricultural policy was conducted. However, the problem of agriculture and of state policy towards it must be understood in relation to the prevailing conception of the NEP.

The economic basis of the alliance – namely, commodity exchange between industry and agriculture – was frequently seen as a fragile one, because such market exchange would give rise to a capitalist differentiation of the peasantry which might undercut the allegiance of the peasantry to the proletarian revolution. It was felt that the 'kulaks' (peasant capitalists) were vital on the marketing of a grain 'surplus' which would provide the necessary investment funds for industrialisation. Consequently it was feared that they would be able to hold the regime to ransom if they withheld their grain from the market. This fear of a 'kulak grain strike' first surfaced in public statements by party leaders in 1925, but it was later used to justify repressive measures which extended to the mass of the peasantry when the growing crisis of 1928 and 1929 seemed likely to jeopardise the first Five Year Plan. It was a view shared by the left opposition and by certain sections of the Bolshevik leadership. Such assumptions made it comparatively easy to mobilise support within certain sections of the party and the state apparatus for a policy of very rapid forced collectivisation which developed during the period of October to December 1929.[2] To understand such a response, it is necessary not only to trace agricultural developments during NEP, but also to analyse the problems of the preceding years which NEP was meant to resolve. The preceding years should also be considered as a form of worker–peasant alliance, albeit under different conditions from NEP, but problems similar to those of the pre-NEP years arose again during the crisis of NEP.

Ignoring the first eight months after the Revolution (except for some important agricultural developments), the years prior to 1930 can be divided into the following periods: War Communism (June 1918 to February 1920), when commodity relations were largely suppressed due to the disruption of the civil war; Proletarian Natural Economy (February 1920 to March 1921), when an attempt was made to develop a non-commodity strategy of socialist transition; NEP–Restoration (1921 to 1924), when commodity relations were used to restore agriculture and industry; NEP–Reconstruction (1925 to 1927), when the renovation and expansion of productive capacity was undertaken; and the Crisis of NEP (1928–9), when coercive attempts to secure the 'grain surplus' threatened and finally ended the commodity exchange basis of NEP.

State–Peasant Relations before the New Economic Policy

The black redivision
In 1917, both preceding and following the decree 'On Land' of 26 October, the peasantry had implemented the old dream of a *chernyi peredel* (or 'black redivision') of the land on egalitarian lines, using the village commune (*mir* or *obshchina*) as the 'indispensable technical mechanism for the redistribution of the land'.[3]

While this process had been going on since February 1917, and increased in scale after the harvest, it was carried out on a massive scale after the promulgation of the land decree.[4] Partial readjustments were more common than universal redistributions affecting all the land and all the population of a commune.[5] The landless peasants and small peasants benefited most (in terms of land, but not as will be seen in terms of inventory or livestock),[6] so that the number of landless peasants dropped by 1919 to about half the figure for 1917 (see Table 2.1).

By the spring of 1918 most of the land had been temporarily reallotted for spring sowing. The temporary nature of the redistributions both allowed compromises to be reached quickly and

Table 2.1   Changes in landholding 1917–19

	Without crop land	1–4d*	4–10d*	Over 10d*	Total
1917	11.5	57.6	25.8	5.1	100
1919	6.6	72.2	19.7	1.5	100

* d = desiatina; 1 d = 1.09 hectares = 2.7 acres.
Source: D. G. Atkinson, 'The Russian Land Commune and the Revolution', 1971, p. 158, citing a 1922 report of the Central Statistical Administration.

enabled further changes in land tenure to be made as returning soldiers arrived and subsequently as people fled the deteriorating situation in the towns when the civil war developed in 1918. By 1919, 96.8 per cent of agricultural land was in the hands of peasant cultivators; over 3 million landless peasants had received allotments and gentry property had been virtually eliminated.[7] This had been accompanied by a decrease in the average size of land-holdings and a loss of technical efficiency, both of which contributed to a steady decline in agricultural productivity.[8] These negative economic aspects of the land redistribution were conceded at the time, but were called inevitable, if the revolution was to retain the support of the peasantry, a view which seems reasonable. Socially, the redistribution led to a diminished size and increased number of families,[9] but some of these were ficticious family splits made to lay claim to more land which was still effectively controlled by the head of the former larger household. Politically, the redistribution destroyed the economic base of the opposition to the new government and created active political support for the new regime among the peasantry. Yet the peasants very rapidly lost faith in the 'black redivision' even in 1918. This discontent was highest in the central agricultural region precisely where the greatest amount of land redistribution had occurred, with the middle and poor peasants predominating among those who were dissatisfied.[10] When queried during the 1922 statistical survey, over half the peasants replied that they were dissatisfied with the existing division of lands. This may have been partly because the unequal distribution of inventory and livestock gave different peasants differential capacities to work the land, with the result that the covert *de facto* distribution of land was by no means as egalitarian as the outcome of the 'black redivision' and legal restrictions on the extent of land ownership would lead one to expect. According to one estimate, kulaks comprised 15 per cent of the peasantry in 1918, but held 38 per cent of the land, and accounted for 50 per cent of the marketed grain.[11]

The Kombedy

As a result of these developments, the situation at the start of the War Communism period in the spring of 1918 was as follows. Grain supplies to the towns were very low, partly because of the loss of important grain-producing areas during the war (a situation which continued later with the control of agricultural areas by elements hostile to the government), and partly because of the previous decline in agricultural productivity prior to 1917, which was aggravated by the 'black redivision'.[12] By May 1918, it was clear that the government could not draw grain out of the countryside by barter, and it was obliged to force it out to feed the towns and the Red Army, both of which were vital to the regime's survival. In June 1918, committees of the rural poor (*Kombedy*) were formed to assist local procurement agencies to take grain from kulaks. These were soon supplemented by contingents of urban workers who organised armed foraging bands in the countryside. The *Kombedy* also encouraged the spread of the 'black redivision', especially the *general* redistributions of land which mostly occurred in the second half of 1918.[13] The *Kombedy* and the armed food detachments were an effective supply agency, and the state received two and a half times more grain in the second half of the year than it had in the first half. However, the *Kombedy* came into conflict with the rural soviets, conflicts which were often related to the resistance of the wealthier peasants to this policy of grain requisitions. There was also the implicit challenge which was posed by the *Kombedy* to the village commune, 'given the gap between its theoretical egalitarianism and its actual stratification'.[14] According to Atkinson the potential challenge of the *Kombedy* to the entire system of soviets was the reason for their fusion with the soviets after the harvest of 1918, when it was announced that the *Kombedy* had fulfilled their function. She also argues that having helped to transform the bulk of poor peasants into middle peasants, the Party had to transform its policies to keep up. Committees of poor peasants alone were too exclusive, so the Party switched from a policy of neutralising the middle peasant to a policy of 'firm alliance' with the middle peasant which was to continue as the official line for the next decade.[15]

This explanation (whatever other merits it has) is not sufficiently clear on the relation between the *Kombedy* and the 'black redivision', and on the effect of this on the proportion of the harvest which could be marketed (or requisitioned). It is important to ask why the committees of the poor (*Kombedy* and *Komnezamozhi*) were formed initially in the central agricultural areas and industrial areas, the former being precisely the areas where even before the *Kombedy* were formed, the 'black redivision' had been most extensive and where the village commune was apparently strongest. While admitting there was a gap in the commune between its apparent egalitarianism and its actual stratification, Atkinson then argues as if by the harvest of 1918 the bulk of peasants had already been transformed into middle peasants. Even assuming that this was true in the above areas which formed the Bolshevik heartland during the civil war, it could hardly be said that this was necessarily the case in, say, the Ukraine, in which peasant capitalist relations had been more developed since the 1890s.[16] The fight against kulaks developed in the Ukraine much later than in Great Russia, in the form of *Komnezamozhi* committees, which continued in a different form up until at least the mid-1920s.[17]

Consequently, the *Kombedy* were not dissolved in late 1918 simply because they were made redundant by their own success in creating a 'middle peasantry'. Rather they were probably dissolved because there was a real danger (not yet realised in 1918) that they would indeed create a middle peasantry, with consequent disastrous effects on the production and distribution of the *kinds of crops* which were necessary to supply the towns and the Red Army. Kritsman is much clearer on this issue than Atkinson. He points to the economic (technical) basis of the worker–peasant alliance: the socialist means of production could not exist without grain, cotton and other industrial crops, while simple commodity production could not exist without transport, nails and agricultural machinery and implements. The concessions which each side had to make for the alliance to work were very important: hence the Bolsheviks came out in October 1917 with an *agrarian* programme, not a proletarian one.[18] During the first phase of the 'black redivision' (up to mid–1918) it was not only the feudal proprietors which had been expropriated, but also the capitalist non-peasant ones. The latter were not really replaced by large-scale socialist forms of agriculture, since the soviet farms (*sovkhozy*) did not use all the formerly large-scale private estates. In any case these farms and the collective farms only had 10 per cent of the necessary horses and a complete lack of usable equipment. Thus the agrarian revolution effectively extinguished large-scale agriculture, and since the Decree on Land made no mention of agricultural industry, it juridically denied it by nationalising all land. Hence the connection of agricultural industry with large-scale agriculture (such as sugar estates) was broken. This restricted the economic and social base of the proletarian revolution (as opposed to the agrarian revolution) by denying certain agricultural raw materials to industry and by turning millions of agricultural workers into small-scale proprietors. The concession of the proletariat to this alliance was to permit a shrinkage of the agricultural base of industry and the town in the form of a loss of marketed agricultural produce. It is clear that Kritsman is not so much thinking of marketed produce as a surplus over peasant family consumption, but rather he is thinking in terms of the kinds of crops necessary to sustain industry and the Red Army, crops which were partly associated with large-scale agriculture. The concession of the peasantry to this alliance, when faced with the choice of conceding land to the gentry or of giving up free trade in agricultural produce, was to choose the latter, but only so long as it was necessary to defend their land. Thus, according to Kritsman, the worker–peasant alliance at this time consisted of giving land to the peasants, and political power (and the means of conducting the war which meant the suppression of the market) to the proletariat.

The historical and geographical context of the formation and dissolution of the bulk of the *Kombedy* in 1918 can now be more clearly stated. The 'black redivision' had considerably equalised land holdings (at the expense, among other things, of important raw materials for industry) but did not equalise holdings of inventory and livestock. So it did not eliminate class relations within the peasantry (although it did eliminate non-peasant capitalist farming). Doubtless this is the reason for the disillusion with the 'black redivision' which Atkinson notes even by mid-1918. In a situation where marketed agricultural produce was completely inadequate and where organisations of the rural poor were being spontaneously formed, usually on the initiative of urban workers or of armed grain supply detachments, the Bolsheviks gave official encouragement to the *Kombedy* to requisition grain and other agricultural products, thereby suppressing market relations between town and country. The poor peasants benefited from this extinction of commodity relations, since they received bread and some industrial products which they could not have afforded to buy. This spread the anti-capitalist revolution from the town to the countryside (where the revolution had to this point been largely anti-feudal). This rural anti-capitalist movement in 1918 basically took the two forms of (i) *Kombedy* in the (formerly feudal) central agricultural and in the industrial regions, which were net grain-consuming areas, and (ii) armed detachments originating from these grain deficit areas who were opposed to the (relatively) large-scale capitalist peasantry of the grain-surplus areas. Thus the grain-surplus areas with their relatively developed capitalist agriculture became the territory of the counter-revolution and the grain-deficit areas (whose feudal peasantry had been partly recruited into the proletariat of the nearby areas of developed industry, and which retained close links with the proletariat) became the territory of the revolution.

Within the latter area, as already indicated, the *Kombedy* began to implement the more general redistributions within the village communes in the second half of 1918, as well as requisitioning grain, sometimes with the support of armed detachments. Not only did this phase of the 'black redivision' lead to a more complete equalisation of land-holding in the central agricultural areas where it occurred, but it was at times coupled with the compulsory sharing of the implements and draught power of the richer peasants. That is, during the civil war (but not during NEP) the poorer peasants gained access to the means of production necessary to cultivate their land, at least in some areas. In these circumstances, a genuinely 'middle peasantry' was temporarily created, since the poorer peasants were not dependent on the kulaks for access to the means of production, but this situation depended crucially on the political power of the *Kombedy*, or on state support for this compulsory sharing. The problem for the Bolsheviks from the viewpoint of conducting the civil war was that this was 'economically reactionary'[19] because in the absence of large feudal or capitalist estates, the kulak peasantry were the main producers of materials for industry and the towns. The economic effect of this extinction of kulak farming (during 1918) was according to Kritsman probably not much less than the effect of the extinction of non-peasant capitalist agriculture which had proceeded for a year up till then.[20]

Hence rather than a political threat to the rural soviets (*sel'sovety*) being the reason for the dissolution of the *Kombedy* after the 1918 harvest, as Atkinson suggests, it was probably the Bolshevik perception of the further restriction of the agricultural base of industry which the *Kombedy* could have caused that led to the declaration that they had fulfilled their task. This consideration was probably reinforced by the political danger resulting from the fact that pressure from the *Kombedy* contributed to the sharp increase in rural uprisings in the summer and autumn of 1918.[21] The 'challenge' to the *sel'sovety* posed by the *Kombedy* cannot have been the main reason for their dissolution. Had this been the main reason, the method of ending the *Kombedy* would have been rather puzzling. Outright dissolution which might have provoked resistance was avoided; instead they were *fused* with the *sel'sovety* through a process of re-elections held in late 1918 and early 1919.[22] The *Kombedy* at times even succeeded in keeping the kulaks out of the election[23] and were themselves often elected to the *sel'sovety*.[24] The end of the *Kombedy* meant the end of attacks on kulak land tenure during the civil war. However, ending the *Kombedy* did not reverse the effects of the more thorough 'black redivision' of the central agricultural area, and quite apart from the direct effects of the continuing grain requisition policy (which led to successive reductions in the area sown with crops during the civil war), the agriculture in this area would probably have supplied less to industry and the towns, since farms here were much more of a small-scale consumptionist type.

The results of the civil war on agriculture

The main outcome for agriculture can be seen from the fact that, as Kritsman emphasises,[25] while sown area fell and harvests fell during the civil war, there was a particular decline in intensive agriculture, in crops which were normally cash crops, and in livestock of the kinds which were normally reared for the market. This was partly due to the disincentive effect of the continued system of grain requisition, and partly to the disruption of transport during the war (which would make the effort of producing for others seem rather pointless). This reduction in sales of agricultural produce was accentuated by the spread of the 'black redivision' and of the *Kombedy* (even after they had been officially dissolved) into areas such as the Ukraine when the Bolsheviks regained territory. This phenomenon meant that small-scale 'consumptionist' farms would spread, farms which would engage to a lesser extent in 'cash crop' production. However, it is unlikely that this latter phenomenon occurred to the same extent as in the central agricultural area, precisely because the more egalitarian *general* redistribution pursued by the *Kombedy* no longer had official support. In any case, in some of the more developed capitalist areas of the countryside (such as the north-west) the 'black redivision' was more nominal than real, and kulak farms remained intact.

The general effects of the civil war and the associated suppression of commodity exchange between town and country (which was epitomised by the policy of grain requisitions) can be summed up as follows. The requisitions had a direct disincentive effect on sown area, but this was particularly acute in the case of crops and animals which would normally have been most associated with commodity exchange, namely, foodstuffs, certain technical crops such as flax and cotton, and in the kinds of livestock most likely to be sold for consumption as meat. The corollary of this is that peasant farming became more self-sufficient.

The requisitions also had indirect effects (since for example the Red Army requisitioned horses which could otherwise have been used for ploughing and local transport). However, during the civil war such effects were much less serious than the effects of disruption of transport. The terms of trade between town and country moved dramatically from 1919 to 1920 in favour of the towns,[26] because there were even fewer manufactured products supplied to the countryside than agricultural products supplied to the towns. This should not be taken to imply that the peasantry bore the greatest burden of the war in terms of suffering: the towns did, because they were chronically short of agricultural produce, especially food. Town dwellers (according to Atkinson) were getting about one-third less food than peasants. However, the economic basis of the worker–peasant alliance was almost completely broken at the end of the civil war, since the terms of trade between town and country were worst in 1920. The policy of requisitions was continued in 1920, even though the military threat to the regime was much less then, and was virtually non-existent after February 1920. This was a grave mistake, since, as became abundantly clear from the peasant unrest during 1920 (especially after the harvest), the peasantry were only prepared to put up with requisitions while there was a threat to their land in the form of a military restoration of gentry or non-peasant capitalist land tenure. Over the winter of 1920–1, sections of the Bolshevik leadership were preparing to make a move away from the policy of requisitions, despite the support which had grown in the Party in favour of a method of construction of socialism using the continued suppression of commodity relations. The uprising at Kronstadt before the Party Congress in March 1921 effectively silenced any opposition within the Party to the introduction of the New Economic Policy. NEP attempted to use commodity relations as the basis for constructing an alliance with the poor and middle peasantry, as a strategy for the construction of socialism.

Conclusions on the pre-NEP period

The first conclusion that can be drawn on the economic preconditions for attempts at sustaining a worker–peasant alliance is that an appropriate product-mix is a vital technical economic condition of such an alliance. In other words, each side of the alliance must supply the products necessary for the economic reproduction of the other, even if this is done (as socialists might hope) in such a way as to transform one or both sides of the alliance. The second conclusion, which is closely related to the first, is that the agricultural demand for a particular industrial product-mix and the capacity to supply the appropriate raw material product-mix to industry are closely related to the organisational forms of peasant agriculture and, partly through these forms, to the class structure of the peasantry. Altering the class structure of the peasantry may well alter the product-mix demanded and supplied by agriculture. For example, an increase in the middle peasantry may well lead to a reduction in the proportion of cash crops planted. It is for this reason that kulaks, as capitalists who are often more heavily engaged in commodity exchange than other peasants, can by marketing their produce provide a technical support for industry: hence the ambivalence of the Soviet regime towards kulaks even during the civil war (as indicated by the dissolution of the *Kombedy*). Another example of the relation between rural class structure and the product-mix is that the lack of inventory and livestock among the poor peasants after the 'black redivision' created a demand for these means of production which were vital to cultivate the land at their disposal. The failure to supply the appropriate agricultural implements to the poor and middle peasantry was partly overcome by the compulsory sharing which they enforced on the kulaks at times during 'War Communism'. However, this compulsory sharing lapsed completely under the NEP, and the consequent lack of means of production among sections of the peasantry became the source of some of the difficulties of NEP. Where there is some such shortage of means of production, it is clear that collective use of these means of production is a precondition to constructing an alternative source of marketed agricultural products, so that urban and industrial consumption does not have to rely on kulaks. The third conclusion to be drawn from the period of 'War Communism' is that where for any reason (such as military exigency or mistaken state policy) the correct product-mix is not supplied to agriculture, then the technical conditions of the worker–peasant alliance are disrupted and the appropriate product-mix from agriculture is less likely to be forthcoming. This can easily hit the technically advanced sections of the economy particularly hard.

The worsening of the terms of trade from 1919 to 1920 which is noted by Kritsman occurred at a time when grain requisitions were much less a matter of military exigency, and much more a matter of a deliberate attempt to construct socialism along non-commodity lines. This period of 1920 has been designated as one of 'proletarian natural economy' by Hussain and Tribe[27] in order to distinguish it from the disruption of commodity relations caused by the war. It was based on the expectation of a revolution in the West aiding the Soviet state. It was this attempt to coercively implement a policy of non-commodity relations that produced the serious peasant unrest of 1920 and early 1921 and that induced a political crisis related to the difficulties of feeding the industrial workers (and the Kronstadt garrison). Had the Bolsheviks not opted for a restoration of commodity relations, the effects would have been economically and politically disastrous.[28]

State Policy on Commodity Relations with the Peasantry during the New Economic Policy

The important new feature of NEP was not simply the introduction of commodity relations, but rather the way these relations were to be managed by a state policy favouring particular organisational forms in agriculture (collective and state farms), forms which would contain and then undercut the development of capitalist relations of production in agriculture. It is important to realise that, as Hussain and Tribe point out,[29] collectivisation is not necessarily a socialist measure, even when the state is a socialist one. Whether collectivisation is a socialist measure depends on the way in which it is implemented (as part of a strategy of the socialisation of the means of production) and on the conditions of existence of the collectivised enterprises so formed (i.e. briefly whether or not these collective enterprises depend on capitalist relations of production elsewhere in the economy). In the case of NEP, the development of co-operatives was seen by Lenin as a way forward to collectivised production enterprises which would hedge in capitalist development (fostered by commodity relations) so that it would in future grow into socialism. This development of co-operatives (leading to the spread of collectivisation) was seen as a means of confronting petty capitalist production, an aim which was also to be achieved by the attraction of domestic and foreign concessionaires. These advanced capitalist enterprises would later revert to the Soviet state. Thus in a 'pincer movement' on petty capitalism, NEP would create large-scale socialist (state or collective) enterprises in industry and agriculture. As Hussain and Tribe argue,[30] neither of these two prime conditions for NEP developed in a satisfactory fashion, although some foreign concessionaires were attracted. The rest of this chapter will concentrate on the difficulties of developing co-operatives and collectivising agriculture. To understand this, the immediate post-Revolutionary attempts at the socialisation of agriculture must also be reviewed.

Attempts at the socialisation of agriculture 1918–21
As we already noted in the preceding section, one of the main effects of the agrarian revolution of 1917–18 was to eliminate many of the conditions of large-scale production. This even included the destruction of machinery that was only suitable for large farms. The attempt to establish state and collective farms was begun fairly quickly, despite these difficulties. At the end of 1918 it was decided that both state farms and peasant collectives (which had already sprung up spontaneously in some areas) should be supported as forms of socialisation of agriculture, with preference given to state farms (*sovkhozy*).[31] After *sovkhozy*, the next form of production unit in order of priority was the *kommuna*, the most communal form of peasant collective. In this all means of production and land were held in common, in contrast to the *artel*, where part of the land and implements were still held by individual families, and the *toz* (an association for the common cultivation of land), where there was simply joint use of certain means of production on jointly cultivated land at certain times of the year. This encouragement of collective production was initiated at the time when the *Kombedy* were being abandoned. Under war-time conditions and faced with peasant resistance to requisitions (by cutting back on cultivation), the advantages of state control through *sovkhozy* and *kommuny* (which had to conform to regional agricultural plans) were obvious. In addition, such forms encouraged the pooling of inventory and livestock which were in such short supply, particularly among the poor peasantry.

The dynamics of the socialisation of agriculture during the years 1918–21 are given by Atkinson (see Table 2.2).[32] Most of the membership of the *kommuny* derived from the poor peasantry and the rural proletariat.[33] Peasants pooling their own land obviously preferred the greater control they retained in the *artel*. For the reason, the *artely* rapidly overtook the *kommuny* as the predominant form of collective farm, since the state was unable to provide the *kommuny* with much of the necessary

Table 2.2   Dynamics of socialisation in agriculture

	Sovkhozy	Kommuny	Artely	Toz	Total
1918	3101	975	604	—	4680
1919	4063 (516)	1961	3605	622	9251
1920	5928 (1636)	1892	7722	886	16428
1921	6527 (2136)	3313	10185	2514	22539

Source: D. G. Atkinson, 'The Russian Land Commune and the Revolution',
    Ph. D. dissertation, Stanford University, 1971.

means of production from former church or gentry lands. The
kommuny were rarely viable without such state support at the
beginning (the main exceptions being *kommuny* established by
immigrant groups, some of which were relatively prosperous).[34] Because of the inadequate technical basis for a rapid
socialist transformation of agriculture, the official intention to
proceed without compulsion was placed beyond question in
repeated policy directives, with Lenin warning that, in view of
the inadequate material base, too rapid a development could be
harmful or even ruinous.[35] This injunction made during the
civil war was repeated by Lenin at the beginning of NEP, so the
need was obvious to supply the appropriate 'material base' in
the form of means of production to collective farms and to poor
and middle peasants, to encourage further voluntary collectivisation.

From the above evidence it seems that a reasonable start was
made on the socialisation of agriculture by 1921. Why then was
this prime condition for the success of NEP not met? To answer
this question, an account of certain aspects of NEP will be
given, exemplifying the difficulties which any state faces in
implementing policy. Any state is composed of a variety of
agencies, with different priorities and objectives which will be
more or less co-ordinated with each other. Where such objectives are contradictory, it is by no means the case that the objectives most consistent with the official overall strategy on a
particular issue will be the ones most vigorously pursued. This
is because different state agencies have different resources and
capacities, as well as different ways of working out how to
implement policy, and the outcome of the interplay between

state agencies cannot be determined simply by reference to any existing overall official strategy. While to some extent these problems can be *reduced* if a state has a central planning mechanism capable of regulating the implementation of policy, this does not eliminate the problem of co-ordinating the activities of various state agencies. In any case, there was no effective central planning agency in the USSR until the later 1920s, when work was begun on the first Five Year Plan.[36]

The land organisation programme

Ignoring *sovkhozy*, the collectivised sector of the rural economy covered less than 1 per cent of the population by the beginning of NEP.[37] Yet, although 96 per cent of all rural families were in village communes (the *mir* or *obshchina*) by 1920, the state concentrated on a 'land organisation' programme, rather than on the allotment of land to *sovkhozy* and *kolkhozy* (collective farms).[38] This in itself could perhaps be considered necessary to increase agricultural productivity by amalgamating scattered strips, thus constituting a precondition of more widespread collectivisation. However, any such 'collectivist' effect was to some extent countered by a spontaneous move among the peasantry towards consolidated land holdings by individual families in 1920. The result was that in 1920, precisely when the campaign for the 'socialisation' of the countryside was at its peak, land officials 'were caught between pressure from above to implement a collectivist policy and pressure from below to reorganise agriculture on diametrically opposed individualistic lines'.[39] Local state officials had little power to resist this pressure where it occurred since they were financially dependent on the *mir*, whose assembly (the *skhod*) was often dominated by kulaks. Here the importance of the differential resources and capacities of different state agencies (and sub-agencies) becomes clear.

In the face of such pressure and of the resistance to the requisitions of 1920, NEP involved an initial relaxation of state support for the 'socialisation' of the countryside. In the same week that the tax in kind was introduced to replace requisitions, a directive was issued to all land departments prohibiting the compulsory allocation of land for *sovkhozy* or *kolkhozy*, and limiting the land that could be placed in new collectives to the amount previously held by members.[40] While this had the merit of avoiding any compulsion of the peasantry into collective forms of production, it was not coupled with a policy of economic support for collective production. Instead, a series of legal and administrative measures such as the 1922 Land Code sought to limit the chances of households in the *mir* from differentiating along capitalist lines. Some of these restrictions were eased in 1925.[41] Thus even in legislation, never mind the actual implementation of rural economic policy, the official priorities in favour of collective forms of land use did not seriously constrain the commune during the 1920s. Despite the prohibition on redistributions, these increased after 1922, partly due to an attack on the old patriarchal household by younger family members, and partly through the development of capitalist tendencies (including attempts to escape taxation on large farms by fictitious divisions).[42] This occurred despite government instructions to land officials to prevent excessive fragmentation of holdings (indeed, a freeze on land holding as of 22 May 1922 had been declared).

In the face of these problems, the land organisation agencies during NEP attempted to combat the problem of separate strips held by each household in the *mir* (many of which were too distant from the household to be usable) and the problem of the intermingling of the lands of different communes. Despite the fact that the 1922 Land Code required the registration of all land holding, this plan was not fulfilled, due to lack of an adequate organisation, and lack of rural co-operation. The plan called for only half of the land to be registered by 1928 and performance was considerably behind plan, despite constant complaints of slow progress from the land organisation workers themselves.[43] Consequently, even this fairly modest attempt to improve agricultural performance (which could have provided a basis for a subsequent more rapid collectivisation) was inadequately implemented during NEP. Yet the consolidation and broadening of strips was having *some* effect, and by 1927 it amounted to 27 per cent of all land organisation work done.

The scissors crisis

It might not seem surprising that the state did not give stronger support to collective agriculture in the early years of NEP, given the devastating effects of the harvest failure of 1921.[44] However, as Kritsman among others has pointed out,[45] agriculture then recovered fairly rapidly from 1922 to 1923, despite the 1923 harvest being worse than the previous one. The year 1923 was also the year of the re-establishment of livestock and of 'technical' crops, providing raw materials for industry. The contraction of industry during the First World War and the civil war had been much greater than that of agriculture: in 1921, industrial production was about one-sixth of the pre-war level, while agriculture was about three-quarters of the pre-war level.[46] Consequently, industrial prices were higher than agricultural prices in 1921, although the harvest failure of 1921 and the famine of 1922 raised agricultural prices, but only for seven months.[47] By July 1922, industrial prices started to rise above agricultural ones again (relative to their pre-war ratios). This process continued throughout 1923, and it became known as the 'scissors crisis' because of a graph produced at the time by Gosplan showing the agricultural prices declining and industrial prices rising, looking like the two blades of a pair of scissors. Kritsman treats the opening of the scissors as a result of the good 1922 harvest (although the scissors opened in July to August 1922, before the harvest) and consequently he treats it as an indication of the strength of market forces, coupled with the weakness of the marketing apparatus of the state and co-operative organisations.[48] As Dobb points out,[49] while these were aggravating circumstances, it was the measures taken to limit the competition between the state agencies themselves which by the summer of 1922 meant that state industry was able to face the peasant buyer and seller across the market more or less as a monopolist, and hence could turn the terms of trade with the village more or less in its own favour. Whereas Kritsman treats the period from the autumn of 1921 to the autumn of 1923 as a period of opening up of market elements, and of co-operation with the new bourgeoisie, and the period after the autumn of 1923 as a period of struggle with the capitalists to end their factual monopoly of the means of circulation, it is probably more appropriate to analyse the scissors crisis in other terms. The absence of centralised supply organisations to ensure raw materials and food for state industry meant that, after the harvest failure of 1921, sections of state industry were forced to compete with each other for raw materials and food, by selling any industrial goods they could make or could lay their hands on. This unco-ordinated competition of state enterprises made it possible for private traders to fulfil a supply role through the market. These traders came to be called *Nepmen*. Their conditions of existence were not the mere existence of commodity relations under NEP, but the failure adequately to regulate those commodity relations. In other words, state agencies were not made to conduct themselves in a manner that was roughly consistent with the overall strategy. Rather than there being effective regulation of the terms of trade between industry and agriculture (town and country) in a manner which supported the poor and middle peasantry, and fostered the socialisation of agriculture, it is clear that from the very start of NEP there were continuing problems with the relation between industry and agriculture. The result was that the terms of trade and the product-mix of trade were never adequately regulated because state agencies were capable of pursuing policies of their own to the point where a series of crises was produced, culminating in 1928 and 1929 in the effective abandoning of NEP.

While Kritsman was correct to point to the weakness of state marketing, this was really only true until mid-1922. What is important for the understanding of the 'scissors crisis' is that when state agencies in this area were strong enough to function effectively, they did so in a semi-autonomous manner which was partly determined by their own organisational form and objectives, rather than in a manner which met the economic preconditions of the worker–peasant alliance. We have seen that a similar problem had already arisen with the movement of the terms of trade in favour of industry between 1919 and 1920, before the start of NEP. When an attempt was made in 1921 to use the supply commissariat to meet the technical conditions of agriculture, many of the goods were totally unsuitable for village consumption.[50] This attempt by state industrial and marketing agencies to supply the peasantry with what were effectively luxury urban goods (such as talcum powder) was also repeated later in the 1920s. As has already been shown, what the peasantry really needed were means of production, especially in the form of inventory. The evidence available indicated that even the poor peasants were prepared to market their produce to be able to buy means of production, when these were available.[51]

In this sense, the difficulties at the start of NEP caused by the 1921 harvest failure cannot be said to explain the lack of state support for the poor and middle peasantry, or for collective and state farms. The recovery of agriculture in the harvests of 1922 and 1923 meant not only that agriculture was capable of supplying industry with raw materials, but that the shortage of means of production among the poor peasantry became relatively more acute, thus increasing their dependence on kulaks and fostering the development of capitalist relations in agriculture. The scissors crisis of 1923 was 'resolved' by lowering industrial prices (a policy endorsed by the Thirteenth Congress of January 1924), but the argument that the 'real' problem was the weakness of industry persisted (especially but not only among the Left Opposition). In addition, as Dobb points out, the 'scissors' continued to persist, but on a much reduced scale: that is, the real terms of trade continued to favour industry.[52]

Agricultural marketing and the rural class structure

More important than the terms of trade, however, was the neglect of the policy of fostering the organisational and technical conditions of the socialisation of agriculture: the development of co-operatives, and the supplying of means of production to the poor peasantry.[53] Under these circumstances the poor peasantry continued to market their produce, partly to meet the tax in kind (or in money), and partly for a variety of other reasons (including paying debts to richer peasants for loans of grain). The result was that the mass of the peasantry marketed the bulk of their grain in the autumn. In absolute terms this was most of the grain that was marketed. The state procuring agencies took advantage of this to lower the price in the autumn, thereby keeping down raw material or urban food prices. This policy reduced the capacity of the poor and middle peasantry to buy the means of production, thereby maintaining their dependence on kulaks. Such dependence was further reinforced by the fact that the kulaks could afford to delay their marketing until spring when the price was higher. At springtime they could sell both to the state purchasing agencies and to the poorer peasants whose requirement for money had forced them to sell beyond their own consumption needs in the autumn. Sometimes the poorer peasants even got into debt in the very process of autumn marketing, because they needed to hire their horse and cart from the richer peasants to transport their produce to market.

Apart from repaying debts and paying taxes (the tax in kind, later changed to a monetary tax, the incidence of which was reduced in 1925), the main motive for marketing agricultural produce was to purchase means of production. Rural producer co-operatives were supposed to facilitate this by providing credit to the poor and middle peasantry, but many such co-operatives had high entrance fees (effectively restricting their membership to kulaks), and even among their membership the richer peasants benefited disproportionately from credit.[54] This is a good example of the difficulties of implementing the strategy of NEP actually fostering capitalist relations in the countryside. Kritsman was to some extent aware of this possibility, pointing out that merchant capital had benefited from the raising of industrial product prices in 1923. During 1923 almost half of all wholesale trade and almost all retail trade was in the hands of merchant capital. However, Kritsman tended to see the solution simply as consisting in a state struggle with merchant capital, i.e. in the strengthening of state and co-operative trading organisations. There is a lot of truth in this argument with respect to the early years of NEP (up to about 1924), since in the absence of state and co-operative trading agencies merchant capital could take over such trading functions. Yet such an analysis overlooks the extent to which capitalist relations can be fostered inadvertently in the implementation of state policy, even when capitalist competition has been restricted, undermined or otherwise countered by a series of administrative measures. This is why the *Nepman* continued to function even after 1925, and indeed it is why various aspects of the 'informal' economy exist in the present-day Soviet Union. However, state control of retail trade meant that, especially after 1925, urban merchant capital was incapable of posing any serious threat to the economic policy of the state. Indeed, even writing in 1924, Kritsman did not see how indigenous capital could become a danger all that quickly. Instead, he correctly saw that the greater internal danger was the huge mass of impoverished peasantry, swollen by the *batraki* (rural wage labourers) who had received land and by the urban workers fleeing the hunger of the towns during the civil war. In 1923 the poor peasants not paying any tax were one-quarter of all households, but in the year 1922–3 they had only one-seventh of the land, and produced only one-fifteenth of all production, judging by the returns made under the tax in kind. All of this mass had land, but nothing to work it with.[55]

As a result some of the poor peasantry were coming into the towns, attracted by the rising living standards of the urban proletariat, so that while the numbers employed by industry were rising, industrial unemployment was rising faster.[56] This movement into towns was already by 1924 freeing land which had in any case been poorly used (due to the lack of means of production). These lands could readily be taken over by kulaks, and many of the land redistributions which took place before completion of the legally permitted minimum nine-year interval were of this kind. There was also a growth in the number of *khutors* (capitalist peasant farms not subject to redistribution within a *mir*), particularly in the west, the north-west (both areas of stronger capitalist relations before the Revolution) and in the central industrial region (where it was easier to migrate to a city).[57] Kritsman argued that this internal danger, where a strengthened bourgeoisie could seek to use the (unwilling) unemployed, would weaken. However, because he considered in 1924 that such a danger existed, he argued that one of the most important tasks of the party was to work among the impoverished peasantry, attracting it to the side of the proletariat, and to the creation of the quickest growth of industry, on which also depended the improvement of the position of the poorest peasantry – the possibility of using its labour power in industry itself, and in forest and construction work.[58] He argued that the necessary precondition for the resolution of this task was the freeing of the poor peasantry from the influence of trade capital and its agents in the countryside – the kulaks – and the non-admission of the latter into peasant organisations (in particular, co-operative organisations) which could otherwise become in the hands of merchant capital an instrument for the organisation of the peasantry around capital and under its command. The latter outcome could be the result of implementing the slogan of replacing the attachment to the land by an attachment to the market as a slogan for the whole peasantry. In reality the slogan of the development of market relations among the poor peasantry – which was interested in the market for agricultural products not as a seller but as a buyer (it was only interested in selling the commodity labour power) – this slogan could only mobilise the poor peasantry under the command of the peasant bourgeoisie. According to Kritsman, NEP had begun as a retreat (not in the sense of running away, but to build up one's forces, which was inescapably connected with the chance for one's opponent to build up his forces). This retreat had permitted from the autumn of 1923 a strictly methodical advance on market elements and on trade capital. The reasons for this strictness consisted in the fact that the basic tasks of the Revolution in Russia had been solved and the class revolutionary tasks now confronting the Russian proletariat were on the world arena.[59]

The conceptualisation of socialist transformation under NEP

This view of NEP as a retreat, following which an advance would be made on capitalist relations by the strengthened forces of the state, was extremely common among the Bolsheviks in the 1920s. It was related to a view which favoured War Communism (and the 'proletarian natural economy') as suppressing commodity relations, thereby undermining the basis of capitalism. Such an approach, which Kritsman to some extent shared, was based on a two-sector conception of the interrelation of capitalist and socialist relations, in which one sector would grow at the expense of the other.[60] Such a view can easily lead to a 'statist' conception of socialism, in which it is assumed that the only way that the state can effectively regulate the conditions of capitalist and socialist relations to secure a socialist transformation is to supplant capitalist forms wherever possible. Where this is not immediately possible, this approach tends to rely on administrative and legal restrictions on capitalist relations. Without denying that such measures have their place, I would argue that the danger of this emphasis on state ownership coupled with legal and administrative restrictions is that measures designed to support other methods of socialist transformation (such as consumers' and producers' co-operatives) tend to be neglected. Kritsman's discussion of the poor peasantry as only interested in selling their labour power comes close to such a position, since it makes it difficult to treat co-operatives as a means of encouraging poor and middle peasants to produce the kinds of technical and cash crops needed for industry and for urban consumption. Such developments could conceivably be encouraged by price policy and priority allocation of means of production to co-operatives. It is certainly true that among the Bolshevik leadership such measures were not adequately supported. The main reason for the growth of capitalist relations of production probably lay in the manner in which the state organisations themselves functioned (which shows the weakness of a Preobrazhensky type of 'two-sector' approach). It is likely that the issue of the lack of effective support for the poor peasantry, co-operatives and collective farms was never seriously raised as an issue among the leadership, prior to the Fifteenth Congress of 1927, because of the prevalence of such a statist conception of socialist transformation. While there might be differences among the adherents of such an approach as to the precise form of the relation between the state and the capitalist (or state and market) sectors, such differences of opinion should not be allowed to obscure the fact that capitalist and socialist relations of production were frequently identified as two distinct sectors. There might have been dispute about the manner in which one sector would grow at the expense of another (for example, dispute over the rate of extraction of a surplus from agriculture for industrial investment, a surplus that was presumed to be at the disposal of kulaks unless it was taken away from them). However, there was no real dispute over the distinctness and antagonism of the two sectors. The two sectors might occasionally be extended to three by sub-dividing the market sector into a capitalist and a petty commodity producing sector, but this did not really alter the main terms of this conception. This approach should be distinguished from an approach which treats socialist transformation as a process of accumulation in which the socialist state's policy is to encourage the growth of investment funds in both 'sectors' (state industry, and agriculture plus rural industry). Such a policy implies the direction of investment funds to production units, whether state, collective or capitalist, in such a way as to provide a rapid rate of growth of productive capacity and to transform the relations of production. Hence rather than socialist accumulation implying the development of state industry (especially heavy industry) at the expense of agriculture and (private or co-operative) small-scale rural industry, such an approach implies the direction of investment funds to both 'sectors' in a way which favours the socialist transformation of state and collective enterprises. In other words, it favours the internal transformation of such enterprises so that they are subject to greater democratic control, thereby mobilising local support for such a strategy and local initiative in solving 'tactical' production problems. At the same time, it implies the generation of a capacity to implement the investment strategy at a national level by developing an effective planning apparatus. Rather than one sector 'feeding off' the other, such an approach implies that *reorganisation* can itself increase productive capacity and generate further investment funds. Consequently some investment should be devoted to providing the conditions for such reorganisation (for instance, state credits to co-operatives to stimulate the conditions for the collectivisation of peasant farming). This strategy of socialist transformation entails the view that investment priorities can be decided in a context of progressively altering the conditions of existence of units of production (and transforming the units themselves). It implies an analysis of the reproduction of the national economy which treats the various branches of industry and agriculture, each with a range of different production units, as providing one another's conditions of existence. Transformation of certain production units should thus be related to transformation of others. This approach is very different from one in which an 'active' state can control a 'passive' or 'recalcitrant' peasantry to industrialise the country.

The latter conception tends to treat the state apparatus as a coherent means for the realisation of socialist relations of production, and ignores the problems of the incoherences in the relations between the state agencies themselves, with their diverse resources, diverse organisational forms and diverse objectives. Rather than a strict and methodical advance being made on capitalism, as Kritsman suggested in 1924, state agencies *both* restricted and undermined merchant capital *and* generated some of the conditions of its existence. In the countryside, agrarian policy was also contradictory in its implementation. It was not just that there was a clear inconsistency between the lip-service paid to the support for the poor peasantry and co-operatives on the one hand, and the lack of action to implement this policy on the other. Rather, it was that the measures designed to counter the development of capitalist relations of production in the countryside were administrative and legal restrictions on kulaks, rather than positive economic support for the poor and middle peasantry to reduce their dependence on kulaks, and to provide alternative sources of the agricultural product-mix required for industrial development. This meant that, since it was assumed that the kulaks produced most of the marketable surplus, the state policy towards them was ambivalent, and variable, as it had been even in 1918. Perhaps the most well-known example of such ambivalence is Bukharin's famous injunction in 1925 to the peasantry to 'get rich', an injunction which he retreated from soon afterwards, but which was used against him in later political struggles. However, the failure to support co-operatives adequately had another effect, which should not have surprised those who had read Lenin's 'On Co-operation'. Lenin clearly linked the cultural work necessary to establish well-run co-operatives to another task – namely, the transformation of the state apparatus. Clearly the development of non-state organisational forms of production was for him linked to the struggle to democratise the state, whereas a statist conception which identifies socialism with the growth of the state sector at the expense of the non-state sector makes it much more difficult to problematise the 'bureaucratic' restriction of the 'commodity' sector.

A good example of the attempts to limit capitalist development by legal and administrative means is the 1924 circular which was sent round by the People's Commissariat of Agriculture (*Narkomzem*) informing land offices that, despite the 'juridical neutrality' of the 1922 Land Code on forms of land tenure, official policy was opposed to the formation of individual farms (*khutors*) out of the village communes.[61] However, the prohibition on land organisation work aiding the formation of *khutors* did not mean that efforts were shifted to the formation of collective farms. Instead, work was done on 'other forms of land tenure from which the transfer to collectives would be less difficult', as the 1924 circular instructions put it. So large unwieldy communes were broken up into smaller ones, and crop-rotation improvements were made. Such developments intensified in 1927 and 1928, which must have helped to improve agricultural productivity, and could be seen as providing some of the preconditions for a transfer to collective farms.

The formation of collective farms in the 1920s

The work of land organisation in support of collective farms actually declined from 2.7 per cent of the work in 1922 to 1.4 per cent in 1925. By 1927 this percentage had risen again, but only to 2.4 per cent of the total land organisation work. Most of the collectives were located in the Volga region, and an exceptional number of them were formed in Samara. *Narkomzem* had instructed its agents to see to it that the poorest peasants received the best land under organisation work, and in 1925 the government assumed the costs of all land work done for the poorest peasants.[62] Thus it would be untrue to say that no work was being done to help the poor peasants, but the scale of such aid was completely inadequate. In general, the poorest peasants provided the largest contingent for collectives, which is not surprising, since if they were going to leave the village commune it would have been difficult for them to set up *khutors* without substantial means of production. Even richer peasants found that they sometimes had to give up the *khutor* and revert to the commune.[63] Consequently, it is not surprising that many collectives came to be formed in Samara in the latter 1920s, since capitalist relations were particularly strong there, and hence a relatively high proportion of the population were *batraki*.[64] This participation of poor peasants in collective farms as a result of land organisation work is in contrast to the low participation of poor peasants in co-operatives, where the entrance fee was often an effective barrier and additional barriers were often erected.[65]

If land organisation work and the officially supported co-operative movement were doing little to promote the development of collective farm production, what determined the process of collective farm formation during the 1920s? It will be remembered that there had been a programme of support for state and collective farms during the period 1918–21, a policy which was linked to grain requisitions. Many of the state farms were directly linked to other state enterprises, to secure supplies of food or raw materials in priority sectors of the economy. With the start of NEP, this position changed. Official support for collective farms (*kolkhozy*) ended, and there was a 'massive collapse' in their numbers.[66] Not only did their numbers fall off with official support, but almost one-quarter of all *kolkhozy* continued to dissolve each year, though usually they were replaced by new ones. What seems to have been happening was the replacement of more complex collective organisational forms by simpler ones, because the necessary investment and other preconditions for complex collectives were absent. This would explain the growth in the number of *tozy*, the simplest form of *kolkhoz*, as well as the rapid growth of 'simple producers' associations', which were not strictly speaking *kolkhozy* at all. According to Lewin, this was an increasingly noteworthy feature of the *kolkhoz* movement up until the end of 1929.[67] This survival of the *kolkhoz* movement was particularly a response to the desperate situation of the poor peasantry. Many poor peasants were prepared to try a collectivist solution to their problems, especially as the land allocated to the *kolkhozy* came from the state reserve. In 1924–5 the number of *kolkhozy* increased again, but, astonishingly, this was mainly due to the fact that further land had become available as a result of the liquidation of state farms (*sovkhozy*) at this time. In 1926 there was a decrease again in the number of collective farms, which was probably related in part to the diminishing supply of new land from the state. By 1927 there was no more free land, and this source dried up.

However, in March 1927, a decree was introduced broadening the advantages to *kolkhozy* in credit and taxation, and turning over to them land that had previously been rented from the state land fund.[68] This signalled a new phase of expansion in the number of *kolkhozy*. Whereas there were around 12 000 in 1926,[69] the number rose to 15 000 in June 1927 and to 33 000 in mid–1928.[70] This still involved below 2 per cent of all peasant households, but the growth rate was impressive. This growth was, as indicated, accompanied by a change in the proportions of different types of *kolkhoz*: whereas in 1921 *kommuny* were about 20 per cent and *tozy* 15 per cent, the remaining majority being *artely* by around 1927, *kommuny* fell to 8.5 per cent and *tozy* rose to 40.2 per cent, while by 1929 *tozy* were 60 per cent of all *kolkhozy*.[71] All the *kolkhozy* were very small agricultural enterprises, the average consisting of about 50 people, 50 *dessiatines* of crops, five or six horses and seven cows. In 1928 the average size of the *kolkhozy* was declining, and it was suggested that their size would have to be increased as a matter of urgency. With low labour productivity, the *kolkhozy* had made little investment in their own development and had largely 'eaten up' the funds allocated by the government in the period up to 1927.[72] Despite the relative ineffectiveness of the credit and other aid granted under the March 1927 decree (or perhaps because of the criticisms of these inadequacies) credit to *kolkhozy* expanded during the period 1927–30. In 1927–8 *kolkhozy* received less than 12 per cent of state credit, while individual farms received 44 per cent. In 1928–9 the two sectors claimed 24 per cent and 33 per cent respectively. In 1929–30, *kolkhozy* received 63 per cent of all credit, while individual farms received less than 4 per cent.[73] Further support was given in the form of orders issued in the spring of 1928 that 'surplus' land be taken from kulaks and given to poor peasants. Any peasants willing to form a collective were given preference in land organisation work.[74] The land law issued at the end of 1928 emphasised this point and made it possible for peasants interested in organising a *kolkhoz* to leave the *mir* at any time, and additional advantages were given in terms of taxation, allocation of machinery and allotment of land. Paradoxically, work on the break-up of larger *miry* (village communes) into smaller ones proceeded at an unprecedented rate in 1928, while work on collectivisation simultaneously accelerated the establishment of large agricultural production units.[75] The smaller *miry* improved their output, probably because of changes in land use, while it was becoming clear that *kolkhozy* were marketing 50 per cent of their output. (This was only 3.7 per cent of total marketed grain in 1927–8, but it was probably interpreted in some quarters as showing how to secure an investible surplus from agriculture.) In 1929 the number of *kolkhozy* rose to 57 000, the area under their control doubled and by the end of the year almost 4 per cent of all households were in *kolkhozy*.[76] Thus the effects of NEP on the *kolkhoz* movement can be summarised as a fourfold rise from 1921 to 1929, but this overall rise included an initial severe decline from 1921 to about 1924, followed in turn by recovery and decline again to 1926, with a final rise from 1927 to 1929.

It is clear, then, that, at least prior to 1927, *kolkhozy* survived despite government neglect largely because of the efforts of poor peasants who needed even the little support which the state gave to them in the form of land. After 1927, when at least some more effective measures were introduced, the rate of collectivisation increased. Indeed, according to Narkiewicz, the percentage of peasant households which had been collectivised by 15 December 1929 was much higher than 4 per cent, being somewhere between 12 and 29 per cent.[77] What were the reasons for this poor performance in socialising the countryside? The reasons often given are a series of political and organisational failures in the countryside itself. These will be discussed in the next section, but failures to organise correctly at the grass roots or weaknesses in the analysis of the party leadership are not sufficient to account for this flaw in NEP. Consequently, the section after the next will deal with the implementation of macroeconomic policy by various state agencies. The final part of the chapter will deal with the crisis of NEP and its demise.

Political work in the countryside
The main agency which was supposed to implement the policy of collectivisation during NEP was the rural soviet (*sel'sovet*). The rural soviets lost the administrative support of the *volost'* (district) land departments, since these were eliminated in 1921–2.[78] This loss of administrative support from the *volost'* soviet (the next rung up the ladder from the rural soviet) reduced the rural soviet's capacity to conduct any land organisation work in favour of collectivisation. Local land affairs were left under the supervision of the *volispolkom* (executive committee of the *volost'* soviet), which was responsible for the observance of all laws by the population within its territory, and so could hardly concentrate on land use. In any case, there was little incentive to develop an expertise in problems of land

use when a system of Land Commissions was set up in 1922, serving as land courts adjudicating land disputes at various administrative levels. This weakening of state agencies capable of implementing agricultural policy at grass-roots level began to be reversed in the latter half of 1924, when the functions and authority of the lower soviets were extended. The supervisory functions of the *volispolkom* were made more specific in matters of land organisation, land rental and the execution of the decisions of the Land Commissions.[79] The range of functions and the maximum number of members of a rural soviet were also expanded at this time. Relations between the rural soviet and the assembly (*skhod*) of the village commune (*mir*) were left somewhat vaguely defined, for the rural soviet was supposed to act as the agent of the *skhod* in some respects, yet the *mir* was subject to all legal rulings of the rural soviet within the latter's territory. This legal ambiguity was effectively resolved in favour of the rural soviet, but only in 1927. Even after that, official reports were still referring in 1928 to a situation of 'dual power' in the countryside, showing that the weak legal position of the rural soviet was only one determinant of its low capacity to implement agricultural policy.

It was clear by the summer of 1924 that the political situation in the countryside was not good, with discontent in Georgia, which was followed by a wave of violence against rural news correspondents in the autumn. The elections for soviets held at the end of the year were characterised by unpopular techniques, including obligatory recommendations for appointment. Voter participation declined to 29 per cent of the qualified electorate from a 1923 level of 37 per cent. At this point it was decided to invalidate all elections where less than 35 per cent had participated.[80] The result of this campaign, despite a slight increase in the proportion of the electorate disqualified (still under 2 per cent), was that 45 per cent of qualified rural voters participated in the election. This attempt to win rural support early in 1925 should be related to the legalisation of limited forms of labour hiring and land leasing (which were extended in 1925), as well as of private trade. Such measures could be summed up in the injunction (mentioned above) of Bukharin in 1925 to 'get rich'. Clearly the attempt to disenfranchise richer voters and mobilise the rest of the elector-

ate was intended to offset politically the concessions which
were being made economically to rural capitalism. Such moves
were evidently a response to the political events of 1924, and are
related to the adoption of the slogan 'face to the countryside' in
1925 and to the attempt to start a campaign to revitalise the
rural soviets in the same year. Yet the situation did not improve
much in the rural soviet elections of 1925–6. It is true that they
produced broadly the same rural response in terms of turn-out,
but the party was rightly concerned at the lack of evidence of
political activity of poor peasants, and about the social composition of the rural soviets.[81] Party membership was not very
high either, rising from 6 per cent of rural soviet members in
1922 to 10 per cent in 1926. Less than 30 per cent of women
qualified to vote in the 1925–6 *sel'sovet* elections had done so,
but this was an improvement over the 20 per cent of the
previous year. The number of women serving on rural soviets
rose to 10 per cent.[82] The number of non-peasants in rural
soviets was about equal to the number of party members. In the
elections held early in 1927 over 3 per cent of the population
were disenfranchised, in an attempt to control the political
activities of the kulaks.

Having established that the legal position of *sel'sovety* was
weak, at least until 1929, and that election campaigns did not
mobilise a great deal of political participation in them, it is
necessary to consider how the rural soviets actually functioned.
The average *sel'sovet* in the RSFSR (the main constituent
republic of the USSR) in 1926 had about 16 members, and
covered 8 villages with a total population of about 1700; 90 per
cent of its members and 95 per cent of its presidents were
peasants.[83] It was supposed to meet every fortnight, but this
was often ignored, and *sel'sovety* met much less frequently than
communal assemblies (*skhody*). Neither the *sel'sovet* nor the
volost' executive committee exercised effective control over the
village commune.[84] The commune decided virtually all
questions, so that nothing was left for the *sel'sovet* to do. While
there was often duplication in terms of the problems dealt with
by the two bodies, the range of problems dealt with by the commune was generally far more comprehensive. While the soviet
was assigned the function of convening the village assembly,
this only occurred when the two units coincided territorially

and the soviet was the executive of the commune. Rarely did the soviet exercise any direction over the commune, as was being pointed out in 1928, three years after the launching of the campaign to revitalise the rural soviets. Similarly the *volost'* executive committee (*volispolkom*) exercised little or no effective control over the commune. Keeping a watch on the manifold activities of the commune was physically impossible for the *volispolkom*, which was poorly staffed and which had to deal with an average number of 93 village settlements each in the RSFSR.[85]

This fact alone shows that it would not have been sufficient to improve the quality of the personnel of the rural and district soviets (for example, by raising their pay), which was often the only remedy suggested for the widely recognised weakness of Soviet rural state administration. The problems were not only those of bad personnel (including corrupt officials) or of peasants' unwillingness to lose work-days to attend meetings. There was a range of meetings and conferences held by a whole series of organisations (party, non-party activist, soviet, trade union, co-operatives and others) which made it impossible to run so many activities with any degree of efficiency at a time when the rural soviets were sometimes incapable of even preparing such elementary materials as lists of voters.[86] One of the major burdens on the *volispolkom* and the *sel'sovet* was tax work. The weak financial position was a continuing problem for these bodies. According to a report published in 1928, the budget for rural soviets was 16 million roubles, whereas the budgets for the communes totalled 80 or even 100 million roubles.[87] The same pattern as in other areas can be seen in the development of rural tax policy to support rural state administration. A 1922 law on local finances gave the *volost'* and rural soviets broader rights of taxation and turned over to them certain state taxes and properties, but it was not until 1923 that provision was made for regular *volost'* budgets, and these were not widely established until 1925. These budgets, mostly based on local taxes, were to take care of local needs, while the central government was to provide basic state requirements, such as defence and communications. The modest *volost'* funds were to maintain state enterprises, provide or rent buildings for public agencies and institutions, establish social services, build roads, and so on, as well as to support the *volispolkom* and to aid the *sel'sovet*. These *volost'* budgetary problems were however minimal compared with those of the *sel'sovet*. In the years 1926–8 only 3 per cent had their own budget.[88] Under a 1925 ruling the rural soviet could not levy a local tax to carry out its public duties without the consent of the communal assembly. The Commissariat of Finances (always a financially conservative organisation) refused to countenance rural soviet budgets except on an experimental basis, and when in 1927 an attempt was made to widen the practice it had little effect. The village commune assembly usually refused to pay taxes for a rural soviet budget because of the agricultural tax. Although in 1924–5 this tax had amounted to 5 per cent of peasants' income, it amounted to 17 per cent of their purchasing power. Such complaints about the agricultural tax may have been connected with the easing of the tax in 1925. However, this had adverse effects on the produce marketed in that year, and did not lead to any greater willingness to pay taxes to the rural soviet. Yet it was clear that the communes were engaged in self-taxation. Apart from land rentals, this was the main source of the 80 to 100 million roubles at their disposal.

This meant that by the end of 1927 many village communes were providing the rural soviets with regular or irregular budgets, thus inducing a financial dependence of the rural soviets on the communes. Furthermore, only rural soviets with their own budgets had the status of a corporate body (which all village communes had by law). Consequently the great majority of rural soviets could not own property, arrange trading transactions or sign a contract. That is, they could not carry on any economic activity or use the funds they were allowed after 1927 from the *volost'* executive committees for economic purposes. Hence there was no way in which they could become politically independent of the commune (which in some cases even chose the president of the *sel'sovet*),[89] nor could they provide economic support for either the co-operative or collective farm movement, though they were supposed to foster these movements.

The financial dependence of the rural soviet provoked considerable discussion at the Fifteenth Party Congress in December 1927. This debate continued throughout 1928 with the participation of agrarian experts and institutions, following which a new land law was promulgated in December 1928:

> The commune was now to include among its members, not only the members of households using its lands, but all village residents participating in its economic life (labourers, herdsmen, blacksmiths, etc.) not previously recognised as having a right to vote in communal assemblies. Only those with the right to vote for, or be elected to, soviets could participate now in the land assembly. The rural soviet was to direct the work of the commune in areas of land tenure and land organisation, and to take over all functions where its own activities paralleled those of the commune. Decisions of the commune on basic land matters were subject to confirmation by the soviet. If the soviet considered any decision of the commune inimical to the interests of cooperativism or of the poor peasantry it could subject the question to re-examination by the next assembly and, failing to secure agreement, could then annul the decision. This clearly went beyond any previous Soviet challenge to the commune. Yet it was still only a matter of paper tigers: all the legislation of the decade had not seriously affected the commune's position.[90]

Clearly, while the village commune had the economic and administrative resources, the rural soviet could not have any decisive impact on the countryside. One can agree with Narkiewicz that the root cause of these problems lay in the government's failure to pay enough attention to local administration before 1925, and its lack of financial aid after 1925.[91]

The other main candidate for mobilising support at a local level for the socialisation of the countryside was the party itself. In 1929, only one-tenth of the communists who were members of rural organisations had already been party members in 1917 or before. The number who had joined during the civil war was one-sixth of the membership, many of whom were workers living in rural areas. During 1922 and 1923 very few peasants joined the party. By September 1924 there were roughly 153 000 rural party members, as opposed to over half a million in the towns. This situation was related to distrust of the rural party cells, whose actions were arbitrary and difficult to distinguish from those which should properly have been undertaken by the state.[92] After 1925, with the slogan 'face to the country-side', the party managed to recruit more peasants, numbers increasing to 333 000 by 1929. These members were not motivated to any great extent by socialist ideals, and in any case the party had roughly only one cell to three *sel'sovety*, and they were scattered over too wide an area to be very effective. Agricultural workers and peasant farmers were in a rather small minority, and most of the cells consisted of officials, even after a recruitment drive to attract agricultural and other workers in 1928. Party membership could bring additional income and other advantages, and among the rural population as a whole, the 'better-off categories were increasingly strongly represented'.[93] During periods when there was a focus on the quality of party membership, the only measures taken were either purges or large-scale campaigns for the recruitment of new members. Nothing was done to provide any basic training for members. Not only the local cadres but also the upper echelons of the party structure were weak. The small party cells were thus incapable of fulfilling the leadership role expected of them, and resorted to 'campaign tactics' (bursts of activity directed towards some specific end, alternating with periods of complete inaction) or to 'administrative methods',[94] a reliance on organisational position and prerogatives as a means of exerting pressure for compliance, rather than political work analysing the situation and persuading people of the benefits or necessity of a particular course of action. Such methods at best generated indifference, and at worst hostility. Consequently, as Lewin puts it:

At this period, the rural sector was undoubtedly the weakest and most vulnerable point in the Soviet system. In this sector the greatest danger lay in wait for the regime, and it was in this sector that the boldest policies, and the most unremitting efforts, were called for. And yet this was the very sector in which the fewest forces were deployed, and to which the Party gave least attention.[95]

The implementation of national economic policy
By 1925–6 agriculture was back to the same level of production

as 1913, though with a different crop pattern.[96] There was a regional specialisation in grain production, similar to the pre-war pattern. The west and north-west were 'grain-deficit' areas with intensive techniques of grain production (combined with industrial crops), while the south, south-east and (of growing importance) Siberia were 'grain-surplus' areas with extensive production techniques. The central 'Black Earth' region (where the 'black redivision' had been strongest in 1918) provided a mixture of the two kinds of agriculture. The recovery of agriculture, following the 'scissors crisis' of 1923, and the measures to restore financial stability in 1923 and 1924, made it seem that the problem of grain production was resolved. In conjunction with the recovery of industrial production, which also reached pre-war levels at this time,[97] this meant that the Soviet Union had re-established itself economically: the period of restoration was complete. However, industrial capacity was now being almost fully employed and was already quite old, most of it dating from the nineteenth century. The renovation, or reconstruction, of industry was thus a fairly urgent matter.

The policy of using foreign concessions as an investment source had clearly failed. Consequently the first Soviet general economic plan, developed during 1925, envisaged the use of grain exports to pay for the importation of machines and raw materials. As it happened, the year 1925 provided what was to be a unique chance to re-enter the world grain market. Russia's dominant position of the pre-war period had been taken over by the USA, Canada, Argentina and Australia, but the 1925 American and Canadian harvests were poor and Australia had transferred its sales to the Asian market. Argentina never sold on the European market before February, so there was an opening for Soviet grain between October 1925 and February 1926. However, precisely at this time, the purchase price of grain rose in the Soviet Union, rendering export unprofitable, and only came down again in January 1926. This failure to export, with a consequent reduction in imports, slowed the growth of industry, worsened the balance of payments, and increased inflationary tendencies.

This was the kind of difficulty that provided the economic background to the debate over industrialisation. Our concern, however, is not so much with that debate but with how such economic difficulties were engendered and dealt with. The 1925 grain crisis was largely an effect of poorly co-ordinated planning. This was hardly surprising in what was effectively the first attempt to construct a national plan in the Soviet Union, but the point is worth emphasising because the crisis was interpreted in some quarters at the time as a 'kulak grain strike', a phrase that was to reappear during the crisis of NEP in 1928 and 1929. However, the causes of the 1925 grain crisis were factors which lay within the planning and regulating capacity of the state. These factors can be divided, following Grosskopf,[98] into causes stemming from the distribution of marketed grain, and causes at the level of grain production which affected the timing of its marketing.

First of all, with regard to the distribution of marketed grain, the government did not develop a plan designed to meet the internal needs for marketed grain before fixing the level of grain exports. Because of state price policy, the peasants of the 'grain-deficit' areas had specialised in industrial crops, producing less grain for their own needs. Hence their demand had increased. Urban demand grew in 1925 due to wage increases and an increase in urban employment of 400 000. Demand by state distilleries had also increased. These were all factors related to state policy. Furthermore, as should have been expected after the poor harvest of 1924–5, peasants were building up their grain reserves. It was in this situation of increased demand that the state attempted to divert grain for export purposes, and prices rose, especially in the grain-deficit areas. Since state reserves were also low, it became profitable for private capitalist traders (*Nepmen*) to sell grain over long distances. (Without such state reserves, it is in general extremely difficult to overcome the effects of poor organisation, natural disasters or price fluctuations.) Furthermore, the costs of marketing had gone up, largely because of bureaucratic organisation. Finally, there was a shortage of sacks and the rail network in areas such as Siberia and Kazakhstan was insufficient, even though it had been re-established at the pre-war level, because these more distant areas were of growing importance in the wheat market.

With regard to the production of grain, and its effects on the timing of marketing, it is clear that many poor peasants were normally obliged to sell their grain immediately after the harvest, even though this meant that they did not have enough grain left to meet their own food requirements for the year. This was to pay the 'single agricultural tax' (the old 'tax in kind' transformed into a monetary tax) and to be able to buy industrial goods (in particular, means of production, which the poor peasants badly needed, as has already been indicated). State encouragement of this grain marketing in the autumn by levying most of the tax then meant that the period October to December was normally the period of lowest prices. Richer peasants could pay their taxes, buy manufactured goods and still afford to delay their grain sales till January, when the price started to rise. Some even brought grain in the autumn from poor peasants to resell in the spring at higher prices. Thus the conditions of production, in terms of access to the means of production, affected the timing of sales. However, the time of sale was more important than before the war because the price differential between autumn and spring was greater: a clear effect of state pricing policy. Furthermore, this low autumn price was achieved by means of the monetary agricultural tax (creating a need for money) and by the timing of the supply of manufactured goods to the countryside. It was for such reasons that the terms of trade remained poor for the countryside throughout almost all of NEP: the 'scissors' never quite closed. This combination of factors meant that the poorest terms of trade were offered to the poor and middle peasants who sold in the autumn. Consequently they could buy fewer means of production with which to escape their dependence on the kulaks. This normal state of affairs was known, and should have been a particularly important element in national planning, since around 80 per cent of the marketed grain came from the poor and middle peasants.

The amount of grain produced and marketed could thus have been increased by offering a higher grain price in the autumn and ensuring that most of the manufactured goods sold (especially means of production) went to poor and middle peasants. This was not done, partly because of a mistaken feeling about the economic incapacity of the small peasant farm (as opposed to the larger kulak farm) which implied that investment of that kind would not yield very good results. In addition, as we have already seen, the view was widely held that the 'goods famine' of 1923 had been caused by the fact that industry was weak and needed in effect to be subsidised by cheap imports of agricultural raw materials. (It should be noted that the failure to support poor and middle peasants completely negated Lenin's conception of providing them with access to the means of production, within a framework of commercial co-operatives, as part of the strategy for collectivisation and industrialisation.)[99] These mistakes were compounded in 1925 by the lowering of the agricultural tax, which meant that, despite the high prices of that autumn, many poor peasants had no incentive to sell. Roughly one-quarter of the grain marketed in the autumn normally came from peasants who were cutting into their own foodstocks and had to buy back grain at higher prices in the spring.[100]

It was precisely in the autumn of 1925 that the state offered only a few manufactured products, mostly of low quality, and mostly sold in an 'obligatory lot', where they were mixed with products such as perfume and wine glasses that could otherwise not be sold.[101] The result was that the majority of peasants covered their own needs, including rebuilding their depleted reserve stocks, instead of selling. The real purchasing power of the peasantry remained lower than before the war, but that of the working class was higher. Consequently the so-called 'goods famine' which recurred in 1925–6 was due to the absorption of manufactured goods in the industrial cities of the north and north-east of European Russia and the surrounding agricultural areas. In other parts of the countryside, the shortage of such goods was an absolute one.[102] This lack of goods largely explains the apparent economic incapacity of the small-scale peasant farms, a situation exacerbated by the fact that agricultural implements were simply wearing out by the mid-1920s. The conditions of a technical alliance between agriculture and industry, which could have resolved the problems of both, were simply not being met. In particular, small-scale rural industry was being neglected, even though it could have supplied agricultural means of production in a way which reduced transport costs. Furthermore, the production of larger-scale industry had not been devoted to replacing these means of production, though this should have been possible even prior to the establishment in 1925 of a national economic plan. Instead, large-scale industry devoted to *consumption goods* had been given priority in the period 1922–5. The 1925 grain crisis was thus largely the result of the failure to supply agricultural means of production to the peasantry.[103] The lesson that the correct price structure and the correct product-mix were necessary to stimulate grain production and marketing was not lost on some agricultural commentators, or on some party leaders.[104]

The measures taken to resolve the problems indicated by the 1925–6 grain crisis confirm that the main causes of such problems lay in factors which the state was capable of regulating methodically. Apart from the immediate economy measures taken early in 1926, the 1926–7 grain procurement campaign shows that this lesson had been learned. The agricultural tax was raised again, and it was collected mostly in the autumn and winter months. Urban wage increases were avoided, so that urban demand for manufactured goods did not grow, while the supply of such goods was increased, and it was directed to the villages of the grain-surplus areas. Furthermore, state and co-operative costs of grain marketing were reduced considerably as the number of such agencies were reduced and their organisation improved. This meant that such agencies could compete with private traders, forcing the latter to reduce their prices. Finally, the difference between winter and spring prices almost completely disappeared, undercutting the main basis for grain speculation. Marketed grain reached a post-war record, but unfortunately grain reserves were not built up. There were criticisms at the time that the purchase price from the peasantry had been too low, encouraging the sale of other products (especially those from livestock rearing).[105] Such criticisms were based on the idea of exporting grain as a source of investment funds (to pay for imports of machinery). However, having missed its chance in 1925, the Soviet Union was in no position to base its export strategy on grain, since the world demand was already being largely met from other countries. There was every reason to export wood and butter instead. In this sense the Soviet concentration on grain production for exports was misplaced.

Yet, accepting that grain was in fact the main focus of export efforts, the measures adopted during 1927 were at first sight astonishing. Although it was known that grain reserves had not been built up at the beginning of 1927, no attempt was made to do so when more grain came on the market during the summer of 1927. Furthermore, instead of supplying manufactured goods to the countryside, especially to the grain-surplus areas, in the autumn of 1927 the rural markets were emptied of such goods to supply the towns, where real purchasing power had gone up again. At the same time private trade in industrial products was severely limited by administrative measures (instead of state competition in terms of supply and price) so that there was no alternative source of such goods for the countryside. This meant that the 'goods famine' reappeared in worse form than ever. Finally, the agricultural tax, which had been raised, was again lowered to celebrate the tenth anniversary of the Revolution. Hence all the conditions for a grain crisis were again present. The monthly pattern of grain sales for the second half of 1927 shows that from July to October they were very similar to the same period for 1926, but this was a time when stocks should have been rebuilt. Even by October sales were down slightly on October 1926. For November and December the sales were much more like the pattern for 1925.[106] Hence at the time of the very important Fifteenth Party Congress, when the policy for industrialisation and collectivisation was being debated, a new grain crisis was developing. However, this was not clear to the majority of the delegates to that Congress.[107] The problem only became clear when the December figures were made more widely available in January 1928.

The Crisis and Demise of NEP

One of the reasons for the difficulty in building reserve stocks of grain during the summer of 1927 had been a war scare, which had emptied the shops and markets. This may also explain why rural markets were emptied to supply urban ones, but such feelings of panic do not seem to have affected the grain procurement agencies. They appear to have imagined that problems of grain marketing could be readily overcome. The reaction of the Central Committee was different. Under Stalin's direction a series of 'extraordinary measures' were taken to ensure that the planned amounts of grain were collected. Such coercive administrative measures effectively bypassed the normal grain procurement agencies. It is important to realise that such agencies could well have resolved the problem by raising prices, a solution ruled out as one which would encourage speculation the following year. However, there had been a bad harvest in the grain-surplus areas (except Siberia) and a very good harvest, even of grain, in the grain-deficit areas where industrial crops were grown. Contrary to the directives of the plan (which envisaged encouraging grain production) the gap between (higher-priced) industrial crops and (lower-priced) grain had scarcely been reduced. So the good grain crop from what were normally grain-deficit areas was not marketed, since the peasants preferred to sell the higher-priced industrial crops and build up their grain reserves. This possibility of resolving the problem by economic means was disregarded. Despite the earlier improvements in their organisation, the grain procurement agencies were accused of inefficiency and of engaging in cut-throat competition, thereby contributing to a rise in prices. There was probably still a lot of truth in such accusations,[108] but this was hardly a reason for handing over their functions to the party. Instead of adjusting prices of grain, the 'extraordinary measures', supposedly directed only against kulaks, were introduced. These involved requisitions using methods reminiscent of War Communism.

These requisitions had three important effects in the first half of 1928. First, peasants even in the (normally) grain-surplus areas were able to buy a lot more grain than was usual. Such village purchases were 40 per cent greater than in the previous year. Second, the 'extraordinary measures' led to unexpected losses of grain. The result of these two effects was that the 'grain surplus' reaching the state and the towns declined more than did grain production, and instead of increasing by the 14 per cent originally planned, this surplus went down by 18.5 per cent.[109] The other main effect was a reduction in sown area, accompanied by serious peasant unrest as the majority of the peasantry (not just the kulaks) saw their grain reserves and even their consumption stocks being requisitioned. The way to avoid this, it seemed to many, was to sow less in the hope that those with no grain reserves would be left alone next time. Consequently there was a reduction in winter grain sowings and in livestock holdings in 1928, since without grain livestock could not be fed over the winter months.

There were attempts to counteract this vicious circle of coercion. A campaign was begun in 1928 to increase sown area, and it involved *sel'sovety*, district executive committees and party organisations. During this campaign, a new method was tried, which had been started in 1927 for industrial crops. There had up to now been three main channels for obtaining grain from the peasants: purchase at market price by state agencies; procurement, where the peasant sold to a nominated government agency at a state-fixed price; and 'contracta-tion'.[110] The use of the latter method was now intensified, being spread from industrial crops to other crops. Yet it did not help to counteract the tendency for sown area to be reduced. The 'contractation' method had the potential to help improve agriculture. In return for agreeing to supply the state with an agreed minimum of grain at fixed prices, which were subject to increase according to quality and date of delivery, the state or co-operative undertook to make payments on future sales, lend seed grain, and facilitate the purchase of equipment. The state might also supply agronomic aid. It was believed in the Polit-buro that the contractation system would serve as an excellent lever for collectivisation.[111] However, the state did not fulfil its side of the contracts, and in 1928 the effect of contractation on agriculture was negligible. Yet although it was related to con-tractation, a drive to encourage the growth of *kolkhozy* and *sovkhozy* in 1928 proved much more successful. It had been noticed that these marketed almost half their production, which was four times more than the average peasant farm. The supplying of various advantages to the rural poor attracted thousands of them into *kolkhozy*, showing how such a policy could have worked earlier in NEP if some resources had been provided to back it up. Even at this point, the financial re-sources allocated were only some 60 million roubles, the cost of building a single factory.[112] The size of this movement caught the *sel'sovety* and party organisations offguard, and the pro-cess of developing a national administration for *kolkhozy* took place only gradually during 1928. Within the *kolkhozy*, there was still a lot of private production, due to a lack of means of production which could be used collectively, as well as due to inexperience and an inability to organise properly. Nevertheless such *kolkhozy* could have increased their production with continued state help, and the movement continued to grow on a voluntary basis until about the middle of 1929 (after which it becomes difficult to distinguish between the effects of voluntary and forced collectivisation, until the end of the year, when forced collectivisation was clearly predominant).

The other measure taken in 1928 to stimulate production was the decision to set up huge *sovkhozy*. This was followed in 1929 by a decision to rehabilitate the old *sovkhozy* as well, under a new administration with considerable resources. However, these measures to counteract the reduction in sown area and in production did not on the whole produce the intended results. The 1928 harvest was again a poor one. The crisis produced a series of splits between different state agencies, and was associated with a growing split within the Politburo. Since the Five Year Plan was not yet ready, there was no overall framework within which to co-ordinate policy implementation, apart from the control figures for 1929. Consequently the Politburo more and more took on the role of adjudicating between, say, the Commissariats of Agriculture and Trade. It took the initiative in an increasing number of fields of economic policy, but was also preoccupied with the struggles between agencies responsible for planning, notably struggles between *Gosplan*, *Vesenkha* and *Sovnarkom*.[113] These struggles were related to the struggle within the Politburo itself, between Stalin on the one hand and Bukharin and Rykov on the other.

Owing to a dearth of seed corn, the poor harvest of the autumn of 1928 was accompanied by a drop in the winter sowings of wheat. This meant that an attempt had to be made to make up the loss in the spring sowing of 1929, but the campaign to do so had only limited success. Rationing was tightened up in February 1929, but the rations were inadequate, forcing workers to buy on the free market. Pressure on *Nepmen* forced many of them to close down, but they then operated illegally, further disrupting the supply system. The worsening urban situation was combined with rural unrest and passive resistance. These were related to the use of 'Urals–Siberian methods', which were the continuation of the requisition methods of the previous year. Rural party and state agencies were also disrupted by a series of purges which had been going on since the beginning of 1928.[114] New higher prices for grain were introduced in 1929, but in the highly price-sensitive field of agriculture this had the effect of leading to a reduction in industrial and other food crops, with the result that parts of the food industry and light industry were adversely affected, at a time of increased urban demand for food and raw materials created by the incipient process of rapid industrialisation.[115] The private sector, rather than state pricing and procurement policy, was once again blamed for this and for the decline in livestock production.

A way out of these problems seemed to be presented by the growing success of the collectivisation programme, especially between June and October 1929. This was largely due to a June reorganisation of the co-operative and *kolkhoz* administrative structures. However, a major instrument in this growing collectivisation was the contractation system, which increasingly became merely an instrument of state coercion. Coupled with this was the concentration of agricultural credits on the collective and state sectors, but the bulk of this credit and of tractors went to the new large *kolkhozy* and *sovkhozy* (the 'grain factories') rather than the peasant *kolkhoz* associations. Yet despite these efforts (which were in any case accompanied by much administrative confusion), the grain procurements campaign did not go all that well, at least in the early months. There had been a serious attempt to improve the efficiency of the procurement campaign, with a reorganisation of the procurement agencies to prevent the kind of cut-throat competition and mutual obstruction which had frequently characterised their actions in the past. Furthermore, there were large stocks of consumer goods ready to be released on fulfilment of delivery quotas.[116] However, by mid-September, *Pravda* was reporting that autumn sowing was going badly because peasants were afraid to bring the seed to government cleaning stations, for fear that it would be confiscated. In addition, in some districts only 17 per cent of procurements were being fulfilled, partly because of black-market selling, but partly because of poor organisation of local authorities, which were slow with grain procurements, and had not prepared enough storage space, transport or technical facilities (including weighing machines).[117] Thus the reorganisation in the centre seems to have had only limited effects in the rural localities, which is perhaps not surprising since local levels of party and state administration had suffered a series of purges. This lack of organisation became fully evident at the end of September, when the first report appeared of wheat rotting in railway sidings. Even *kolkhozy* and *sovkhozy* were hiding their stores from the procurement brigades, and some *kolkhozy* were disbanded as a punitive measure. The crisis worsened in October, with *kolkhozy* being the worst defaulters in fulfilling their quotas, this being one indication among others that poor peasants were hit hardest by the requisitions.

While grain was rotting in the open or in railway wagons all over the country, and while resistance of peasants and sometimes local party authorities grew, workers' brigades were reorganised into large armed detachments. This was around mid-October, and was a response to the growing number of outbreaks of violent resistance to the requisitions. In this context, collectivisation took on a punitive character as a response to the resistance to forced requisitions. Beginning in November *Pravda* started to announce that whole districts were being collectivised, and it published an article by Stalin on 7 November. The main victory for Stalin's line occurred in November, with the removal of Bukharin from the Politburo, and the decision of the Central Committee to set up a commission to develop full collectivisation. This commission met on 8 December,[118] the day after Mikoyan, who was in charge of state procurement policy, announced that procurements were up to 16 million tons, compared with 10.8 million tons in 1928, even though the harvest had been poorer in 1929.[119]

Clearly there had been a dramatic turn-round in procurements, showing that the armed detachments had been highly effective. This task force could now be used for collectivisation. However, it was not immediately clear that it would be. The commission did not submit its first draft to the Politburo until 22 December. Interestingly, this was two days after the start of the First All-Union Conference of Agrarian Marxists in Moscow[120] at which the rural class structure was being debated. Since there were divisions within the commission as to the pace of collectivisation and the severity of treatment of kulaks, the Agrarian Marxist Conference could conceivably have supplied academic support for those urging a slower pace and more lenient treatment of kulaks.[121] It was almost certainly for this reason that Stalin appeared at the end of the Conference on 27 October 1929 to announce that the kulaks were to be liquidated as a class. At about the same time, the commission was being told to redraft its proposals to recommend a maximum pace and severe treatment of kulaks, including deportation to the worst districts where they might not even receive the smallest plot of the worst soil. The relevant decree was issued by the Politburo on 5 January 1930.

The decision to proceed with mass forced collectivisation, probably taken by Stalin in late October, thus required two months of manoeuvring to get it accepted by the rest of the Politburo. The increased coercion was necessary in November to overcome peasant resistance to forced requisitions, but this could not be admitted since (not surprisingly in view of the experiences of 1920 and 1921) some Central Committee critics and the expelled opposition leaders had been predicting just such an outcome – hence the excuse that peasants were rebelling against collectivisation and not against requisitions. It should be clear by now that a voluntary collective movement had been gaining support up to about June 1929. Yet the requisitions rather than the *kolkhozy* had delivered the goods. The problem was that the process of breaking peasant resistance could not be continued by requisitions, whose negative economic effects had been repeatedly shown. This is the reason for the move, from late October onwards, to reorganise agriculture radically to 'ensure' that the planned deliveries would take place during the industrialisation process.

Conclusion

The situation at the end of 1929 was very different from that just before the beginning of NEP. First, while agriculture only had 80 per cent of its 1913 level of traction power, because of the livestock situation (a problem that was to worsen as livestock was slaughtered during the forced collectivisation process), it

had finally attained its 1913 level in machinery and implements.[122] It had already been demonstrated in 1925 that
roughly the 1913 level of agricultural production could be
reached with fewer means of production. Consequently despite
all the problems agriculture was not in the catastrophic and
declining condition that it had endured at the end of 1920. In
this sense it could 'afford' to some extent the setback caused by
forced collectivisation. Nevertheless, after collectivisation rural
consumption declined dramatically and state procurements
were no better and were possibly worse than they had been
before collectivisation. Thus collectivisation contributed
nothing to the industrialisation strategy of the First Five Year
Plan. Second, despite the difficulties in drawing up the plan and
in constructing state agencies capable of implementing the plan
in various economic sectors in a reasonably co-ordinated way,
the plan did have a significant impact. Not only did it generate
its own investment funds by developing various measures for a
more effective use of existing productive capacity (such as cost
reductions, productivity increases, widening basic supply
bottlenecks), but it was also a sufficiently effective allocating
mechanism to be able to replace, in effect, the 'free-market'
commodity relations between agriculture and industry which
had characterised NEP. In other words, it was able to secure
the technical reproduction of the economy, despite the damage
to agriculture. Thus it achieved the aim of the policies which
had been tried and failed during the 1920 experiment in 'proletarian natural economy'. The knowledge that this was technically and administratively possible clearly encouraged those
impatient with NEP to end the dependence on small-scale
peasant agriculture. The tragedy is that these industrialisation
measures *and* voluntary collectivisation could probably both
have been achieved, if only market interventions and rural
political work had been better planned and implemented, as
functions of the original NEP strategy. Instead, the development of an apparatus capable of pushing through forced collectivisation in the early 1930s had a disastrous effect on the
development of democracy. The Soviet Union today still bears
the marks of this experience.

Notes

1. See M. Harrison, 'The Soviet Economy in the 1920s and 1930s', *Capital and Class*, no. 5, 1978; S. Grosskopf, *L'Alliance Ouvrière et Paysanne en URSS: Le Problème du Blé*, Maspero, Paris, 1976; A. Hussain and K. Tribe, *Marxism and the Agrarian Question*, vol. 2, Macmillan, London, 1981; G. Littlejohn, 'The Agrarian Marxist Research in its Political Context: The Soviet Rural Class Structure in the 1920s', *Journal of Peasant Studies*, vol. 11, no. 2, January 1984.

2. See O. Narkiewicz, *The Making of the Soviet State Apparatus*, University of Manchester Press, Manchester, 1970; and M. Lewin, *Russian Peasants and Soviet Power*, Allen & Unwin, London, 1968, ch. 16.

3. D. G. Atkinson, 'The Russian Land Commune and the Revolution', unpublished Ph.D. dissertation, Stanford University, 1971, p. 149. I am grateful to Colin Darch for lending me his microfilm photocopy of this invaluable work. The commune was indispensable at this time because it provided the only available mechanism for confiscation and redistribution of land which could offer a hope (not always realised) of avoiding violence. There were effectively no other competent agencies.

4. Ibid, pp. 150–1.

5. Ibid, p. 155.

6. Ibid, p. 157.

7. Ibid, p. 160.

8. Atkinson, 'The Russian Land Commune', p. 160. Atkinson attributes the loss of technical efficiency partly to the lack of inventory of the smallholder peasant, and partly to the loss of economies of scale (presumably due to the break-up of gentry property). This corroborates the arguments advanced by L. Kritsman, *Proletarskaya Revolyutsia i Derevnya*, Moscow, 1929, by Grosskopf, *L'Alliance Ouvrière*; and by Hussain and Tribe, *Marxism and the Agrarian Question*; M. Dobb, *Russian Economic Development since the Revolution*, London, 1928, p. 340, also states: 'In the village the redistribution of land after the October revolution had considerably equalised peasant land holdings; but inequalities in ownership of stock and implements remained; and NEP gave possibilities for these inequalities to increase and for the rise of a class of rich peasants, cultivating more land because they had more equipment, and lending stock, implements and seed at onerous rates to their needy brethren.' Atkinson later (p. 193) reiterates the point that many peasants who had received land during the 'black redivision' were without the tools and animal power necessary to work it.

9. Atkinson, 'The Russian Land Commune', p. 161.

10. Ibid, p. 162.

11. Ibid, p. 168.

12. Ibid, pp. 166–7.

13. Ibid, p. 171. For a further discussion of the effects of the *Kombedy*, see the extracts from Kritsman's *Geroicheskii Period Velikoi Russkoi Revolyutsii* (1925), which are reprinted in Kritsman, *Proletarskaya Revolyutsia*, pp. 79–106. Unfortunately, the full Russian version is not

available to me, but for those who read German, it is available as Kritsman, *Die heroische Periode der Grossen russischen Revolution*, Verlag Neue Kritik, Frankfurt, 1971. The Russian version is referred to (along with a book by Larin and Kritsman) both in Dobb, *Russian Economic Development*, and in Dobb, *Soviet Economic Development Since 1917*, Routledge & Kegan Paul, London, 1966.

14. Atkinson, 'The Russian Land Commune', p. 173. According to Kritsman, this challenge of the *Kombedy* to the domination of the village commune by the wealthier peasants was not only implicit; at times it was explicit, as can be seen, for example, in L. Kritsman, 'Class Stratification of the Soviet Countryside', *Journal of Peasant Studies*, vol. 11, no. 2, October 1984.

15. Atkinson, 'The Russian Land Commune', p. 174.

16. For the geographical distribution of Lenin's famous 'two roads' of capitalist development, which clearly locates the 'capitalist peasantry' road in the Ukraine and the South in general, see the maps in S. M. Shipley, 'The Sociology of the Peasantry, Populism and the Russian Peasant Commune', unpublished M. Litt. thesis, University of Lancaster, 1979. Atkinson, 'The Russian Land Commune', p. 68, in her discussion of the Stolypin reforms, shows that within Great Russia the provinces which had the highest land prices and the highest proportion of separations from the commune following the Stolypin Reform were in the Southern Steppe provinces. This can be taken as a rough index of the extent of peasant capitalist development in these areas between 1906 and 1914, and fits well with the map of the percentages of private agricultural property in 1916 which is provided by S. Grosskopf, *L'Alliance Ouvrière*, p. 71. C. Darch, 'Saddle Rugs for Shrouds' (unpublished, n.d.) points out that the 'anarchist communes' of Nestor Makhno during the civil war were located in the Ukraine, an area where capitalist relations were quite developed. The 'landlord's transition' road, which was the alternative form of capitalist development mentioned by Lenin, being a slow capitalist transformation of the 'feudal latifundia' (or gentry land, as Atkinson calls it), was located mainly in the central agricultural areas, where the village commune was strongest. The pre-revolutionary association of village communes with large semi-feudal estates was by no means accidental: see Shipley, 'The Sociology of the Peasantry', and Atkinson, 'The Russian Land Commune'.

17. Kritsman, *Proletarskaya Revolyutsia*, p. 91.

18. Ibid, p. 85.

19. This is Kritsman's phrase: ibid, p. 93.

20. Ibid, p. 94.

21. Atkinson, 'The Russian Land Commune', p. 174. She points out that in the central agricultural area, where the communes were strongest, the poor peasants were most radical and the potential for rupture (with the kulaks) was greatest.

22. Ibid, p. 173.

23. Kritsman, *Proletarskaya Revolyutsia*, p. 91, footnote.

24. Atkinson, 'The Russian Land Commune', p. 178.
25. Kritsman, *Proletarskaya Revolyutsia*, p. 94–106.
26. Ibid, p. 102.
27. Hussain and Tribe, *Marxism and the Agrarian Question*, p. 104. They acknowledge that the term derives originally from Kritsman, but point out that they are deviating from Kritsman's original use of the term.
28. In the absence of aid coming after a revolution in the West, either the Bolsheviks would have lost control of the state, or they would have somehow managed to implement their policy of 'proletarian natural economy' in the face of the peasant resistance. If the latter course of action had been successfully pursued, presumably the consequences would have been worse than the forced collectivisation of the early 1930s: perhaps the tragic catastrophe in Kampuchea of the Pol Pot regime's attempt at what might be called a 'peasant natural economy' is a guide as to what could have happened if the Bolsheviks had continued with a policy of forcible suppression of commodity relations, in the face of peasant resistance. It is difficult to see how the voluntaristic suppression of commodity relations, in the absence of adequate planning and supply mechanisms to replace them, can lead to anything other than disaster.
29. Hussain and Tribe, *Marxism and the Agrarian Question*, p. 116.
30. Ibid, p. 110.
31. See Atkinson, 'The Russian Land Commune', pp. 187–201 for details.
32. Ibid, p. 193. The figures in brackets refer to *sovkhozy* which were directly 'ascribed' to other institutions or enterprises for the purpose of supplying them with foodstuffs or raw materials essential for industrial operations.
33. Ibid, p. 196.
34. Ibid, p. 197.
35. Ibid, p. 188.
36. This is not to deny that certain techniques of planning, such as material balances, had already been developed to some extent. Groman had begun work on this in 1923 and continued the work in Gosplan until 1928 or 1929: see N. Jasny, *Soviet Economists of the Twenties: Names to be Remembered*, Cambridge University Press, 1972, ch. 6. The point is that such techniques were not being used in an institutionally effective manner until the drafting of the first Five Year Plan.
37. Atkinson, 'The Russian Land Commune', p. 200.
38. Ibid, pp. 207–8. 'Land organisation' involved the allotment of lands to *volosti* (administrative sub-units of Provinces) and to village communes. Work on the elimination of narrow strips and land holdings distant from the peasant households who held them was a relatively minor part of the early efforts of *Tsentrozem* in 1919–21. This was the agency under *Narkomzem* (the People's Commissariat of Agriculture) which was responsible for land organisation work. By 1921, however, in addition to an existing official prohibition on redistributing land, *Tsentrozem* increased this programme elimination of narrow strips and distant lands. This work became its most important activity in terms of

the area involved. At the same time, the allotment of land to *sovkhozy* and *kolkhozy* remained a minor though steadily increasing function.

39. Ibid, p. 211.
40. Ibid, p. 227.
41. Ibid, p. 230. Atkinson describes some of these measures, but does not treat them as limiting the prospects of capitalist development within the *mir*.
42. Ibid, pp. 233–4.
43. Ibid, pp. 239–40.
44. For a discussion of the 1921 harvest and a comparison to the harvest failure of 1891, see Grosskopf, *L'Alliance Ouvrière*; see also Hussain and Tribe, *Marxism and the Agrarian Question*, on the effects of the 1921 famine as well as Kritsman, *Proletarskaya Revolyutsia i Derevnya, passim*.
45. L. Kritsman, *Tri Goda Novoi E konomicheskoi Politiki*, 1924, an extract of which is reprinted on pp. 106–16 of Kritsman, *Proletarskaya Revolyutsia i Derevnya*. See also Dobb, *Russian Economic Development*, on the recovery of agriculture up to 1925.
46. Kritsman, *Proletarskaya Revolyutsia i Derevnya*, p. 109.
47. Ibid, pp. 109–10. See also Hussain and Tribe, *Marxism and the Agrarian Question*, pp. 110–11.
48. Kritsman, *Proletarskaya Revolyutsia i Derevnya*, pp. 110–12.
49. Dobb, *Russian Economic Development*, ch. 8, and Dobb, *Soviet Economic Development*, ch. 7, p. 156. See p. 222 of Dobbm *Russian Economic Development*, or p. 164 of Dobb, *Soviet Economic Development*, for the Gosplan graph of the 'scissors' crisis based on the figures provided by S. Strumilin. Dobb provides an excellent discussion of the debates at the time on the nature and causes of the 'scissors' crisis and general inflation in 1923.
50. Hussain and Tribe, *Marxism and the Agrarian Question*, p. 110. In addition, there was a loss of goods through theft, which was made easier because of transport dislocation.
51. Ibid, p. 121. On the supply of machinery and implements to agriculture, see Grosskopf, *L'Alliance Ouvrière*, pp. 238–46.
52. Dobb, *Soviet Economic Development*, p. 176. See also the graph in Grosskopf, *L'Alliance Ouvrière*, p. 195, which shows the extension of the scissors crisis up to at least 1927.
53. Dobb is aware of the lack of means of production among the poor and middle peasantry at this time: see note 8 above. However, he does not relate the product-mix of trade between industry and agriculture to the problem of the terms of trade. It was not cheap goods of any kind that the poor and middle peasants needed and wanted, it was cheap means of production.
54. For illustration of this, see Kritsman, 'The Class Stratification of the Soviet Countryside', *Journal of Peasant Studies, passim*. According to Solomon, Kritsman developed this point at greater length in another book published in 1925. See S. G. Solomon, 'Controversy in Social Science: Soviet Rural Studies in the 1920s', *Minerva*, vol. XIII, no. 4,

1975, p. 568. I am grateful to Professor Solomon for sending me an offprint of this article. For further evidence of low participation rates by poor peasants in co-operatives see Narkiewicz, *The Making of the Soviet State Apparatus*, pp. 69–71, and Grosskopf, *L'Alliance Ouvrière*, pp. 292–7.

55. Kritsman, *Proletarskaya Revolyutsia i Derevnya*, p. 114.
56. C. Bettelheim, *Class Struggles in the USSR*, Harvester, Brighton, 1978, vol. 2, implies that these unemployed should have been taken on anyway by industry, but it is not clear that this would have done anything other than raise the costs of industry, leading to a 'scissors'-type pressure on industrial prices.
57. Atkinson, 'The Russian Land Commune', p. 242. She points out that the journal *Kollektivist* in 1925 referred to 'khutormania' in Byelorussia.
58. Kritsman, *Proletarskaya Revolyutsia i Derevnya*, p. 115.
59. Ibid, pp. 115–16.
60. Thus Kritsman in his 1924 article pointed out that NEP was not only a period of 'primary socialist accumulation' but also of 'primary capitalist accumulation'. He did not make it clear who the target of this criticism was, but it was presumably Preobrazhensky. The point is that while he disagreed with such a position as that of Preobrazhensky, it is clear that Kritsman's own analysis deployed similar concepts and was consequently only able to conceive of *one kind* of development of market relations, favouring the kulaks. A similar tendency towards a sectoral analysis is evident at points in Kritsman's 'Class Stratification of the Soviet Countryside', which suggests that Hussain and Tribe, *Marxism and the Agrarian Question*, p. 144, may be misleading when they suggest that Preobrazhensky initiated the line of analysis based on distinct sectors, which has certain theoretical affiliations with the 'articulation of modes of production' approach. Preobrazhensky may well have been simply the most systematic exponent of a line of thinking among the Bolsheviks which identified the process of socialist transformation with the growth of the 'state sector' at the expense of the 'capitalist sector'. For a discussion of Preobrazhensky's position see K. Smith, 'Introduction to Bukharin: Economic Theory and the Closure of the Soviet Industrialisation Debate', *Economy and Society*, vol. 8, no. 4, November 1979, pp. 446–72.
61. See Atkinson, 'The Russian Land Commune', p. 242. She points out that *khutors* and *otrubs* nevertheless continued to grow in the north-west (around Pskov) during the 1920s. By 1929 they covered 44 per cent of land in the Pskov district.
62. Ibid, p. 244.
63. Ibid, p. 245. Special regulations for this process of reversion from *khutor* to village commune appeared from *Narkomzem* in 1927.
64. See L. Kritsman, *O Samarskom Obsledovanie* (1928), reprinted in *Proletarskaya Revolyutsia i Derevnya*, pp. 342–57. This work (*On the Samara Research*) was the introduction to the book by I. Vermenichev, A. Gaister and G. Raevich, *710 Khozyaistv Samarskoi Derevnyi* (*710 Farms of the Samara Countryside*) Moscow. In the Introduction,

(on p. 344 of the 1929 reprint) Kritsman notes that 19 per cent of farms were either taking on or hiring out time workers, while the total for this (if one included hiring of daily and seasonal wage-labour without livestock or inventory) was 58 per cent of farms. Relations of renting or hiring out of livestock and inventory included 91 per cent of farms. Renting in and leasing out of land covered 45 per cent of farms and credit relations covered 27 per cent of farms. This evidence indicated very strong capitalist relations in the countryside in Samara *Gubernia* (Province).

65. See note 54. See also Lewin, *Russian Peasants*, pp. 93–102, on the weak development of rural co-operation. He states 'There is agreement among reliable sources that the cooperative movement mainly served the interests of the better-off peasants' (p. 99). He points out that simple forms of collective production, and even the *kommuna, artel'* and *toz*, were flourishing *outside* the co-operative movement (pp. 100–1).

66. The phrase 'massive collapse' comes from a 1927 Communist Academy report on *kolkhozy*, quoted by Atkinson, 'The Russian Land Commune', p. 304. Lewin, *Russian Peasants*, p. 107, also mentions a decline in *kolkhozy*, but attributes part of this to a deliberate liquidation of some *kolkhozy* by local authorities who only 'imperfectly understood' NEP. According to Lewin, there was an appreciable drop in the number of *kolkhozy* in 1923, this being most marked in the case of the *kommuna*, and less so in respect of the *artel'*; on the other hand, the *tozy* continued to increase in number and in proportion to the total.

67. Lewin, *Russian Peasants*, p. 108, from which the account in the rest of this paragraph is taken.

68. Atkinson, 'The Russian Land Commune', p. 305. Lewin, *Russian Peasants*, pp. 117–18, discusses the same decree, pointing out that in practical terms the help given was small. Yet it does seem to have been a turning-point.

69. Lewin, *Russian Peasants*, p. 108. Lewin estimates that there was around 18 000 *kolkhozy* by the end of 1927. Both Lewin and Atkinson draw attention to the differences in official estimates by different agencies of the number of *kolkhozy*.

70. Atkinson, 'The Russian Land Commune', p. 306.

71. Lewin, *Russian Peasants*, pp. 109–10, and Atkinson, 'The Russian Land Commune', pp. 193, 304.

72. Lewin, *Russian Peasants*, pp. 111–12. The 50 people amounts to about 12 families. Atkinson, 'The Russian Land Commune', p. 308, puts the average size of *kolkhozy* at about 13 members (families or individuals) in mid-1927 and barely 18 members two years later.

73. Atkinson, 'The Russian Land Commune', pp. 306–7. Admittedly the last year must also include credit to collectives during the period of forced collectivisation.

74. Ibid, p. 306. It is not clear what the effect of this measure was.

75. Ibid, p. 309.

76. Ibid, p. 312.

77. Narkiewicz, *The Making of the Soviet State Apparatus*, p. 193 and

appendix IV, pp. 220–23. However, these higher figures seem to be related to the beginning of forced collectivisation from October 1929, before the official decision of the Central Committee commission on 'complete collectivisation', in January 1930.

78. Atkinson, 'The Russian Land Commune', p. 247.
79. Ibid, p. 249.
80. Ibid, p. 250. Narkiewicz, *The Making of the Soviet State Apparatus*, pp. 135–7, provides further detailed evidence from Smolensk on the weakness of the election campaign and points out that the second elections sometimes produced a poorer turn-out than the first. However, the general result was a higher turn-out of around 47 per cent in this area.
81. Atkinson, 'The Russian Land Commune', p. 251.
82. Ibid, p. 252.
83. Ibid, p. 253.
84. Ibid, pp. 253–4. Atkinson provides comparative data showing ratios of 12 rural soviet to 96 village commune meetings, 119 to 802, 8 to 22, 278 to 1039, 3 to 71, 13 to 82, and so on. See also Narkiewicz, *The Making of the Soviet State Apparatus*, pp. 137–8, for corroborative material on the Smolensk area. Lewin, *Russian Peasants*, ch. 4, pp. 81–93, also discusses these issues.
85. Atkinson, 'The Russian Land Commune', p. 254.
86. Narkiewicz, *The Making of the Soviet State Apparatus*, p. 138.
87. Ibid, p. 139, and Atkinson, 'The Russian Land Commune', p. 258. Lewin, *Russian Peasants*, p. 89, also mentions the figure of 100 million roubles.
88. Atkinson, 'The Russian Land Commune', p. 256, and Narkiewicz, *The Making of the Soviet State Apparatus*, p. 132.
89. Atkinson, 'The Russian Land Commune', p. 255.
90. Ibid, p. 260.
91. Narkiewicz, *The Making of the Soviet State Apparatus*, p. 140.
92. See Lewin, *Russian Peasants*, pp. 119–20 for details.
93. Ibid, p. 122.
94. Ibid, p. 125.
95. Ibid, p. 126.
96. Grosskopf, *L'Alliance Ouvrière*, pp. 119–20. Overall production was 104 per cent of the volume of 1913, but the area sown in grain was only 90 per cent of the pre-war figure, while the area sown in industrial and intensive crops was 128 per cent of the 1913 figure. Livestock production was also increasing.
97. Ibid, pp. 120, 123.
98. Ibid, pt II, ch. 2, on which this account draws heavily, as does the account of Hussain and Tribe, *Marxism and the Agrarian Question*, ch. 4. A review of the Tribe and Hussain work (P. Bew and C. Roulston, 'Land and the European Left', *Economy and Society*, vol. 11, no. 1, February 1982, pp. 60–8) considers it strange that they claim that the crisis of NEP began in 1925. In my view this is not what they are arguing. Rather, they are using Grosskopf's analysis to show that the *kind* of problem which characterised NEP did not arise for the first time in the

winter of 1927–8, when NEP entered a period of serious crisis which ended in it being abandoned.

99. Grosskopf, *L'Alliance Ouvrière*, pp. 156–9. This lack of support turned to open support of the kulaks, with the 'Provisional Ordinances' of April 1925. These 'Provisional Ordinances', associated with Bukharin's 'get rich' slogan, allowed kulaks to close down the farms of the poor peasants and to employ them as wage-labourers. This was presented as an 'enlargement of NEP' (neo-NEP) but was in fact a negation of the prior policy of support for the mass of the peasantry against kulak exploitation (ibid, pp. 316–17). This showed that the fears of Kritsman (discussed earlier) concerning lack of support to the poor peasantry in 1924 were well founded. With the promulgation of the 'Provisional Ordinances', as the poor peasants well understood, purchase of the means of production became very important. Conditions of wage labour for the kulaks were very hard (ibid, p. 317).

100. Ibid, p. 141. In 1923–4, 23.7 per cent of the marketed grain came from peasants with a 'negative grain balance'. Since the sown area of grain and the number of livestock were counted for tax-assessment purposes, while inventory (implements) was not, poor peasants had a further incentive to seek manufactured goods as a way of increasing production, rather than extending sown area or livestock. However, Grosskopf shows (on pp. 142, 169–71) that poor peasants sold most of their production to buy manufactured goods, rather than simply to pay the agricultural tax. In some grain-surplus provinces, this phenomenon reached the point in 1923, the year of the 'scissors crisis', where average consumption was only 60 per cent of the physiological minimum.

101. Ibid, p. 171.

102. Ibid, pt II, ch. 3, where Grosskopf produces a considerable amount of evidence to demonstrate this.

103. Ibid, p. 262.

104. Ibid, pp. 172, 260–1, for the analyses of the commentator Pistrak and party leader Dzerzhinskii respectively. Interestingly, Dzerzhinskii's remarks were in April 1925, before the autumn crisis.

105. Ibid, p. 329.

106. Ibid, p. 333.

107. According to Lewin, *Russian Peasants*, p. 210, only Mikoyan spoke openly of the bad news coming in from the rural areas, though the entire Politburo knew the facts.

108. Narkiewicz, *The Making of the Soviet State Apparatus*, p. 173, provides evidence on this.

109. Grosskopf, *L'Alliance Ouvrière*, pp. 337–9. See also Lewin, *Russian Peasants*, pp. 242–3.

110. Narkiewicz, *The Making of the Soviet State Apparatus*, p. 182.

111. Lewin, *Russian Peasants*, pp. 268–9.

112. Ibid, p. 271. Some of the movement into the *kolkhozy* in this year was because kulaks were no longer lending means of production to or renting land from the poor peasants, so their plight was unusually desperate in 1928. This was a repercussion of the grain requisitions, it seems.

113. See ibid, ch. 11, and Smith, 'Introduction to Bukharin', for differing views on the *Gosplan* and *Vesenkha* Five Year Plan drafts.
114. Lewin, *Russian Peasants*, pp. 383–95.
115. Ibid, p. 399.
116. Ibid, pp. 412–13.
117. Narkiewicz, *The Making of the Soviet State Apparatus*, pp. 189–90.
118. Ibid, p. 193.
119. Lewin, *Russian Peasants*, p. 414.
120. Solomon, 'Controversy in Social Science', pp. 554–82.
121. See Narkiewicz, *The Making of the Soviet State Apparatus*, pp. 192–8; and Lewin, *Russian Peasants*, ch. 16.
122. Grosskopf, *L'Alliance Ouvrière*, pp. 248, 249, 262. The number of tractors in 1929 was only around 35 000 as against 24 million horses and 4 million cattle. It was not until the mid-1930s that tractor production had any real impact on Soviet agriculture.

3
Economic Units and Economic Calculation: The Basis of Production Relations

Introduction

The purpose of this chapter is to explore the relative capacities of various economic agents. It was argued in Chapter 1 that a theory of the class structure could only demarcate the boundaries between economic agents on the basis of specifying important differences in their capacities for action, deriving from their relation to the means of production. Thus the relations of production, i.e. the relations operating between economic agents deriving from their differential access to the means of production, must be examined in some detail if one is to have adequate grounds for either claiming or denying that class relations exist. The relations between the agents concerned need not be exclusively interpersonal relations; indeed, they cannot be exclusively interpersonal if some of the economic agents are collective agents. If a monastic order can be a feudal landowner, or a joint-stock company can be a capitalist, then a theory of the relations of production which restricts itself to relations between human agents runs the risk of missing vital aspects of the social formation in question.

However, if it is accepted that non-human agents are potentially important in the relations of production, then the conditions of such agents must be analysed. If one is to avoid treating them in a rationalist manner, as a collective subject capable both of recognising the appropriate means to realise its ends and of acting on those means (for example, in the manner of Talcott Parsons's collectivities), then the following features of collective agents are pertinent to the formation of their objectives and their capacity to conduct a course of action in pursuit of those objectives.

First, *the internal form of their organisation*. Collective agents cannot be treated as unitary entities, and sub-agents within them may be crucial in affecting the relations of the collective agent with other agents.

Second, *their means of calculation*. Concepts which may be widely available in the social formation, or specially developed for the collective agent in question (or some admixture of the two) are necessary if the agent is to monitor its own internal state and to calculate courses of action with respect to other agents (for example, struggle over access to the means of production). Unless the means of calculation are treated as having some effects of their own, then the collective agent will in effect be analysed as if its objectives were the result of its 'consciousness', and as if the means of realising its ends were somehow directly observable in the real.

Third, *the resources at its disposal*. These resources may be 'internal' (that is, directly at its disposal) or may be accessible because of the economic location of the agent.

In addition to these considerations, which seem to be implicit in accepting that collective agents are pertinent to the relations of production, the examination of the relations of production in a planned economy carries other implications. Not only must one pay particular attention in such an economy to relations between non-human agents, examining their respective capacities, but one must consider whether class relations might operate directly between such collective agents, or between collective and individual agents, or finally between individual agents as a result of the relations between collective agents. Furthermore, in any economy with an advanced division of labour, one must assess the relations between units of production in agriculture and in industry, as well as retail distribution units, and units of social consumption (the latter is a category which includes families, as well as hospitals, schools and, in the case of the Soviet Union, cultural and holiday centres). However, as well as these kinds of collective agents, in the case of the Soviet Union one must also examine the capacities of the various state agencies involved in plan construction, and in the regulation of plan implementation. This is because Soviet national economic planning involves the attempt to co-ordinate the division of labour at the level of the overall social formation. If it is at all effective, it must have a major impact on the relations of production, either exacerbating or mitigating class relations. The means of economic calculation within all these various kinds of agencies involved in the construction and implementation of the overall economic plans will thus be a concern of this chapter, though units of consumption will be more the concern of Chapter 5.

The concern with the means of economic calculation in this chapter is not simply because it is relevant to the organisational forms of collective agents, but also because it is important for the analysis of policy formation and hence to the analysis of struggles between agencies. Ultimately, it is such struggles which determine the relative capacities of agents, so without neglecting both resources and organisational forms as determinants of the capacities of agents a particular concern of this chapter will be with forms of economic calculation. This is because different economic units (agents) use different means of calculation, and these cannot be totally unified (otherwise the distinct economic functions of different units would be nullified, i.e. there would be no division of labour).

This chapter is divided into two main sections: agriculture and industry. This is primarily because conditions in Soviet agriculture have historically 'lagged behind' those in industry, largely as a consequence of the policy of forced collectivisation of the peasantry at the beginning of the 1930s. Consequently the organisational forms and the capacities of agricultural economic units are different from those in industry. It is also important to examine agriculture carefully to be in a position to evaluate the official Soviet theory of the class structure, according to which collective farmers are in a different class from state employees. Because some agricultural units, the private plots and the collective farms, have a particular relation to urban consumption, there is a discussion of retailing units at the end of the section on agriculture. However, most of the chapter is devoted to industry, where the main units discussed are the state enterprises, production associations, Ministries and the central planning agencies.

Agriculture

The condition of agriculture in the Soviet Union is still a serious cause for concern, some half a century after the forced collectivisation of the peasantry. Partly this is due to the difficulties of making good the neglect of a generation, a process which really only started around 1965. Partly it is due to the positive damage done, not only by the forced collectivisation itself, but also by the 1941–5 war ('The Great Patriotic War') and later by Khrushchev's voluntarist attempts at a sudden improvement in agriculture. The inadequate performance of agriculture is also partly because of current policies, forms of planning and economic organisation, even though these have been improved since the fall of Khrushchev. Since this is not a book on Soviet agriculture, the developments before the 1960s will only be mentioned in passing, even though their impact on contemporary agriculture is still evident.[1]

The main changes in agriculture under Khrushchev were the abolition of the Machine Tractor Stations (MTSs) in 1958 and the conversion of many *kolkhozy*/(collective farms) into *sovkhozy*/(state farms), mostly between 1955 and 1962. The other related change was the increase in the size of the *kolkhozy*, often produced by amalgamating them into a single large one. However, as Stuart points out, structural change in agriculture has been going on since 1950.[2]

Table 3.1 provides a picture of the structural changes in agriculture.[3] At the end of 1981 there were 25.9 thousand *kolkhozy* and 21.6 thousand *sovkhozy*. The *sovkhozy* in 1977 had an average area of 5600 hectares each, whereas the average for *kolkhozy* was 3800 hectares, so although there were fewer *sovkhozy* in 1977, they formed 52.6 per cent of the agricultural area, with the *kolkhozy* forming 46.2 per cent and the remaining 1.2 per cent being constituted by the 'personal plots' of *kolkhozniki* (collective farm workers), workers and employees. The personal plots produce just over 25 per cent of all agricultural output, specialising in vegetables, meat, milk and eggs. An adequate class analysis of Soviet agriculture must confront the issue of the interrelation of these three forms of property, as well as their relation to other agencies such as the planning and supply agencies, the *kolkhoz* market, and so on. Unless this is

Table 3.1   Number of enterprises and agricultural organisations

	1927	1940	1950	1977	1979
Kolkhozy (in thousands)	14.8	236.9	123.7	27.1	26.4
Sovkhozy (in thousands)	1.4	4.2	5.0	20.1	20.8
Enterprises, organisations, unions associating *kolkhozy* and *sovkhozy* (in thousands)	—	—	—	7.7	9.3
Individual farms of poor and middle peasants (in millions)	23.7	3.6	0.7	—	—
Farms of kulaks (in millions)	1.1	—	—	—	—

Source: M. Lavigne, *Les Economies Socialistes*, Armand Colin, Paris, 1979.

done, it will be impossible to evaluate the distinction within agriculture between *kolkhozniki* and state farm workers.

The kolkhozy

To start with the *kolkhozy*, the changes in size of the *kolkhozy* and the conversion of some of them into *sovkhozy* have been related to other practices that have changed the internal structure of the *kolkhoz* as an economic unit. It has grown bigger, and the amount invested has gone up. Farms have become more complex internally as they have grown in size, but there is still regional variation in their internal structure. These internal structural changes became increasingly evident after 1958. This was the year when the MTSs were abolished. They had been introduced in the late 1920s in association with collectivisation measures, and their abolition marked the end of a policy of constraint towards agriculture. The period 1958–65 could be characterised as a period of liberalisation in agriculture, but the policy of intensification of agriculture was not well conducted since the *kolkhozy* did not have enough resources. The period from 1965 was one of considerable growth of investment in agriculture.

The internal changes in *kolkhozy* really began around 1958, when brigades (the main sub-unit within the *kolkhoz*) began to grow in size and importance and were reclassified according to the structure of output and the method of handling mechanisation:

(a) the *complex* brigade (crop and anumal production);
(b) the *branch* brigade (field brigades, tractor–field brigades, potato brigades, and so on);
(c) the *specialised* brigade (single product);
(d) the *tractor–complex* brigade (after 1958).

The complex and tractor–complex brigades grew from just over 14 per cent of all brigades in 1957 to 34 per cent in 1962 and remained about that proportion until at least the late 1960s.[4] This form of brigade is used where production is not highly specialised, and where both field crop and animal-breeding sectors are relatively highly developed.

At times a complex brigade may be called a 'department', as it would be if it were on a *sovkhoz*. A department closely resembles an entire collective farm of the late 1940s. This diversification within complex brigades may be related to distribution difficulties (poor roads, poor-quality vehicles, inadequate storage facilities and an insufficient number of retail distribution points). Specialisation now takes place at the level of sub-units within the complex brigade. It is not at all clear how far this specialisation within a multi-product brigade has helped to raise productivity. Low productivity may also be related to the low level of formal education at brigade level, though qualifications are higher among *kolkhoz* chairmen.[5] Certainly it is becoming difficult to explain comparatively low production levels by low levels of investment, since this has been increasing since the early 1960s. Yet it has not apparently been very productive investment. A rough indication of this can be seen from the figures cited by Lavigne[6] on the growth of agricultural production: in 1950–4 it grew by 22 per cent, in 1955–9 by 49 per cent, but in 1960–5 it only grew by 14 per cent. This latter period was precisely when the relative investment in *kolkhozy* was increasing.

The link betweeen the relatively low educational and skill levels, the pattern of specialisation and the low productivity of investment seems to be as follows. Complex brigades form only about one-third of all brigades. The *kolkhozy* rely much more on specialist brigades, where a technician (often with higher educational qualifications than the farm chairman) can oversee the work of unskilled workers within a relatively narrowly specialised 'span of control'. The organisational rigidity produced by the proliferation of relatively narrow specialisations among heads of different *kolkhoz* sub-units may well account for both the limiting of the spread of complex brigades and for the apparently continuing high cost of certain aspects of farming, such as livestock rearing, which creates the economic opening for the 'personal plots' (the 'private sector'). This picture of comparative stagnation in terms of the 'formal organisational blueprint' within the *kolkhoz* since the early 1960s is consistent with Stuart's suggestion[7] that the 'good' *kolkhoz* may be less a function of the organisational form as such and more a function of other factors, for example natural conditions and state credits. It would also explain the poor wage incentive system which makes it difficult for *kolkhozniki* to calculate the relation between effort and reward and subjects them to very detailed supervision.

This organisational rigidity has created an unnecessary demand for investment, as well as a labour shortage. The inflexible labour supply within the farm means that administrative pressure on the *kolkhoz* to increase agricultural production cannot be dealt with by internal reorganisation, but only by increased investment. According to Nove, agricultural investment rose from an average of under 3 milliard roubles a year in 1951–5 to 7.27 milliards in 1961 and then to 23.7 milliards in 1973 – over 24 per cent of total investment in that year. Nove provides an excellent analysis of why 'unbalanced planning' of inputs makes much of this investment inefficient,[8] but to his analysis must be added the effects of this organisational rigidity, which makes it very difficult for the *kolkhoz* to calculate its own investment priorities. When these problems are added to difficulties over obtaining state credit, and a state tendency to plan inputs according to technical norms which do not dovetail well with brigade-level plans, it is clear why *kolkhozy* accept state inputs, yet need a high level of overall investment to be able to deal with their own particular production bottlenecks (which may not be registered in terms of the state's technical norms for investment). Ironically, because of maintenance problems, 15 per cent of tractors stand idle every year due to technical inoperability.

The central planning agencies also face problems with the

planning of inputs: the technical norms used have regional scales for the cost of particular inputs. But it is up to the individual *kolkhozy* to decide how much of its land falls into a particular category. Consequently it is difficult for the central agencies to compare costs within a region, since these are defined in terms of these technical norms, and there is no way to ensure that different *kolkhozy* are applying these norms in the same way. Interregional comparisons of costs are even more difficult. Furthermore, these norms only change slowly, despite constantly changing conditions. Without a form of measuring costs in a manner that does not perpetuate existing practices, but rather helps indicate how costs could be reduced, the poor performance of agriculture is likely to continue, and agricultural investment is likely to remain a high proportion of total investment.

The convergence of kolkhozy and sovkhozy
Many of these problems apply also to the *sovkhozy*, since the administrative and operational differences between the two kinds of farm have diminished over the years, as both Nove and Stuart indicate. This raises the issue of the extent to which they can be conceived of as distinct forms of property. The greater dependence of *kolkhoz* incomes on financial performance, and the poorer pension rights, poorer state aid for investment, and so on, are only juridically possible on the basis of the distinction between co-operative ownership and state ownership. Yet as Stuart makes clear, the *kolkhoz* chairman is not really elected, and the autonomy of the *kolkhoz* is limited within the planned economy, even though, as Stuart puts it, 'the mechanisms utilised to integrate the *kolkhoz* into the planned economy have differed from those utilised for other organisational forms in the Soviet economy'.[9] Furthermore, there have been a series of measures to assimilate the two forms of property, as part of the efforts to improve agriculture since 1965.

These measures, which have improved the profitability of *kolkhozy*, reduced the differences between them and *sovkhozy*, and have been associated with a very large investment programme, are aimed at producing a convergence between agriculture and industry. However, these attempts have been marred in the second half of the 1970s by a return towards voluntarist planning methods, which were a response to the mediocre results of the 1971–5 Five Year Plan. These attempts to use administrative pressure to increase *kolkhoz* sales did not meet with any great success, and in 1981 greater concessions to 'personal plots' were made in an attempt to stimulate further marketing of agricultural production. Nevertheless, attempts are continuing to industrialise agriculture. Apart from changing agricultural technology, one way of doing this since 1965 has been the creation of 'agro–industrial complexes' integrating industrial and agricultural activities. In 1978 there existed 8000 enterprises of this type, associating 90 per cent of the *kolkhozy* and 60 per cent of the *sovkhozy*, many of them participating in several enterprises. These enterprises employed 1.6 million workers in 1978. The ultimate aim seems to be the urbanisation of the countryside. The idea of the *agrogorod* (agro-town) seems to have been resurrected, though in a different form from that advocated by Khrushchev in 1950 (and later). This could have adverse effects, as Wädekin has pointed out,[10] on the 'personal plots', which is one of the reasons why, as Lavigne remarks, *kolkhozniki* seem to be attached to their individual houses. Indeed, many of these ambitious hopes for agriculture could well imply a transformation (or even eventual abolition) of the 'personal plots'. Consequently this third form of agricultural property must now be examined.

Personal plots

As Wädekin makes clear, 'personal plots' do not simply belong to *kolkhozniki*, but also to workers and employees. The latter are often thought to be employed in *sovkhozy*, but, as both Nove and Wädekin make clear, they also consist of state-employed persons working in suburban or urban areas. The distinction between those plots on *kolkhoz* land and those on *sovkhoz* land is of very little significance, except that *sovkhoz* plots are usually smaller, which is related to the higher wages of *sovkhoz* workers. In contrast to earlier times, the income of *kolkhozniki* from 'personal plots' is now only a secondary income.

   The main impression given by Wädekin's painstaking work to glean evidence from a large variety of sources is of the *interdependence* of *kolkhoz* (or *sovkhoz*) and 'personal plot' sectors.

This interdependence applies to mutual aid (not all of it legal) between the *kolkhoz* and 'personal plot' in terms of inputs, and what is effectively a division of labour between them in terms of products, with the 'personal plots' concentrating on what the *kolkhozy* do badly – potatoes, vegetables, eggs, fruit, meat and dairy produce. This division of labour has become more evident with rising living standards, so that the private plots did not just produce means of consumption for the *kolkhozniki* but began to cater for developing urban markets for the above products rather than for the staple foods based on grains.[11]

The interdependence between *kolkhoz* and personal plots both helps to explain why the latter appears so productive (for example, it receives feed grazing and young animals for its livestock rearing) and why such plots continue to exist. They compensate (or have in the past) for the under-investment in agriculture by producing output for very little investment. Furthermore, in adapting to the market, they have provided the kind of flexibility which has been precluded, it seems, by the organisational rigidity of *kolkhozy*, but which is required in the face of varying harvests, often voluntaristic approaches to agriculture and, more recently, the changing demand for agricultural products. However, the role of the personal plots appears to be declining: in 1950 they amounted to 5.1 per cent of total sown area in the USSR, by 1959 they were 3.7 per cent, and by 1969 they were 3.2 per cent.[12] In the last decade the decline has continued; thus, according to Lavigne, in 1979 they were only 2.7 per cent of total sown area.[13] The decline in the private plot may be in part simply a demographic effect, as old people in *kolkhozy* and *sovkhozy* die, while the household rights to their plots are not transferred to a new household because younger people have been moving from the countryside. If this is so, it may in intself be the cause of a slight deterioration (or stagnation) in overall agricultural performance in the Soviet Union, because of the (admittedly slight) economic support which the private plots give to *kolkhozy* and *sovkhozy*.

Yet this decline in sown area devoted to personal plots has not been matched by a proportionate decline in output. They still produced, in 1979, 25.5 per cent of total agricultural production (and sustained 21 per cent of the livestock), according to

Lavigne. The output of the urban plots producing directly for urban markets seems to have been increasing, which may be why the value of output from personal plots has remained so high, despite the diminishing area devoted to them: produce for urban markets commands higher prices. It is probably to satisfy this growing demand that concessions to personal plots were made in 1981: with a decline in rural plots, the effects on production of food were being felt quite strongly then. This link between personal plots and urban food consumption raises the issue of retail trade in food.

Retail trade

Nove says that turnover statistics show that retail sales in rural areas have been rising steadily, but argues that, judging from criticisms, there is ample scope for improvement in marketing, particularly by the rural consumer co-operatives. He mentions the most pressing physical problems – poor roads, inadequate transport, a serious lack of packaging materials and of storage space. In 1977, according to Lavigne, state commerce and retailing co-operative commerce were responsible for 69.6 per cent and 28 per cent respectively of all retail turnover, both food and non-food. Hence the *kolkhoz* market in 1977 accounted for 2.4 per cent of all retail turnover. The *kolkhoz* markets provide a retail outlet for the output of the *kolkhozy* which is not taken up in the state procurement plan. In addition, they provide a retail outlet for some of the produce from the private plots. If one takes *kolkhoz* market sales as a percentage of *all food* sales, then the share of the *kolkhoz* market was 4.5 per cent in 1969, 4.3 per cent in 1977, and 4.7 per cent in 1979. Consequently, after a period of relative decline in the 1950s and 1960s, the *kolkhoz* retail markets have stabilised their share of the food markets in the 1970s. Clearly, even in the case of personal plots, most of the produce is marketed through state and co-operative agencies.

Overview of agriculture

It is now possible to discuss agriculture as a whole. Clearly the distinctions between *kolkhozy* and *sovkhozy* are diminishing, a task which requires a massive allocation of resources to agriculture both to invest and to subsidise agricultural prices. As Nove points out, the geographical and climatic features of the Soviet

Union mean that for a particular volume of output it will probably always require greater investment than, say, the USA. Nevertheless, many of the resources devoted to agriculture must be wasted because of forms of planning and because of the organisational forms of the 'socialised sector' and their inadequate means of calculation. As Lavigne has pointed out, it is astonishing and disturbing that the Soviet Union cannot cover its needs for agricultural products, nutritional produce and raw materials when 22 per cent of its population is engaged in agriculture and such a high proportion of total investment is devoted to it. This global underdevelopment leaves the way open for the activities of the 'private sector', which, even if it is selling to consumer co-operatives, is still very prosperous and produces one-quarter of total agricultural output. Unless and until organisational forms and means of calculation can be developed that will enable the *sovkhozy* and *kolkhozy* to produce as efficiently as the 'personal plots' on the same products, agriculture will continue to be a chronic problem. The distribution of agricultural products (as of industrial ones, as well as services) will similarly have to improve if the agricultural organisations are to have the means of planning starting from calculations as to likely consumption. This may well require a radical alteration of both priorities and planning techniques in the Soviet Union.

Industry

It is not very easy to separate agriculture from industry. Not only do agriculture and industry produce means of production for each other, but they share common problems in many ways with regard to relations between the units of production and the ministerial authorities and planning authorities themselves. However, the greater importance attached to industry in the USSR, and the organisational differences between industrial and agricultural economic units, make it easier to discuss them separately.

State enterprises
As with agriculture, I propose to start with the units of production before discussing other economic units. Whereas in the

case of agriculture the main works referred to were those of economists, it is possible to begin by discussing an explicitly sociological account of enterprises, or at least of the social location of their directors, namely that by Andrle.[14] The main theoretical mode of analysis used by Andrle is role theory and, although no attempt is made by him to defend its use, the defects of this mode of analysis are limited to some extent by his distinction between theoretical and empirical work.

Andrle begins his analysis of the position of the manager in the relations of production (conceived of primarily as inter-personal relations) by positing two basic types of state intervention in the economy – regulative and directive planning – or, put another way, market regulation *v*. administrative planning. The main arguments which I would raise about this conception of the 'dialectic' (as Andrle calls it) between managerial initiative and plan discipline are as follows: first, that it does not stem from any gap between the conceptual and the real,[15] but from differences between different discourses; second, that the problems of Soviet planning should not be analysed in terms of the mutual interaction of two organising principles which define the range of variation of the structure. Andrle quite explicitly does the latter by positing regulative and directive planning as two polar opposites defining the 'gravitational field' within which all proposals to set individual interests in harmony with a specific notion of 'general interest' would have to fall.

Yet, despite what I consider to be the weaknesses of Andrle's mode of analysis of planning, he is able to give a reasonable account of the basic problems facing Soviet planning:

> the centralised planning of complex diversified industrial production is based on inadequate knowledge of the minutiae of specific conditions under which decision makers at the production level have to operate. Centrally formulated prescriptions tend to become ambiguous or inconsistent (depending on how specific they are) by the time they arrive on a factory manager's desk. From the central planner's point of view, the response of managers – and by chain reaction of all those affected by managerial decisions – is insufficiently determinate, with consequences which may contradict some of the planner's objectives.

Therefore, the administrative structure of directive planning must be such as to offer the central planner some way of salvaging at least some of the objectives which appear to be denied in the process of implementation. In the Soviet Union the central organs of the state, with the central organs of the Communist Party playing the crucial co-ordinative and policy-formulating role, fight for control over the productive process by continuous issue of corrective directives, multiple checks on their fulfilment, and periodical, large-scale campaigns against whichever managerial policies are brought to the attention of the central authorities as detrimental to the national goals. The efficiency of these efforts of course requires that no managerial decision-making is protected by autonomously enforcible legal status. However, as a consequence of the inadequacy of centralised information, the whole system would simply grind to a halt if factory managers did not have the initiative to arbitrate between conflicting directives and cut corners by officially unblessed practices in their pursuit of the chosen goals.[16]

Andrle then analyses the relations between state enterprises and the higher organs of state economic planning and management in terms of the directive and regulative principles of control over the economy, but his close adherence to the empirical sources enables him nevertheless to make a series of useful points. The 1965 Enterprise Statute did not provide for the legal enforcement of enterprise rights *vis-à-vis* the higher organs, a problem which is exacerbated by the difficulty of distinguishing between a law and an administrative directive, which means that complaints against higher authorities' 'unlawful decisions' are rare. Reversal of higher decisions is more likely to be successful on the grounds that they were made on an 'unscientific basis', i.e. without due regard to, say, the calculated or reported productive capacity of the enterprise. There is no system of accounting whereby the damage caused to an enterprise by its higher organ can be assessed. Despite the pressures to interfere at enterprise level, it is in the interest of officials of the higher organ that the enterprises under their jurisdiction appear to work well. Relations with superior organs are likely to be better if the industry is high on the priority scale and thus gets scarce supplies, if there is a direct link between the enterprise and its Ministry, if the primary production of the enterprise is central to the brief of the Ministry, and if the higher organ has a broad scope and is wealthy. These latter points, of course, all relate to the problems of supply. Despite the importance of Gossnab (which is of the same order of importance as Gosplan), some of the Ministries have managed to organise their own supply offices. External control of the supply of raw materials and instruments of production is of course an important limitation on enterprises, but the partial Ministerial control of supplies clearly enhances the Ministries' own autonomy in plan implementation *vis-à-vis* the central planning agencies such as Gosplan. With regard to financial autonomy of enterprises, Andrle makes the interesting point that the enterprise accountants are often better qualified than the Ministry of Finance inspectors. (This is in sharp contrast to the position in agriculture.) The State Bank inspectors are probably more effective, and have a wider range of sanctions, but Andrle makes the same point as Lavigne that extreme financial sanctions against enterprises are exceptional.[17] Some powerful enterprises even keep State Bank inspectors off the premises! Finally, Andrle makes the important point that

> the structural circumstances of directive planning based on imperfect knowledge make mutual trust a scarce and highly valued commodity which can be obtained through the exchange of personal favours extended at personal risks. Thus there emerge cliques whose members use the resources to which they have access through office for preferential treatment of each other's interests. Woe to the director who does not manage to develop personal bonds across institutional boundaries.

Leaving aside criticisms of the use of the concepts of 'directive planning' and 'imperfect knowledge', Andrle is right to stress the importance of informal interpersonal relations, but apart from indicating that these are related to supply difficulties and success indicators his analysis is of little help in analysing the determinants of the formation of these cliques.

The effect of this is to make the formation of alliances to which Andrle refers a matter of the subjective decision of the managers themselves: it is a matter of role-playing, with the choice as to how to play the role being determined by the 'symbolic environment' and by membership and reference groups which help to create their own symbolic environment or sub-culture and which may not fit in with the official or dominant culture. Andrle's analysis is noticeably lacking in any detailed specification of the consciousness of the local power elites, nor does he specify the structural determinants which give them (as opposed to some other agency) their apparently pivotal role in sustaining enterprise autonomy while integrating it with directive planning. Consequently one is forced to turn elsewhere for an analysis of the relations between enterprises and other economic units.

However, before doing so, it is worth mentioning that Andrle's analysis of relations *within* the enterprise is much more adequate in terms of its specification of the determinants of the kinds of struggles which take place there. While the principle of one-man management was reaffirmed in the September 1965 Enterprise Statute, there are a number of well-known formal and informal limitations on the capacities of enterprise directors. These limitations stem in various ways from the CP, the trade unions, labour legislation and the rank-and-file workforce. The CP attempts to retain political control over production by various means – mobilisation of the masses, and supervision by higher party organs (both of which tend to be formalistic and inadequate); Party Commissions and Commissions of People's Control, both of which make it hard for the rank and file to criticise superiors in ways which are not called for. However, there is effective party control of recruitment and selection of managers, but in-service training seems to be very ineffective – indeed, in municipal, light and food-processing industries, managers seem to get by with no effort to raise their qualifications, which seems to be (at least nominally) a worse situation than in agriculture, where at least token attempts are made, as described by Stuart.[18] The main form of party control of enterprises is through the co-ordination of and arbitration between managerial interests: in reallocating resources in ways not envisaged in the plans, and in arbitrating between managers the party retains some control over production. This political reconciliation of the disparate planned objectives is clearly important, but, in my view, precisely because it is not clear how or to what end these objectives should be reconciled, and because local party officials are judged by their ability to help enterprises meet their plan, even this form of party 'supervision' of enterprise directors is limited in its effects. Andrle reports that the secretaries of enterprise party organisations rarely disagree with the directors, even when the latter are criticised from above. Similarly, there are generally good relations between directors and the secretaries of regional and district parties.

The trade unions are in some respects quite a good defensive organisation (from the viewpoint of the manual work-force), though they can be lax on safety and legal standards, and they tend to take a softer line in the bigger enterprises. However, more than half the cases referred to the Commissions for Labour Disputes are won by workers. Similarly, the labour legislation provides a reasonable defensive support, but that is not the same thing as participation in management. Only a few sacked employees seek redress in court when dismissed (but this could well be because they are genuinely in breach of factory discipline, which is poor). Of those who do go to court, more than half are reinstated. Of the 'agencies of mass participation', the Production Conferences, whose acts are judicial or quasi-judicial, do limit the directors' autonomy to some extent, but the Production–Technical Councils do not constitute a serious limit on one-man management. The poor discipline, poor motivation and high labour turnover are serious limits on the capacities of directors and can only be effectively countered by official and unofficial incentive schemes, for example when management takes over the basically trade-union function of allocating flats. There is little that is surprising in this picture painted by Andrle, but it is the kind of evidence which must be borne in mind in the analysis of relations between economic agents.

Production associations and Ministries

At the beginning of 1973, there began a process of reform of industrial organisations. The original intention was to set up a system in which the basic production unit would no longer be the industrial enterprise but would be the 'production association' or 'union' (*proizvodstvennoe ob'yedineniye*) or 'combine' (*kombinat*). This was to consist of a number of factories plus a research and development institute or similar functional organisation. The 'centre' or 'top' of each state–management hierarchy was to be the sectoral Ministry, as before, but with the departments (*glavki*) abolished. The higher organ of the production association or union was to be an 'industrial association' or the Ministry itself. The industrial associations were to work on a *khozraschet* basis but with strict centralised discipline in price formation. *Khozraschet* (economic accounting) is a form of calculation which is supposed to give the agency using it a greater degree of financial autonomy, and hence decision-making autonomy.

This partial reform (which was only partially implemented) occurred in the context of 1965 reform and its implementation. As is well known, the 1965 reform attempted, among other things, to tackle the 'success indicator' problem, a problem which could be characterised as an effect of the disparity between planning on the basis of aggregated information and implementation on the basis of disaggregated information. The aggregated planning information is discursively distinct from the information necessary to operate an enterprise (or other sub-unit) of the agencies of plan implementation (the Ministries). Crudely, the disparity could be overcome by (i) laying down only a few targets whose pertinence to the operation of the sub-units is problematic but which allow substantial autonomy to the enterprises in calculating how to meet those targets (a procedure which may lead to the serious 'subversion' or failure of the overall economic plan), or (ii) laying down a whole series of detailed targets or norms which ensure greater subordination of enterprises to the Ministries (a procedure which, since the detailed norms are likely to be mutually inconsistent and ambiguously related to the overall plan, usually leads to 'subversion' or failure by a different route). The danger is that if the first option is taken enterprises may meet targets in a way which ignores or even endangers other objectives of the overall plan not specified in the targets laid down, whereas if the second option is taken the enterprises lose the very decision-making capacity necessary to operate the plant flexibly under changing conditions, so that some targets are met at the expense of what might for the time being be more important targets in the priorities of the overall plan. The 1965 reform attempted to resolve the problem of the most appropriate form of success indicators by reducing the number of compulsory indicators. These were, in outline: output sold, total profits, profitability, contributions to and receipts from the state budget, the size of the wages fund, norms establishing the size of centralised investment and the introduction of new productive capacity, the fulfilment of basic tasks for the introduction of new techniques, and supply of raw materials and equipment.[19] However, the reform also attempted to retain Ministerial control of the enterprises, despite the increase in enterprise autonomy apparently implied in the reduction of the number of success indicators. The result of the 1965 reform was that the Ministries effectively won the struggle to retain a substantial degree of control over the enterprises.

The partial reform of 1973–5 must consequently be analysed in the context of this re-establishment of Ministerial capacity to regulate enterprise activities despite the 1965 enterprise reform. From 1970 the extra success indicators which had been informally imposed by the Ministries began to be imposed officially. The development of the 'production associations' and the so-called 'industrial associations' (that is, administrative associations within Ministries) must be seen as yet another attempt to enhance enterprise autonomy in relation to the Ministries, and the gathering of enterprises into associations was certainly opposed by the Ministries, doubtless with the collusion of some of the enterprises protected by them. The enterprises were not supposed to be subordinated to their associations as they otherwise were to their Ministries. Rather, there was supposed to be a division of labour, with the association centralising certain communal services, while the enterprises had room for manoeuvre in daily management. However, with the development of a variety of forms of association, the industrial associations remained an administrative relay, federating juridically autonomous enterprises, while the production associations ran their component establishments in a variety of ways, even within the same Ministry, sometimes interfering in the plans of constituent enterprises. The net result, according to Lavigne, was that there was less enterprise autonomy in 1977 than in 1965, despite the partial industrial restructuring from 1973 to 1975.

This raises the issue of why the Ministries struggle to retain control of the enterprises, and the means by which they regularly succeed. In analysing this issue it may be possible to show what the determinants are of the informal connections mentioned by Nove and emphasised (at local level) by Andrle. Nove analyses the Ministerial system of plan implementation in terms of 'centralised pluralism', by which he means that the central decision-making of the planning agencies such as Gosplan, Gossnab and Gosstroi is modified by the disparate decisions taken by the Ministries, even though the latter are operating within state plans which they must enforce on their subordinates. Nove argues:

> In practice the sheer volume of work and of decisions in Gosplan places very considerable powers in the hands of the ministries. They are more likely than the planning agencies to have information about the existing situation and future possibilities. Their proposals, and their reaction to proposals made by 'their' enterprises, affect the plans and instructions which they receive. Those with experience of these matters speak of a constant tug-of-war between the ministries and Gosplan.[20]

While this indicates that the Ministries are not simply passive instruments of plan implementation (a feature which would only surprise adherents of a rationalist conception of planning),[21] Nove's concept of 'centralised pluralism' is couched in terms of empire-building by Ministerial interest groups. However familiar this may appear as a 'motive' for certain kinds of action in large-scale organisations, Soviet Ministerial struggles with the planning agencies, with other Ministries and with 'their own' enterprises still need to be explained. The much-cited supply problem is certainly part of that explanation, but it is generally agreed that problems over supplies are also an *effect* of these struggles. Why have attempts to modify Ministerial control over enterprises failed?

One answer to this problem, considered by Andreff,[22] is that the Ministries (and, secondarily, production associations) are 'autonomous centres of appropriation', i.e. effectively private properties in the sense used by Bettelheim.[23] In this kind of argument Ministries would be like monopoly-capitalist properties with subordinate production enterprises. However, Andreff points out that to be sustainable such an argument would entail the relegation of the central state agencies to the role of supporting the decentralised accumulation of capital, by collecting savings which were redistributed to the monopolies, in a manner analogous to the role of the state in certain analyses of 'state monopoly capitalism'. Such an analogy would appear to be supported by the de-specialisation of Ministries, which do not restrict themselves to a single branch of industry but appear to have moved into the production of more 'profitable' and highly demanded goods, such as consumer durables. However, Andreff rejects such an analysis, even for Western economies, on the grounds that (i) it assimilates capitalist relations of production to property and distribution relations, which leads to the lack of an analysis of the foundations of the relations of production, wage-labour, (ii) there is no demonstration that production, including monopolist production, is production of surplus value, and consequently, (iii) an ambiguous status is given to profit, which is not treated as transformed surplus-value, and hence there is no study of that transformation. Even if one does not accept the labour theory of value, one must agree with Andreff that the capitalist nature of this 'monopolism' is simply presumed or postulated in such an argument, due to an inadequate theorisation of capitalist relations. In addition to Andreff's criticisms, one could add that it would be difficult in such a conception of Ministries as independent capitalist properties to explain their resistance to the development of production associations, since their development would simply be an indication of the concentration of capital; in the usual Marxist conceptions of capitalism, this would be quite compatible with the centralisation of capital in monopolistic properties controlling a series of large-scale production units.

Clearly the resistance of the Ministries to production associations and administrative associations is related to the latter's potential as an organisational mechanism for an alternative mode of intervention in plan implementation by the central planning agencies. The development of such organisational alternatives by the central planning agencies would reduce their dependence on the Ministries for accounting information on past performance and would provide a certain flexibility in plan implementation, since it would be possible for certain purposes for the central planning agencies to bypass the Ministries in laying down targets or norms, and enterprise autonomy from the Ministries would be enhanced to a certain extent. Precisely because the Ministries are not capitalist properties able to control a 'decentralised' series of production units by means of financial accounting procedures, Ministerial control of 'their' enterprises must take the form of administrative regulation by setting detailed targets and norms. If such control is lost or reduced, Ministries would be in the position of being nominally responsible for the performance of a particular sector of the economy, while losing some of the armoury of weapons which are used to secure 'adequate' performance of that sector: crudely, they would have responsibility without power. This approach to the reaction of Ministries to attempts to provide alternative or supplementary modes of intervention in the economy implies that it is precisely because they are effectively subordinated to the central planning agencies in certain respects that they evade or resist attempts at control or at bypassing of their functioning in other respects. It is the fact that they are effectively responsible for the performance of a certain sector in an uncertain supply situation that accounts for the 'interference' in enterprise management, and for the Ministerial hoarding of supplies, while it is the combination of taut planning with inevitably inadequate indices of plan fulfilment which helps create the uncertain supply situation.

The characteristic features of the supply system – slowness, incoherence and lack of precision (in the specification of what is to be supplied) – generate a 'seller's market' where supplies are the main condition of a sub-agency (such as a Ministry or enterprise) fulfilling the plan. The failures of the supply system in a planning system which prioritises physical production determine both the scope and the need for inter-enterprise arrangements, and for other forms of politicking to secure supplies. These, then, are the conditions for Andrle's 'local power elites' and for Ministerial resistance to alternative modes of intervention in the economy, but these conditions can only be fully

understood in terms of the forms of regulation of plan implementation which ensure that the priorities established by the
central planning agencies and the upper levels of the party are
indeed effective to some extent.

The regulation of plan implementation

The problems of central regulation of plan implementation are
raised in Tartarin.[24] His article represents an attempt to escape
from the formal oppositions and abstract dichotomies which
characterise much work on the Soviet Union. For example, the
oppositions between rationality and irrationality, plan and
market, centralisation and decentralisation,[25] official economy
and parallel economy are common. It also attempts to avoid
overall structural characterisations such as command
economy, state capitalism or bureaucratic socialism, and
concentrates instead on organisational forms and their mode of
functioning in a way that attempts to break with the idea of a
unity or homogeneous totality which many earlier analyses
have retained. The approach to the regulation of the economy is
in terms of the ways of measuring results without denying structural constraints determining the capacities of sub-agents.

The regulation of the economy is conducted by the setting of
norms for sub-agents within a sphere of supervisory competence of an agent. These norms (using the term in a broad
sense) are of a variety of kinds: ratios, norms (*normativy*),
standards, assortments, indices, scales, legal rules, instructions, organisational models to be followed, and so on. They relate to diverse domains, yet there is a strong unity between
statistics, planning indices and accounting data, a unity which
is ensured by their subordination to planning objectives. There
are various organisational means of ensuring this unity, but the
effect of the unity is that accounting norms are the means of
controlling the execution of the plan. Relations between agents
consist of the exchange of orders or information relating to the
norms. The reconciliation of conflicts is achieved by the modification of norms. Reforms consist in the suppression of some
norms and their replacement by others which are thought to
lead to better behaviour by 'decentralised units' (or, as I prefer
to call them, sub-agents or sub-units). If an economy defines its
functioning by a system of norms, this is not just a matter of

relations between particular levels of the administrative hierarchy, nor of optimal calculation. The increase in the number of norms in 1979 was not just about economic calculation, but about control.

Tartarin introduces the concept of 'accounting value' (*valeur comptable*) to refer to the abstract properties of the rules, and statistical and accounting practices, in so far as they serve as a basis for the functioning of Soviet-type socialist economies. Norms establish external control over hierarchically organised units. There is a hierarchisation of units of decision-making and a 'normalisation' of orders and controls. What is produced is not commodities but *items* on a list. This requires a classificatory system, a system of accounting and recording. In a socialist economy, the centre, enterprises and users are differentiated as agents, according to Tartarin.

The relations between these agents are asymmetric, with the centre in a dominant position. The relation between enterprise and user is never direct, unless the centre itself is the user: enterprise–user relations are mediated by centre–enterprise relations. For the enterprises, norms are constraints which delimit the possible behaviour, since they must produce accounting values corresponding to the imposed norms. So a part of total production is only produced as the real condition of producing accounting values. For the centre, norms are objectives which must be respected by enterprises. However, these objectives concern *both* the results and the means of achieving them, so often accounting values (for reporting results) are identical to parameters (for regulating plan implementation).

Apart from the satisfaction of the use-values of the centre, results are measured by norms (on paper). The conformity with norms is not absolute; it depends on the quality of inspections used by the supervisory agents (*organes de tutelle*). These inspections are rare, superficial and conducted by services of little competence whose interests are not independent of the 'decentralised units' and whose sanctions are excessively weak. There is a large margin of interpretation of norm fulfilment even without fortuitous error and deliberate fraud. This process of inspection occurs at each level of the hierarchy for information going 'up' and 'down'. So in addition to accounting in terms of planned tasks by an accounting chief, there is economic accounting for internal goals by an economic chief. But the latter is effectively a palliative since the accounting validation of task performance leads to a *formal* execution of tasks, a form which admits to a certain play in relation to reality. The outcome of attempts to overcome this play is a perpetual oscillation between a paralysing over-centralisation for both the controlled and the controller, and a reduction on controls destined to give enough room for manoeuvre for the controlled and an effective focus for the controller on the really high priority objectives. The cyclical movement is an effect of the universal character of any modification which leads to a different bias, to different organisational costs, and so on. It is not just an effect of the limits of language: the interdependence of higher and lower levels leads to negotiations and informal conflicts over the fixing of tasks and their evaluation and over the reciprocal rules which superiors and subordinates should respect. This leads to informal solutions such as mutual exoneration. Autonomy also occurs when norms which are interdependent in ways unknown to the centre are fixed in a mutually contradictory fashion, imposing partially unrealisable results. (It is at this point that a manager might claim, as Andrle indicates, that a plan is 'unscientific'.) The more the network of norms attempts to be comprehensive, the more the superiors must tolerate (partial and local) violations. Periodic reforms of indices clarify and reaffirm the fundamental criteria of the actions of decentralised units.

These lead to a circular causality in which the norms lead to an artificial reality created to satisfy the fulfilment of norms; it has a conservative effect because the sole guarantee of the coherence of norms is past reality. This is the essential justification for planning from the level achieved. On the other hand, it also explains the downward revision of plans on the basis of actual performance, as a way of obtaining 100 per cent plan fulfilment.[26] The formal and informal aspects of 'accounting value' are thus intrinsically related. There is not a 'second' or 'parallel' economy, but a series of economic activities at each level between which (activities) the law traces the limit of the legal and the illegal, the permitted and the forbidden. But for various reasons the disjunction between these aspects cannot be retained because of the ideology of accounting value where the real is retraced as a series of gaps in relation to the norms. The legality to be set in motion is incoherent and practically inapplicable. Almost all economic activity necessarily entails an infraction, so the execution of orders can only be illegal. This is scarcely surprising: incoherence and lack of precision mean that legality gives way to arbitrariness, or rather to the sovereignty of the superior level which goes with all administrative subordination. Since each level is not a passive agent in the hands of the superior level, objectives are pursued which are added on to the goals whose execution the system of norms is supposed to ensure. The importance of these individual objectives is all the greater since the organisation considers itself impersonal and only the centre is supposed to know which objectives need to be sought.

This gap between reality and 'normativity' is not constant. If the centre tries to reduce it, the adaptive behaviours of all levels, taking account of the relative stability of the system of norms, tend to augment it. When a new system of norms is set up, it takes a certain time for agents to discover all the potentialities of autonomy which it conceals. It also requires a certain time for the necessary compromises to be reached with superior levels, to regulate litigious interpretations, and to establish the exact significance of diverse measures. The efficiency of a new system relates less to its specific content and more to its novelty in so far as it authorises a readjustment and clarification of all the controls, benefits which disappear little by little in the long term. In so far as deviations are recorded at the centre, *ad hoc* norms are introduced. This 'rampant centralisation' is accompanied by a progressive jumbling of commands which presses little by little towards a new general reform.

The specific character of crises in Soviet-type economies is thus related to accounting value. With exchange-value there is a crisis of overproduction. With accounting-value there is an *a priori* valorisation of 'normed' tasks, and workers are paid for a rate of success of over 100 per cent. Products do not exchange against products or money, but at best (with a coherent outcome) the rates of realisation of norms condition one another, the reciprocal accomplishment of tasks being the condition of realisation of the plan. Yet it is a formal accomplishment, the neglected aspects sometimes being the condition for fulfilment of tasks by other units. In attempting to resolve the crisis once it has been revealed by the accounting values, despite the specific dissimulation which they engender, the centre has the choice of abandoning or reinforcing the rules which constitute the system. Solutions are conceived of either as a partial or total abandoning of the system of norms or as a profound reorganisation of the system (to reinforce their effectiveness).

The decree of July 1979 is an example of the latter kind of solution – a return to directive methods, reinforcing massively the control of execution, in seeking to eliminate the reducible incoherences. It shows that the way followed by the authorities, despite its intrinsic faults, is that of the amelioration of the system of norms in a way which increases the ability to foresee the results and increases the conformity of the results (with the plans). It confirms the importance of this system with respect to the fundamental structure of Soviet-type economies.

Leaving aside an appraisal of the 1979 reform for the moment, it must be said that Tartarin's distinction between 'accounting value' and 'use-value' is difficult to accept. It rests on a distinction between the calculated objectives of state agencies and the directly experienced needs of individuals. However, *any* calculation of needs involves the use of concepts, and in an economy with an advanced division of labour giving rise to both human and non-human agents (loci of decision-making and loci of means of action) the calculation of needs will not be conducted by a single means. A variety of forms of discourse will necessarily be used by different agents, and discursive forms of regulation and co-ordination of the activities of these diverse agents need not be identical to the forms of discourse used for internal purposes within such agents.[27] Nor can there be a single form of regulation of the various agents, precisely because of the varying relations of the agents to the overall plan. The same agent will simultaneously have a variety of relations to the objectives of the plan, even if these objectives are consistent with each other. Much of the value of Tartarin's paper consists in its drawing attention, not to the problems of 'accounting value', but to problems of regulating the economy in any conceivable form of socialist planning. The discursive incommensurability between, on the one hand, the means by which agents calculate their own objectives and regulate their own practices more or less according to these objectives and, on the other hand, the means by which various relations between agents are handled is a disjunction which is endemic in any advanced (and changing) division of labour, whether capitalist or socialist.

Economic calculation and central planning

Whereas the rationalist conception of planning implies a single means of calculation, for example in terms of 'time' in many conceptions of socialism, the position just outlined by way of a critique of Tartarin's concept of use-value implies a variety of means of calculation, each with its own conditions and effects. The calculation of needs or wants (or, if this terminology is preferred, of socially useful effects) must take account of the needs of the agencies which implement the planned objectives, i.e. various administrative exigencies and exigencies of production and distribution (including intermediate or 'productive' consumption). Even within, say, a productive enterprise, these needs are not directly experienced, so it is impossible to counterpose the 'real' characteristics of production against their measurement in terms of norms or indices. The 'real' characteristics of a mechanical spare part are defined in terms of an engineering discourse which specifies those characteristics by means of concepts and measurements within certain ranges of tolerance. The latter are no less parameters than the parameters of performance specified for a productive enterprise by another agency. It is for this reason that discursive disjunctions rather than a real/conceptual disjunction have been stressed at various points in this chapter.

The collapse of the real/conceptual distinction (which is related to the conceptualisation of use-value in terms of experience) may appear to undermine much of the force of Tartarin's critique of the use of norms in Soviet-type economies. However, problems such as the non-registration of salient characteristics of products by the centrally determined norms, or the redefinition of the norms in terms of 'practical necessities', can be explained in terms of the different discourses operative in the various arenas of plan construction and implementation. The decision that certain characteristics not registered by the norms are salient, or that certain 'practical necessities' must be taken into account, can only be made in terms of an alternative mode of calculating. Such alternative calculations could either be made by agencies other than the ones which established the official norm, or they could in principle be made by the same agencies. The official deployment of alternative modes of calculation would certainly make possible a greater disjunction between monitoring and regulating the performance of the economy on the one hand and the provision of economic incentives to sub-agents on the other hand, which could ease the 'success indicator' problem as analysed by Nove, Lavigne or Tartarin. It would certainly make it easier to estimate the extent to which the 'official' regulating measures were effective. For example, to take Tartarin's analysis of economic crisis in such economies as a form of creeping paralysis which takes time to register on official norms because of practices designed to conceal non-fulfilment or 'formal' fulfilment of the plan, such a crisis could in principle be registered earlier by other means of measuring performance. This is not a case of the real imposing itself on the theoretical, but of the deployment of means of calculating the effectiveness of measures to regulate the implementation of economic plans. A good example of this can be found in Seurot.[28] Seurot shows that by using an alternative measure of productivity (a measure, as he is aware, with problems of its own) rather than the official index of productivity, a much lower rate of growth of productivity is registered, and for the 1970s it is lower than the rate of growth of average monthly wages. The divergence is particularly acute in the years 1978 and 1979, at the end of the Five Year Plan period, which is when most of the Five Year Plan is usually fulfilled. The official index shows productivity rising faster than wages for these two years, though it does show 'creeping paralysis' and non-fulfilment of the plan. The decision that all is not well or that there is a crisis is possible on the basis of both the official and unofficial measures, though the problem of stagnating productivity seems more acute on the unofficial index. The decision that a particular measure is inadequate can only be made by a critique of the way the measure is constructed which determines its mode of calculation of the effects which it registers. Such a critique is more readily mounted and accepted if alternative modes of calculation are also available and are deployed. The measurement problems involved in regulating the economy are not a matter of the inadequacy of the conceptual to the real, but of the disjunction between the various discourses which are inevitably present in an economy with an advanced division of labour.

To say that such problems are inevitable is not to say that Soviet indices or norms are adequate or acceptable. Most of the work cited in this chapter implies a criticism of them in one way or another. In addition, even if many of these problems were minimised, the problems of regulating the Soviet economy are not merely discursive, but political. The implementation of plans is not a matter of neutral instruments realising ideas, as the earlier remarks treating intermediate consumption as needs in their own right have already indicated. The means of action, of plan implementation, clearly have their own effectivity. As mentioned earlier, this is related not only to the discourses deployed by them but also to their own organisational exigencies. Relations between agencies of plan construction and plan implementation, and between various kinds of agencies within each category (for example, between Ministries, production associations and enterprises – all agencies of implementation) constitute arenas of struggle. The outcomes of these struggles determine the capacities of the various agencies for the time being – hence the diversity of relations between production associations and enterprises even within the same Ministry, as mentioned by Lavigne. The fact that the struggles by the agencies of implementation take place over reporting productive capacity, reporting results of the last plan period, and over supplies, indicates their effective subordination (despite their struggles) to the central agencies of plan construction which construct plans in a very 'productionist' manner, using material balances.[29] Thus both the means of economic calculation and the related struggles are conditions of the capacities of the various agents. This is important in appraising the 'norms' established, since otherwise there is a danger of treating them in a manner similar to many kinds of sociological theory which sees them as an effect of a 'central value system' (to use Talcott Parsons's phrase). This sort of theory implies a unified centre with norms as a neutral means of realising its aims; failure by subjects to conform to the norms amounts to 'deviance'. At times Tartarin approximates to this position, with the informal individual pursuit of use-values being the 'deviance' in his analysis.[30] Yet Tartarin also begins to show how such action is an effect of inconsistent norms, and argues that the distinction between formal and informal cannot be sustained even by the higher-level agencies of implementation – hence the mutual exoneration of superiors and subordinates. The analysis of the relations between the various economic agents in terms of arenas of struggle takes one further away from the traditional sociological account which treats social structure in terms of norms and treats actors in terms of conformity to or deviance from the norms.

Tartarin is right to say that the problems of regulation of the economy do not only stem from language, but are problems of relations of superiors and subordinates. Unfortunately, his treatment of 'the centre' either as a single unit or as a series of individuals leads him to ignore the problems of the political relations between agencies at 'the centre'. The potential and actual arenas of struggle constituted by relations between Gosplan, Gossnab, the other State Committees, the Council of Ministers, the individual Ministries, etc., mean that 'the centre' cannot be treated as a unity laying down norms; its non-unity is precisely the source of some of the incoherence in the plans. However, the discursive sources of plan incoherence must also be taken seriously. To say, as Tartarin does, that commodity relations do not 'fit in' with the regulation of the economy by means of norms is somewhat misleading. In the presence of commodity relations, some of the norms must be specified in monetary terms. The problems of final consumption are not *necessarily* the effect of planning by norms, or if they are then the prospects for the socialist planning of final consumption are poor indeed. Many of the problems of retail distribution stem from its low priority, poor organisation, inadequate resources, and the form (not the fact) of intervention by the central planning agencies. It is the form of planning which prioritises production and which does not adequately co-ordinate monetary policy with material balance calculations that generates many of the problems of final consumption. No serious attempt has been made to plan from a projected final consumption,[31] but in the broad sense used by Tartarin this would still entail the use of *norms* of consumption. Before I am accused of paternalism, let me ask what the alternative is: it is not 'consumer sovereignty', since even in the West demand is partly generated by the placing of new products on the market, i.e. by supply. Arguing for flexible norms is not the same as arguing for their abolition. In addition, norms of consumption have to be established (however democratic or otherwise the process of establishment) for social consumption in the form of social security, health care, education, and certain kinds of leisure. Finally, there have to be norms for intermediate consumption to define criteria of 'disproportionate' use of resources in this manner. Norms *per se* will only disappear in the utopian world where socialist planning is conducted with reference to the directly experienced needs of the freely associated producers.

The 1979 reform

Considering the 1979 reform in the light of the above remarks, it must be seen as an attempt to improve both planning and the regulation of the economy by increasing the number of calculations conducted by the central planning agencies, by reorganising the system of norms, and by reinforcing the control of plan implementation. If Tartarin's analysis were correct, the benefits of this reform, like others, will disappear little by little in the long run, but in my view the norms used are not neutral. They affect the capacities of sub-agents and thus the scope for evasion of supervision and regulation. This is precisely why reforms are resisted by some agents, such as the Ministries. The ability of sub-agents to evade regulation depends partly on the form of regulation. The simultaneous deployment by the central planning agencies of alternative modes of supervision (accounting indices) would certainly enhance their capacity to regulate the plan implementation, and help combat the progressive dissipation of effective regulation. However, as Tartarin points out, each form of calculation has its organisational costs and this limits the capacity of the planning agencies in this respect. This limitation is exacerbated by the chronic delays in deploying computer capacity.

The reform seems to aim at control of enterprises, effectively attempting to overcome the successful resistance in the 1970s by Ministries to attempts to make enterprises more responsive to central objectives (as opposed to Ministerial ones), thus controlling Ministries from below. According to Lavigne, this is one of the three ways used to try to control the Ministries: from above, from below and from inside.[32] The July 1979 decree attempted to amalgamate these forms of control. In the first place the predominance of Gosplan over the Ministries was confirmed through closer supervision of their plan preparation and of their management of their enterprises: plans cannot now be lowered during the year in order to make plan fulfilment appear better. In the second place, the completion of the restructuring of industry in terms of production associations was retained as an aim to be achieved 'in two or three years', i.e. by 1982, or later. In the third place, the use of *khozraschet* is to be extended among Ministries from 1981, 'in so far as Ministries are prepared for it'.

This reform of the position of Ministries, which are sectoral agencies of plan implementation, has been supplemented by enhanced territorial regulation of plan implementation, though the latter is still subordinated to the central plan. Consequently the reform places a lot of weight on the central planning agencies, i.e. the eighteen State Committees, the State Bank and the Central Statistical Administration. The most important single State Committee is Gosplan, particularly since the July 1979 decree. The application of the measures envisaged by the decree is its responsibility. However, Lavigne points out that this gain in authority is not accompanied by a reinforcing of its powers.[33] Gosplan cannot give orders, either to the Ministries or to other functional administrations (which I call central planning agencies), notably Gossnab, which has so often held Gosplan in check; Gosplan is thus in a situation of being responsible for failure without necessarily being credited with success.

The effect of the reform at enterprise level has been to limit its autonomy, while increasing the technological autonomy of the workshop or brigade, 'in a distinctly productivist vision'.[34] The 1979 reform has also given a certain degree of organisational autonomy to brigades. Thus it has tried to improve productivity in this way by giving workers greater control of the production process, and also by insisting on the demand for consumption, notably for new products and for better quality. The enterprise as a whole, however, is subordinated to a plan defined strictly in terms of physical units. The enterprise, or production association, or *kombinat*, is to function from 1981 on the basis of a Five Year Plan, broken down annually. Its participation in plan construction will be limited. The Ministries themselves will have to operate on the basis of the control figures of Gosplan to present their own plan proposals, and it will be difficult for enterprises or Ministries to hide reserves, since each enterprise will be on file, having a 'passport' giving the details of the state of its productive capacity, its use, and a certain amount of technical-economic data. The effectiveness of the passport is related to the industrial restructuring, since the passports will only be operational when all enterprises are in production associations.

The Five Year Plans will operate using fourteen indices, which, according to Lavigne,[35] are rational and sophisticated, though it raises the question of how the statistical services will cope. The annual plans and the Five Year Plans are to be tied together, so that enterprises cannot impose their own plans and there is less scope for collusion between enterprises and Ministries to obtain advantageous plans. This means that annual plans will not predominate over the Five Year Plans, and Gosplan has more time to construct a coherent and 'scientifically founded' Five Year Plan (because of the enterprise 'passports'). The 1979 decree re-establishes the value of direct commercial contracts, backed this time with judicial sanctions, even against Gossnab. Enterprises will not be able to consent to 'mutual amnesties' for delivery failures, as in the past. The use of long-term five-year contracts between enterprises or production associations is to be generalised. Lavigne rightly asks how it will be possible to control the application of these measures!

This raises the general issue of the appraisal of this reform. There are now a series of plans whose relation to one another is more coherent than in the past. This rationalisation of the plan structure using a refounded system of indices implies a rapid unification of the 'nomenclatures' (classificatory lists) used by different agencies. Lavigne points out that this is no easy task for the Central Statistical Administration.[36] Regional and sectoral planning are more strictly co-ordinated. While the decree gives great importance to plans of social development, it also gives great emphasis to labour resources. These measures clearly indicate that the July 1979 decree is a serious attempt to improve Soviet economic performance by improving both plan construction (particularly in terms of coherence and of lengthening the time scale of the planning horizon) and the regulation of plan implementation.

The potential problems with plan construction are clear: the increased coherence in terms of indices used in various plans is highly desirable, but there are bound to be difficulties in unifying the 'nomenclatures' (which describe the specifications of items) and still retaining manageable lists of items to plan. Aggregation leads to imprecision, but even partial disaggregation will require substantial and sophisticated computing capacity, together with some means of monitoring the appropriateness of the agreed specifications of items. There will, in other words, continue to be liaison problems within and between the central planning agencies. The problems of co-ordination will also continue at an unnecessarily high level if Gosplan cannot give certain 'technical' orders to Gossnab, even though both would continue to be subject to supervision by the party or Council of Ministers. However, the most important problem for plan construction is the dependence on 'passports' of enterprises. The independence of Gosplan from the Ministries as regards information on enterprise capacity is thus postponed until the restructuring of industry, a restructuring whose completion has already been postponed twice since it was started. In addition, the high organisational costs involved are likely to prevent Gosplan from going in for the simultaneous deployment of a variety of indices measuring the same norm.

With regard to the regulation of plan implementation, there are also evident problems: for example, the problems of ensuring that direct commercial contracts are finally effective, which entails an ability to have recourse to civil litigation, as Lavigne realises. The more important problems are, first, those of limiting Ministerial intervention in enterprises, which means completing the transition to production associations, and second, using the increased brigade autonomy and other measures to increase labour productivity.[37] It is impossible on the basis of the information available to predict the outcome of the struggle to bring all enterprises into production associations. It is possible that the improved information at the disposal of Gosplan, even without effective 'passport' files on enterprises, will make it easier to counter certain practices by Ministries, but much depends on the political support behind such restrictions on Ministries.

Conclusion

This chapter has attempted to analyse the relations of production as relations between agents whose capacities are determined partly by the means of calculation available to them, partly by their organisational forms, and partly by the various struggles in which they are or have been engaged. Relations of production are thus not only economic but political. For this reason, various human and non-human economic agents have been analysed in terms of these main determinants of their capacities.

One of the interesting effects of this approach has been that differences in terms of juridical property have been less important in the analysis than might have been imagined. This is partly because of the policy of assimilating *kolkhozy* to *sovkhozy* in various respects, but also because minor juridical distinctions in the status of different personal plots seem to be of little importance in comparison with the economic relation between *kolkhoz* personal plots and the collective output from the *kolkhozy*. The differences between the three types of property in the Soviet Union (state, collective and personal plots) are no longer one of the *major* features of the economy, though they are still important, and will continue to be until the situation in agriculture is much improved. The juridical determinants of organisational forms in agriculture have been much less important than state policy towards the various kinds of agents or economic units in agriculture since 1965. The same is clearly the case for industry, and for this reason the analysis has concentrated on the discrepancies in the means of calculation employed by various agents and on the role of struggle in determining the current relations of production. Consequently the system of regulating the implementation of plans has received a lot of attention, since sub-agents struggle to resist or amend the plan implementation as centrally envisaged.

The 1979 reform is thus particularly interesting as an attempt to modify the relations of production in favour of the central planning agencies in an attempt to improve economic performance. However, even if it were entirely successful, it would do little to solve the problems of planning from final consumption, which would not only imply perhaps changes in social policy, but also imply a capacity to respond to changing demands for consumer durables and retail services. It is not clear how far the 1979 reform will curb excessive intermediate production, since some of the 'excessive' intermediate production may simply result from the priority given to physical production of manufactured goods. It is arguable that 'structural shortages' result partly from the pressure to increase such production (as well as from organisational difficulties over supply), and the pressure to increase such production may be related to military insecurity.

Since some of the low productivity in industry is due to 'spontaneous' labour mobility associated with a search for housing, according to Seurot, the 1979 decree may raise productivity indirectly by its measures to improve housing and working conditions.[38] In the absence of a radical change in economic strategy and forms of calculation in favour of final consumption, the 1979 reform does at least hold out the promise of improved performance by rationalising the structure of industry, curbing the power of the Ministries, increasing the coherence of the overall economic plans, and giving greater autonomy to workshops and production brigades. Yet, in all these areas, there are grounds for doubting the likelihood of its success.

Notes

1. See, for example, N. Jasny, *The Socialised Agriculture of the USSR: Plans and Performance*, Stanford University Press, 1949; and A. Nove, *An Economic History of the USSR*, Allen Lane, London, 1969. For a detailed discussion of developments between 1953 and 1964, see K. E. Wädekin, *The Private Sector in Soviet Agriculture*, University of California Press, 1973, chs 8, 9.

2. R. C. Stuart, *The Collective Farm in Soviet Agriculture*, D. C. Heath & Co., Lexington, Mass., 1972, ch. 4 'Structural Change in the Kolkhoz Sector'.

3. Lavigne, using different sources from Stuart, gives a figure of 123 700 for 1950, as can be seen from Table 3.1, taken from M. Lavigne, *Les Economies Socialistes: sovietique et européennes*, Armand Colin, Paris, 1979, p. 155. The 1979 figures are from *Narodnoe Khozyaistro SSSR 1979*, p. 215 (private communication from M. Lavigne).

4. Stuart, *The Collective Farm*, p. 64. I shall refer to both complex and tractor–complex brigades as 'complex brigades'.

5. Ibid, pp. 177–86.

6. Lavigne, *Les Economies Socialistes*, p. 161.

7. Stuart, *The Collective Farm*, p. 195.

8. A. Nove, *The Soviet Economic System*, Allen & Unwin, London, 1977, pp. 131–7. Lavigne, *Les Economies Socialistes*, p. 164, says that the proportion of total investment going to agriculture was 15 per cent between 1950 and 1960, 18 per cent between 1961 and 1970, and 26 per cent between 1971 and 1980. According to *The Guardian*, 24 October 1980, Brezhnev's proposed remedy for the expected 20 per cent shortfall in the 1980 grain harvest was to increase investment still further and to boost efficiency. How will the latter be achieved?

9. Stuart, *The Collective Farm*, p. 45.

10. Wädekin, *The Private Sector in Soviet Agriculture*.

11. This is described in detail in ibid, ch. 7 'The Interdependence of Private and Socialised Production'.

12. Ibid, p. 45.

13. Private communication with M. Lavigne. Lavigne, *Les Economies Socialistes*, p. 164, mentions a figure of 1.4 per cent of cultivated surface area, an increase over the figure of 1.2 for 1977. This should not be confused with 'sown area', which does not include pasture and other land uses.

14. V. Andrle, *Managerial Power in the Soviet Union*, Saxon House, Westmead, 1976.

15. This is effectively what Andrle argues in ibid, p. 9.

16. Ibid.

17. See M. Lavigne, 'The Creation of Money by the State Bank in the USSR', *Economy and Society*, vol. 7, no. 1, February 1978.

18. Stuart, *The Collective Farm*.

19. For discussion of the 1965 reform, see Nove, *The Soviet Economic System*, pp. 87–92; and Lavigne, *Les Economies Socialistes*, pp. 85–98.

20. Nove, *The Soviet Economic System*, p. 63.

21. For a discussion of the rationalist conception of planning, see G. Littlejohn, 'Economic Calculation in the Soviet Union', *Economy and Society*, vol. 9, no. 4, November 1980. The concept of 'the rationalist conception of planning' is based on the analysis of the rationalist conception of action provided by B. Hindess, 'Humanism and Teleology in Sociological Theory', in B. Hindess (ed.), *Sociological Theories of the Economy*, Macmillan, London, 1977. It could be argued that recent

claims in the journal *Soviet Studies*, that the Soviet economy is not planned, are the product of just such a rationalist conception of planning. The controversy appears in *Soviet Studies* in April 1978, April 1979 and January 1980. There is an intervention by Nove in January 1980.

22. W. Andreff, 'Capitalism d'état ou monopolisme d'état? Propos d'étape', in M. Lavigne (ed.), *Economie politique de la planification en système socialiste*, Economica, Paris, 1978.

23. C. Bettelheim, *Economic Calculation and Forms of Property*, Routledge & Kegan Paul, London, 1976. In this work Bettelheim considered the enterprises, rather than Ministries, as separate properties.

24. R. Tartarin, 'Planification et régulation dans les économies socialistes: pour une théorie de la valeur comptable', *Revue d'Etudes Est-Ouest*, no. 2, 1981.

25. The distinction between *centralisation* and *decentralisation* has already been criticised by Lavigne, *Les Economies Socialistes*, p. 47, who points out that it stems from the influence on American 'Sovietologists' of American juridical discourse. One could add that a similar discursive presence is evident in sociological organisation theory for similar reasons: see, for example, A. Etzioni, *Modern Organizations*, Prentice-Hall, Englewood Cliffs, N. J., 1964, ch. 3. Lavigne argues that another notion, derived from French law, is more appropriate for the analysis of the socialist countries of Europe – *deconcentration*, which is a 'technique of organisation which consists in remitting important powers of decision to agents of central power placed at the head of diverse administrative divisions or of diverse services'. The formal/*khozraschet* distinction, used by Andrle and others, could be considered as constructed by overlaying the centralisation/decentralisation dichotomy with a plan/market dichotomy.

26. I assume the argument here is that granting such a downward revision shows the 'real' conditions for achieving coherence which can guide plan formulation for the next period. If this is what is being argued here, then it must be remembered that downward revision of the plan is also allowed because Ministries wish to report the success of their enterprises.

27. Tartarin mentions the impossibility of using a single signifying (or significatory) index of economic activity, and this is a point which is becoming increasingly widely appreciated among students of the Soviet economy. For example, quite independently of my remarks on this issue in 'Economic Calculation in the Soviet Union', Nove draws attention to the growing appreciation of this point among Soviet economists themselves. See A. Nove, 'Soviet Economics and Soviet Economists: Some Random Observations', paper given to the Panel on the Theory of Economic Planning and Regulation in the Socialist System, Second World Congress for Soviet and East European Studies, Garmisch, 1980.

28. François Seurot, 'Salaires et productivité en URSS: la réforme de 1979', paper given to the Groupe de Récherche sur la Théorie de l'Economie Socialiste, Centre d'Economie Internationale des Pays Socialistes, Université de Paris I, Panthéon–Sorbonne, 24 October 1980.

29. The role of material balances in relation to other forms of calculation used by the central planning agencies such as Gosplan is discussed in Littlejohn, 'Economic Calculation in the Soviet Union'.
30. Indeed, the second part of his paper is entitled 'Deviancies in the System of Value Accounting'.
31. However, there is a discussion of this issue in the October 1980 issue of *Planovoe Khozyaistvo*.
32. Lavigne, *Les Economies Socialistes*, p. 44.
33. Ibid, p. 58.
34. Ibid, p. 78.
35. Ibid, p. 106.
36. Ibid, p. 240.
37. For an excellent assessment of the use of brigades in raising productivity, in relation to the 1979 wage reform, see M. Drach, 'La brigade sous contrat dans l'industrie soviétique et la réforme de juillet 1979', paper read to the Groupe de Récherche sur la Théorie de l'Economie Socialiste, Centre d'Economie Internationale des Pays Socialistes, Université de Paris I, Panthéon–Sorbonne, 24 October 1980. A brief account of this in English can be found in G. Littlejohn, 'Class Structure and Production Relations in the USSR', unpublished thesis, University of Glasgow, 1981. Drach draws attention to the tension between a degree of self-management and central planning of resource allocation, and between the brigade's attempts at wage-bargaining and the role of the party in the enterprise. Seurot, 'Salaries et productivité en URSS', also points out the conflict between brigade wage-bargaining and the 1979 wage reform. He also points to problems within the terms of the 1979 wage reform itself.
38. Seurot, 'Salaires et productivité en URSS'.

4
Law, State and Politics

Introduction

The analysis of the relations of production as relations between economic agents (both individual and collective) has raised various issues whose implications require further exploration. The analysis of the relations of production as affecting the relative capacities of economic agents, capacities which can change as a result of struggle between agents, has raised the issue of the political determinants of the relations of production. These political conditions are important if one treats the relations between agents as being themselves partly political.

In analysing Soviet politics, the most important aspects of which are intimately connected with relations between state and party agencies, it has proved necessary to discuss various theories of Soviet politics which have some currency in the West. This will be done mainly to remove various misconceptions (as I see them) which present obstacles to an adequate analysis of the effects of the law, state and politics on the relations of production, which in the case of the Soviet Union are in a sense more politicised than in the West. The main approaches which will be dealt with are totalitarian theory, elite theory, and Hough's approach to Soviet politics, which eclectically combines the 'directed society' approach, the 'conflict school' approach, and the interest-group approach with an attempt to analyse Soviet politics in terms of 'institutional pluralism'. Thus Hough's approach is useful to the purposes of this chapter because it combines a wide range of approaches (which can thus be quickly discussed) and because it includes a serious empirical discussion of various state and party agencies which are heavily involved in economic policy or supervising its implementation. Consequently, while using his more empirical analysis, the more theoretical aspects of his position are discussed to avoid the danger of simply accepting Hough's empirical analysis at face-value, useful though it is. Hence, prior to the empirical material, the difficulties of totalitarian theory, elite theory and 'institutional pluralism' will be raised. Following on from this an attempt will be made to outline an alternative approach to the analysis of Soviet politics, which will be related to the evidence presented by Hough.

The aim of this chapter is to integrate the empirical discussion of state and party agencies more fully into the analysis of the relations of production presented in Chapter 3, and what might be called the analysis of the relations of distribution presented in Chapter 5. Both relations of production and relations of distribution (of income) are profoundly affected by state policy in the Soviet Union, so the relations between the state and party agencies most heavily involved in state policy formation cannot be ignored.

Law

The previous chapter on economic units and economic calculation has raised the issue of the regulation of plan implementation, and has indicated that the effects of legal forms of regulation are limited. This is because legal norms appear to be mutually inconsistent, because the plan itself, which is a legally enforceable order for each enterprise, is in many ways inconsistent, and because various kinds of *de facto* autonomy of economic units or agents are not legally recognised. Consequently it seems necessary to investigate certain aspects of Soviet law in order both to understand better the nature of legal regulation of the economy and to begin an analysis of the Soviet state and politics.

Law and socialism
Beginning the analysis of the state with a discussion of law does not amount to treating the state as emanating from law. Discussing the law in the context of legal regulation of the economy does not entail accepting the traditional Marxist conception of the law as a *reflection* of the relations of production, i.e. law as defining property rights. The latter conception, which implies

that the law is an effect of ontologically prior economic relations yet is a condition of the effective functioning of those relations, has been subjected to very serious criticism by Hirst.[1] As Hirst points out: 'Law as analysed in Marxist theory is divided into two distinct social functions which it performs: the function of regulation of possession and the function of regulation of the struggle between classes.'[2] Consequently, Hirst argues, the Marxist theory of law has tended to divide into relatively distinct bodies of theory – the theory of property, and the theory of the state. Hirst concentrates his criticism on the theory of property in the text cited, but one of the issues raised by his critique, particularly his critique of Pashukanis,[3] is the adequacy of a discussion of law which is relatively distinct from a discussion of the state. Hirst argues against the 'conception of property right as an "expression" of social relations borne by an individual subject and necessary to his [socially determined] practice'[4] and consequently against Pashukanis's treatment of public law as formed by analogy with private law. The avoidance of treating law as a proprietal right of individual subjects, which makes possible their (intersubjective) economic and social relations, avoidance of this position implies taking public law and the state seriously even in the analysis of private law. The argument is further extended in Hirst's more recent essay 'Law, Socialism and Rights',[5] where the role of law in socialist states is considered.

Among the problems considered by this later work is the question of 'whether the elimination of a certain legally sanctioned class of agents – "private" owners of the means of production – problematises the existence of the institution of "law" itself'. Contrary to Pashukanis, whose position is that socialists must work for the progressive deconstruction of law, the facilitation of its 'withering away', Hirst argues that in a realm of differentiated agents (whether human individuals or not), the scope and limits of these agents' actions must be defined and limited; this is a condition of their having a determinate capacity for decision. Regulation is definitive of agents and imposes requirements of action on them; it also establishes a relation between agents and the 'public power', not merely a relation between agents with the public power as adjudicator. In contrast to Pashukanis, who conceives of law as recognising

prior realities and regulating an already given realm of relations between agents, Hirst is arguing that regulation of relations between agents is a condition of their existence and their
capacities for action. Regulation concerns the form of definition
of agents as agents:

> This necessarily arises whenever a realm of differentiated
> agencies of decision must be constituted, whether or not
> these agents are directly concerned with production, and
> *whether or not the relations between those agents take a*
> *commodity form.*

While I have no reason to disagree with Hirst's critique of
Pashukanis, nor indeed with his critiques of various other legal
theorists, to my mind Hirst does not make it sufficiently clear
why regulation of social relations should take the form of legal
relations.

Co-ordination certainly implies the regular supply of information, so that different agencies can calculate their actions
with respect to each other, but it does not necessarily imply
'external' control. As Hirst points out earlier in the essay (when
discussing the implications of the concept of a realm of differentiated agencies of decision), 'the agent's actions, however much
circumscribed by conditioning factors, are determined in their
form by calculation and not given to them by some other agent'.
While co-ordination may be more likely to work well if it takes
the form of regulation, it need not do so. Hirst certainly indicates the probable costs of a lack of regulation: a plurality of
agencies of decision, dependent on one another's compliance
and goodwill, competition for resources, and multiple performance of functions. They would thus not only be limited by
their own objectives, but by the means at their disposal and
their various (limited) forms of calculation. However, these
costs of a lack of overall regulation of the different agencies do
not impose a *requirement* of a regulatory instance. It is possible
to conceive of a series of agencies working by administrative
regulation of their own sub-agents and co-ordinating their
activities at the level of the overall society by means of an
admixture of *ad hoc* adjustment, regular flows of information
and struggle over resources. Admittedly, the co-ordination

would be much poorer without legal regulation, but there would be non-legal limits on their forms of existence and their capacities for action. It does not require the positing of an ontologically prior realm of diverse agents to construct such an argument, since it does not deny the necessary existence of some regulation in the society; it merely denies the necessity of an overarching regulatory instance successfully making general claims as to its own scope as a public power.

Of course, if there is no ontologically prior realm of agents, then the state and the law cannot be considered as *necessarily* oppressive. This latter conclusion underlines one of the main themes of Hirst's essay, which I support: namely, that if the state and the law are not necessarily oppressive, there is no necessity to abolish them. Even if one does not accept that a general regulatory instance is a *necessary* condition of a realm of differentiated agencies of decision (that is, of an advanced division of labour), the probable costs indicated by Hirst of the absence of a body which makes general claims to regulate other agencies could be considerable. While the state cannot resolve all the problems of regulation and co-ordination, its capacity to resolve at least some of these problems provides a forceful political argument in favour of retaining the state and law in socialist societies. As Hirst makes clear in a section on 'Pashukanis and Socialist Social Policy', Pashukanis's concept of 'social defence' could only be realised (by replacing legal regulation of social policy) at the cost of lower standards of control of administration than are accepted in the West. This is not the same thing as supporting the current forms of law and state organisation in the Soviet Union, as Hirst makes clear. Indeed, one of his arguments in favour of legal regulation imposing limits on state agencies is that this can prevent such institutions from serving as means of suppression of political opposition. He is not arguing for a restoration of 'socialist legality' but for changes in the law, and more importantly for the provision of effective means of limiting certain capacities of state agencies.

Hirst's work on law makes it difficult to ignore the role of public law in analysing the Soviet Union, particularly since, as Hirst among others points out, the Soviet Union has an ineffective legal framework of control. Perhaps the most striking recent example of this is the provision made in the 1977 Constitution for workers' collectives, though the organisational form for implementing them is not made clear. This means that it is conceivable that the 1979 decree enhancing the role of production brigades in the enterprises could be considered as related to the implementation of this provision of the Constitution, even though, as the Lavignes point out,[6] some juridical interpretations treat the workers' collectives as extensions of the trade unions in the enterprises.[7] If the production brigades were to be able to function legally as workers' collectives, their relation to the CP and to the trade unions' factory committees would have to be legally specified. Until some such legal enactment is made, the Constitutional provision for workers' collectives will remain ineffective.

Legal regulation of the Soviet economy

The Constitutional position on the agencies for regulating the economy is clear:[8] the Council of Ministers – the Government of the USSR – is the highest executive and administrative agency of state power, subject to the control of the Supreme Soviet. The various state committees, chief administrations and other departments are attached to the Council of Ministers. However, the legal commentary on 'The Directing and Planning Agencies' provided by Hazard *et al.* is not very enlightening, since it is concerned with historical swings between centralisation and decentralisation, and has no analysis of the contemporary effectivity of the law in the relations between the various central agencies.[9] However, its citation of cases of disputes over plan enforcement and production quality control is helpful. The role of the law in regulating relations between 'The Operating Agencies' of various kinds such as Ministries, production associations and enterprises is clearer. There is legal specification of organisational forms of these relations for separate branches of industry, of enterprise powers, of measures for checking against fraud and mismanagement, and of legal successors in the event of liquidation of an enterprise.

There has been considerable debate in the Soviet Union as to whether the best legal framework for regulating the economy requires the establishment of a special 'Economic Code'. The idea is that this would codify all economic relations, thereby reducing the current legal incoherence in this area. However, both sides in this debate are subject to Hirst's strictures against conceiving of the law as recognising a prior realm of relations between agents which it then sets out to regulate. Since the law partly defines the relations between agents, coherence is a worthwhile objective, and codification is one useful means of achieving this. However, such conclusions cannot automatically enable one to decide which range of laws (or governmental normative acts) need to be codified under one rubric, or what the relations should be between the various branches of law. The argument that, say, a Construction Code and Banking Code would need to be co-ordinated could equally well be applied to relations between the proposed Economic Code and other branches of law. The differentiation of law into various branches occurs because of the problems of unification, and arguments for a single Economic Code of the USSR will need to be conducted on some other basis than the supposed unitary nature of the economy. The broader the span or range of a legal code, the greater the danger of internal inconsistency within the domain which it purports to regulate; the corollary of this is that there is a greater danger of avoidance or evasion of the law by various means, including simple confusion as to which laws are applicable. It would seem, then, that to be effective the law must, like the technical aspects of an economic plan, be capable of specifying agents and relations between them with reasonable precision and be capable of enforcing those relations (or enforcing the conditions for negotiating those relations), while at the same time maintaining a reasonable degree of coherence with other domains being legally regulated and with other forms of non-legal regulation. This is a problem to which there is no final or optimum solution; acceptable solutions will depend on the theorisation of existing social relations and on current political objectives.

Even within the relatively narrow sphere considered here of administrative law and civil law concerned with the regulation of the economy, there is a substantial diversity of legal relations. This diversity, and the legal inconsistency which often accompanies it, should lead to caution in analysing the effectivity of the law in social relations. It is partly for this reason that the Soviet state cannot be treated as emanating from law. Even though legal definitions of institutions partly determine its structure, political determinants of the state structure (forms of struggle between agencies, as well as forms of co-operation) do not simply take place in legally defined arenas according to legally defined norms of conduct. For this reason, the Soviet state and the forms of politics associated with it will be analysed together.

State and Politics

One need look no further than the account of Hough and Fainsod for an adequate institutional account of the Soviet state (the Supreme Soviet, its Praesidium, its Standing Committees, the Council of Ministers, the Ministries, State Committees, and so on).[10] It is not proposed to repeat this account here, though Hough's analysis of both state and party institutions will be discussed, since the effectivity of institutions cannot be ignored. The Soviet state and politics will be appraised from the viewpoint of what such an analysis contributes to an understanding of the formation of economic and social policies affecting the relations of production. This approach diverges from those which analyse the state in terms of the representation of class interests,[11] since the impact of state policy on the relations of production is not going to be treated as an outcome of the successful representation of class interests, but rather as an outcome of struggle between various (state and non-state) agencies whose objectives or interests need not coincide with those of any particular class, however defined. As already indicated in the preceding section on law, the state is not going to be analysed in terms of the developing conditions under which it could wither away, since the concept of a social totality on which such a conception rests has been abandoned. Even in the absence of class relations, the classical Marxist conception of a unitary property at the disposal of the free, associated producers is impossible to sustain, since the diversity of uses to which the property could be put will entail a diversity of agencies disposing of parts of the total social property and a diversity of means of calculating the various objectives and means of securing them: in other words, some division of labour is inevitable.

Thus, without arguing for a structural necessity of the state, the Soviet state will not be criticised for refusing to wither away or to conform to Lenin's conception of a 'semi-state'. However, such a position does not amount to a refusal to consider whether the Soviet state is repressive, authoritarian or in some sense undemocratic. The classical Marxist approach has tended to criticise 'bourgeois' or parliamentary democracy for retaining an institutional separation between the decision-making agencies of the state and the working class or the people, and has proposed that true democracy will overcome this separation.[12] The current Soviet theory of the state, which (according to Hough) is closely associated with Fedor Burlatskii, attempts to treat the Soviet state in the stage of 'developed socialism' or 'advanced socialist society' as an 'all-people's state'.[13] Even ignoring the problematic relationship between this position and the classical Marxist position, the current official Soviet theory of the state, effectively enshrined in the 1977 Constitution, faces the problem that 'the Soviet people' is divided up in terms of workers, peasants and employees, and in terms of nationalities. While the ultimate aim is to reduce or eliminate these differences within the population, the 'all-people's state' is constructed to 'represent' the differences between the nationalities, but not other differences. This lays the state open to the charge that it is being undemocratic in not representing these other constituencies' separate interests, or that it is not doing so adequately.[14]

However, the notion of democracy implied by such a criticism is one in which the interests or desires of an underlying population are represented in the political structures. This conception, which implies that the population is not *already* structured by political institutions, has been criticised by Hindess, who provides an alternative conception of democracy.[15] This approach argues that democratic mechanisms (namely, the use of a 'free' vote within some relevant constituency or constituencies) for the appointment of personnel and the reaching of decisions always coexist with non-democratic forms. Hence the approach concentrates on analysing the scope of the democratic mechanisms and their relation to the non-democratic ones. The theoretical rationale for this position is that the 'interests' or objectives of various parts of the population can only be articulated by specific organisational forms, and that to posit 'interests' as distinct from the organisational forms through which objectives are formulated is to posit an unknowable 'counterfactual' in terms of which expressed interests can be appraised. Where the expressed interests or objectives do not correspond to the counterfactual (the 'true' interests of that section of the population) the forms of articulation of interests or objectives are then criticised from the utopian standpoint of their inadequacy or failure to represent the true interests of their constituency. Hindess argues that a concentration on the organisational forms both avoids this utopian critique and the complacency which ignores both the currently *limited* scope of democratic mechanisms and the extent to which such mechanisms are affected by their relation to non-democratic mechanisms.

It might appear that Hindess's position makes it difficult to describe a form of state as repressive, if the notion of the interests or desires of an underlying population is abandoned. This might also appear to be a conclusion to be drawn from the discussion in the previous section of Hirst's analysis of the law. Yet even if one abandons the notion of the inherent interests of a population arising out of its supposed ontological structure, interests which the state then acts upon to express or repress, one could argue that it is still possible to characterise a state (or other overtly political organisations) as undemocractic or repressive if it actively interdicts the development of voluntary organisational forms for the articulation of objectives which are not officially approved. This is one form of restricting the scope of the 'free' vote, by restricting the issues which can be voted upon. Some states do permit the articulation of illegal objectives while enforcing the law until such time as it is changed. The conclusion that a particular law or aspect of state organisation is itself repressive can only be reached on the basis of an analysis of the relation between democratic and non-democratic ways of appointing personnel and reaching decisions. Far from precluding statements about the undemocratic nature of a particular form of state organisation, the position outlined by Hindess allows one to analyse democratic mechanisms in terms of the conditions under which they operate (including the variously constituted social forces or agencies acting on the democratic mechanisms).

This approach seems potentially much more fruitful than

arguments about whether the Soviet Union's 'failure' to represent certain workers' interests means that it is no longer 'really' a socialist state. Instead, the emphasis here will be on conflicts between and within state agencies. While they are not the only form of political struggle in the Soviet Union (for example, there are also the activities of the dissidents and the feminists), these struggles are probably the most important form of conflict, apart from intra-party conflict, in so far as the latter is separate.

Politics and the relations of production

It seems appropriate to concentrate on struggles between state agencies over economic policy, and to discuss the related differences within the party in conjunction with them, because, according to White, one of the main sources of support for the current political set-up in the Soviet Union is its economic performance.[16] It also focuses the discussion on the political conditions of the relations of production, which is the main reason for analysing the law, state and politics in this book. This approach may seem to have much in common with Brown's brief discussion of Soviet politics in terms of 'bureaucratic pluralism'[17] or the apparently independent and lengthier analysis of 'institutional pluralism' by Hough.[18] Yet, as will be seen, while the analysis here will rely heavily on the work of Hough, the theoretical basis of the analysis will be somewhat different. Furthermore, Hough's analysis is by no means confined to an analysis of the upper levels of party and state, which is what forms the main focus of concern here. Such an approach may appear strange to those unfamiliar with fairly recent developments in the study of Soviet politics, and indeed Hough spends a considerable amount of space discussing alternative approaches, as does Brown.[19] The aim here is to break from such 'conventional' approaches, as well as from the classical Marxist approach, criticised in the previous section.

Totalitarianism

Probably the best-known approach, at least in popular discussions, is analysis of Soviet politics in terms of totalitarianism. This approach has, as Brown indicates, become increasingly difficult to sustain in view of the widely acknowledged changes in Soviet politics since the fall of Khrushchev. The major element in Brown's defence of the concept[20] is that it can be used as an ideal type, which by accentuating certain elements of Soviet reality can provide a classificatory framework for the periodisation of Soviet history. Thus the years 1934 to 1953 would be the period most closely approximating to the ideal type of totalitarianism. However, the use of ideal types, for which Hough also displays a weakness, is by no means as unproblematic as Brown seems to imagine.[21] In addition, the content of the ideal type of totalitarianism itself poses further problems, for there is little to distinguish it from the concept of autocracy as deployed by Friedrich and Brzezinski,[22] except the additional use of modern technology (the mass media and modern forms of effective armed combat) and bureaucratic co-ordination of the whole economy.

The main paradox of the 'totalitarian' approach to the study of Soviet politics is that it emphasises tight central control, yet assigns to the mass party and the mass media the functions of mobilisation of the population for mass participation in politics, while denying that this mass participation has any significant effects on the form and scope of central control. Such a position can only be sustained on the assumption of almost literally total control of the population, so that 'participation' is of the most passive and formalistic kind. Quite apart from the rationalism of such a position (the implicit claim that the means of control are fully adequate to the imputed ends of the political leadership), the evidence produced by Hough[23] and even by White[24] on contemporary political participation and political beliefs is difficult to reconcile with such a view. Even in discussing the Stalin period one need hardly claim that the society was under totalitarian control in order to demonstrate that politics were in many respects conducted in a repressive and autocratic manner:

> for all its popularity as a description of the Stalin era, the totalitarian model always had certain shortcomings. The drive to transform society, to remake man, and to keep the administrators from becoming a privileged elite implies the continuing use of radical reformers against established authority . . . The totalitarian model gained plausibility as a

depiction of the Stalin regime because the policies of the First Five Year Plan period could be cited as evidence of a determination to transform society while the rigid controls in the late Stalin period could be cited as evidence of the authoritarian features. In the process, however, the conservative nature of most of the Stalin period – the immobilism of the Stalin regime in the dictator's last years – was obscured from view.[25]

It could perhaps be argued that Brown's use of the ideal type of totalitarianism and his restriction of its applicability to the period from after the First Five Year Plan to Stalin's death mean that his use of 'totalitarianism' escapes from the above criticism. Certainly Brown distances himself from Friedrich and Brzezinski, but he retains the elements of an all-embracing ideology, police terror on a mass scale, which atomises society, and the technological means to impose central control over an entire country. Brown thus probably does escape the above criticism by Hough, in restricting the use of 'totalitarianism' to the period of 'immobilism', but Brown's position must then be subject to Hough's other criticism that 'the totalitarian model was especially weak in gliding over the implications of the succession', namely that the experience of the terror placed limits on the post-Stalin conduct of politics. In contrast to Brown's use of the ideal type of totalitarianism to draw attention to factors inhibiting more radical political change, Hough's argument implies that 'the totalitarian model' is weak on the 'long-term dynamics of the system' and precludes an analysis of certain sources of change.

Yet important changes have taken place. It would be difficult to claim now, for example, that police terror operates on a mass scale in the Soviet Union or that police activity results in an atomised society. Such a conclusion would be at serious odds with Hough's work, or White's somewhat different form of analysis. There is simply no need to conceptualise the current forms of suppression of opposition, of policy formation or of political mobilisation in totalitarian terms.

Elite theory
Another approach to the analysis of Soviet politics relies

heavily on the use of the concept of an elite, or oligarchy. This approach is only briefly discussed in Hough and Fainsod,[26] perhaps because Hough retains the use of the term 'elite', albeit used in a very loose sense, and is consequently not too critical of it. The notion of an elite refers to a relatively small, self-conscious group which is differentiated from the rest of society by its social location and by its access to esoteric knowledge.[27] It is the common access to knowledge not widely available which constitutes it as a group, and the resulting cohesion is in some sense (perhaps indirectly, depending on the theory in question) related to the successful seizure or retention of power (which is conceived of in a zero-sum sense). Hough sometimes deviates from this position by arguing that the elite need not be unified.[28] He also deviates from the zero-sum conception of power in his criticism of Dahl's definition of power (which, although Hough does not mention it, is identical to Weber's conception): '*A* has power over *B* to the extent that he can get *B* to do something that *B* would not otherwise do.'[29] Hough argues against this by pointing to the difficulties of analysing power in terms of a counterfactual (what *B* would otherwise have done). Since *B* is presumably subject to various influences, the attribution of *B*'s action to the power of *A* (as opposed to *C*, *D* or any other source of influence) is problematic.[30]

These two modifications by Hough (allowing for disunity in the elite, and effectively abandoning the zero-sum conception of power) seriously compromise his (or indeed any other) use of the concept of elite. Hough makes these modifications because he insists that power is a situational and relational phenomenon.

The focusing of the analysis on the situational and relational character of power means that the theorisation of the social location of people or groups thought to be part of the elite must be taken more seriously. The common Weberian approach treating the elite as constituted by the chiefs of bureaucracies[31] shows some of the difficulties of the use of any concept of an elite. At first sight it does seem to specify the social location of the elite, but it is extremely difficult to specify where the elite ends and the mass begins when dealing with a bureaucracy with (in most conceptions) a hierarchical chain of command. It is difficult to restrict the elite simply to the titular heads of the

various bureaucracies while denying that their immediate subordinates are also comparatively powerful in relation to the
mass, and once this is acknowledged it is not clear where the
line should be drawn.[32] It is not drawn in terms of the social
location of the elite, but in terms of its self-consciousness as a
group. The elite is thus treated as a collective subject, and the
esoteric knowledge to which it has access (which may be as
mundane as simply the knowledge of the unpublicised activities
of the other members of the elite) then becomes the main defining feature of the elite: the apparent definition in terms of social
location has collapsed into an almost tautological definition of
the elite as a collective subject. Such a conception is simply not
compatible with a situational and relational conception of
power since the concept of power entailed by such a definition
of an elite is of power deriving from its unity as a group and its
capacity for collective action to realise the collective ends of the
group, thus wielding power over the mass. In other words, the
concept of elite implies a unity of purpose within the elite, and a
zero-sum conception of power, which are precisely the two
aspects of the concept which Hough questions. His attempted
eclectic retention of the concept under these circumstances is
pointless.

Hough's approach to Soviet politics: institutional pluralism
In fairness to Hough, it must be said that he does argue that the
totalitarian approach, the elite-domination approach and the
related 'directed society' approach all suffer from a lack of
serious attention to the complex process of policy formation. It
is to Hough's credit that he does pay serious attention to this
aspect of Soviet politics, without denying the repressive and
authoritarian aspects of contemporary Soviet politics. This is
the basis of his discussion of Soviet politics in terms of 'institutional pluralism'. This position of 'institutional pluralism' conceives of Soviet politics as a series of 'complexes', i.e. complexes
of agencies. Relations within and between complexes are
affected by 'tendencies' whose interaction with other tendencies form 'whirlpools' on particular policy areas. A 'tendency'
consists of an expression of views by a loose coalition of actors,
operating at different levels of the political structure, whose
articulations of views tend in the same direction, but who are

unlikely to be fully aware of the common thrust and consequences of their activity. Hough follows this approach to some
extent, which has the merit of avoiding the need to assume that
the articulation of objectives requires either self-consciousness
as a group or explicit *group* organisation. However, in conceiving of the interaction of tendencies in whirlpools, he adds the
assumption that political conflicts in the Soviet Union, as in the
USA, tend to be compartmentalised, with the debate in such
policy areas being largely limited to those whose careers are
associated with it, those most directly affected by the decision,
and a few who have developed a special interest in it.

Such an approach both attempts to conceptualise struggles
without positing a necessary group cohesiveness to the contending forces (which would imply that personnel always
formed into the same groups on different policy issues) and also
attempts to relate these struggles to the existing structure of
political institutions in the Soviet Union. Consequently it
seems to be the most promising line of analysis among what
might be termed conventional Western political science work
on the Soviet Union, despite the apparent diffidence of Hough
in advocating it and his refusal to give up other modes of
analysis. It is worth seeing what use Hough is able to make of it,
given his command of the empirical material available on
Soviet politics.

In discussing policy initiatives (that is, the beginning of
struggles to change policy or develop policy in a previously
neglected area), Hough argues that the initiation process surely
must include the stream of proposals and pressures impinging
upon the leadership and the apparatus coming from a variety of
directions, particularly from individual specialists writing in
specialised journals who do not necessarily represent any
'interest group's' perspective.[33] However, while such specialists
may (in my terminology) make available new means of political
calculation, Hough makes some interesting points about what
he calls 'agenda-setting and the building of support'. Since
there is a vast range of potential alternative objectives, Hough
asks:

How is attention narrowed to a manageable range of alternatives? How is support built for the different alternatives?

What types of alliances tend to be formed most often in the struggle to achieve policy goals? The answers to these questions will depend in large part on the levels of our analysis. The setting of the agenda and the building of support extends from the first substantial efforts to focus public or governmental attention on a proposal . . . to the movement of that proposal toward a final vote in Congress or the Politburo or a final decision by the General Secretary or President. Obviously these processes are going to be very different in character.[34]

Despite the attempts by the leadership to define the agenda, vigorously using the secret police and censorship to enforce its definition, Hough argues that the leadership's

decision to permit debates implies a willingness to let others try to organise support for their ideas, at least in a verbal way. Its desire to be exposed to information about societal shortcomings and to proposals for improvement implies a willingness to let others influence the setting of the agenda, at least as long as the proposals do not become too threatening. And regardless of the regime's desires, nothing could prevent some of those affected by a policy from attempting to influence it in whatever manner they can.[35]

This, then, is the basis for Hough's concept of institutional pluralism: outside the Politburo there is scope for formulating objectives and struggling for them, but since factional victories and defeats do not coincide with policy decisions (on the evidence presented by Hough) the institutions, such as Ministries, trade unions, regional party and governmental units, and scientific institutes, must be the most important agencies in defining which problems are most important and which solutions are the reasonable policy alternatives. Hough justifies his 'institutional pluralism' (as opposed to some other basis for the development of a plurality of contending agencies) by arguing that

the antifaction rule is fairly effective in curbing the formation of any substantial network of alliances along philosophical

lines among regional and other middle-level political officials. The nature of censorship – especially the restriction of
the more sensitive debates to specialised journals –
strengthens the tendency for the policy relevant alliances to
remain compartmentalised within specialised 'whirlpools'
even more fully than occurs in the West, with the selective
censorship making it difficult to appeal through the press for
outside allies.[36]

The concept of 'institutional pluralism' as used by Hough,
then, is an attempt to deal with what he calls the informal distribution of power. He argues that there has been a major diffusion of power in the Soviet Union in recent decades, especially
since the removal of Khrushchev.[37] The word 'pluralism' is used
to denote this, and the word 'institutional' is intended to indicate that it is different from Western pluralism, not that institutions are the only actors in the political process. One could thus
conclude from Hough's analysis that this limited diffusion of
power and growth of participation has strengthened the hand of
various state agencies in the process of policy formation.

It is this aspect of his position which makes it relevant to the
concern of this book with the analysis of struggles among state
agencies (particularly over economic policy). Hough's analysis
shows that state agencies are in a position to struggle for certain
of their own objectives, and that there are effective limits on the
extent of such struggles, limits which are set by the regulatory
capacities of other party and state agencies. In other words,
Hough begins to analyse the conditions (including the limits) of
struggle between state and party agencies. His analysis avoids
most of the critical remarks on interest-group theory made by
Brown,[38] but there are still problems with the concept of
'institutional pluralism', as Hough in a sense acknowledges
when he asks what aspects of pluralism are associated with the
consequences 'that we associate with pluralism'.[39] The concept
of institutional pluralism (like 'Western' pluralism, or the
concept of totalitarianism) designates what is considered to be
an empirical set of relations that produces certain effects. Since
the concept refers to the *complex* of social relations as a whole
(a 'global definition') the relevance of the definition becomes
questionable as soon as part of that complex of social relations

is no longer considered to be present. Once part of the complex of social relations has disappeared, can the former concept still be used? Which aspects of the complex are 'really' associated with the effects which it is thought to engender? The problem cannot be really avoided by designating the concept as an 'ideal' type. The insistence on attempting 'global definitions' creates this problem and gives rise to the explicit eclecticism that is by no means confined to Hough or Brown. Thus, for example, the 'elite-domination model' is perhaps combined with elements of the 'interest-group model' to deal conceptually with, say, the relatively restricted access to some struggles coexisting with wider access to other struggles. Apart from eclecticism, this mode of conceptualising Soviet politics also gives rise to charges that a particular 'model' is 'outdated' (for example, totalitarianism).

The combination of 'bureaucratic regulation' and struggle against it by sub-agents is what produces the pattern of access to some struggles (and thus access to policy formation) by certain state and party agencies. The varying degrees of openness of policy formation and implementation to proposals, initiatives or simply resistance from subordinate state agencies seem to be related to the priority attached to the policy in question by the most important central party and state agencies. In other words, while the central agencies cannot completely determine the political agenda or determine which state agencies can have an impact on a particular policy, they do preponderate in structuring the access of other state and party agencies to the processes of policy formation and implementation, so that the degree of openness of such processes varies with the issue. This is largely managed by designating certain state and party agencies as the ones to be involved in particular policies. Hough's concept of 'institutional pluralism' is an attempt to deal with the greater openness of policy formation in some issues, while not denying that this is still largely restricted to specific state agencies. However, because the concept functions as a descriptive designation of a historically specific complex of social relations (a global definition), it is vulnerable to historical changes in those social relations.

An alternative approach to Soviet politics: arenas of struggle
What is needed is a mode of conceptualising politics in which concepts do not become redundant once it is conceded that fairly important social changes have taken place. Indeed, the concepts must be usable to analyse the changes themselves. It is for this reason that the concept of 'arenas of struggle' is proposed here as a key element in the conceptualisation of Soviet politics, though it need not be restricted to the Soviet Union, and is by no means used for the first time here.[40] An 'arena of struggle' refers to the conditions under which agencies (or individuals) contend for the realisation of their objectives. The arena *may* be institutionally regulated, i.e. legally, administratively or customarily regulated. The extent of the arena is defined by the range of issues, the scope of the various struggles and the nature of the contending agents; in addition, the extent of the arena may be determined by other conditions of its existence, such as the outcome of struggle in another arena. Precisely because some arenas are institutionally regulated and defined, and societies are institutionally differentiated into a variety of agencies of decision, struggles cannot all take place in the same arena. The articulation of arenas of struggle is thus an important area of analysis, since the relations between arenas may change, and arenas may appear and disappear. Thus arenas cannot be considered in complete isolation, though the extent to which the conditions of struggle are taken into account in a particular analysis will vary in terms of what is pertinent to that analysis. Thus outcomes of parliamentary struggles in Britain may affect, say, trade-union struggles with individual employers, but for some aspects of trade-union struggles little reference may be necessary to their legal conditions.

This mode of analysis does not attribute in advance any particular set of qualities to any arena or to the agents engaged in struggle in it. Agents may be involved in more than one arena. The precise nature of the agents and the alignment of forces engaged in an arena is a matter for analysis in each particular situation. The outcome of the struggles could include a change in the nature of the agents engaged in the struggle, a change in the alignment of forces, a policy change, a change in the extent of the arena, its mode of operation or its relation to other arenas, and so on. The analysis of struggles taking place in an arena requires reference to the socially available means of calculation of political objectives and of ways of achieving them. This aspect of the analysis implies recourse to at least some of the material used by Brown and White in their analyses of 'political culture'.[41] Without recourse to currently available means of calculation, the analysis of the formation and pursuit of objectives or 'interests' would be adversely affected by the common tendency to reduce 'interests' or political objectives to the social location of the agents pursuing them, whether it be class position, location in the bureaucracy, nationality or whatever. The available means of calculation may be fairly slow to change on some issues or in some arenas, but may change rapidly in others (where specialist policy debates may be taking place, where there are continual shifts in alliances, or where the arena is in a 'subordinate' position making it very susceptible to the outcomes of struggles in other arenas). One of the problems of the concept of 'political culture', even though it refers to relatively distinct sub-cultures of various kinds, is that it provides little means of analysing the conditions of such differential changes in the socially available means of political calculation, though White's work does indicate that some such changes may be taking place in the Soviet Union.[42]

The legal or administrative regulation of the arena may well mean that the contending forces also have to co-operate as well as struggle with one another (for example, in British parliamentary struggles over legislation). For this reason analyses of 'power' which treat it as a quality or attribute inherent in a particular social location run into difficulties: such a conception implies that the agent occupying that social location exercises power *ipso facto* over other agents and tends to treat co-operation by other agents as compliance. However, if the capacities of agents in an arena are conditioned by the actions of other agents (that is, if, as Hough points out,[43] power is always situational and relational), power cannot be considered as a capacity to act which inheres in the social location of a certain agent (or class of agents): that capacity to act must always be related to conditions within (and outside of) the arena of struggle. Co-operation need not be merely compliance, since it may create dependence on the 'less powerful' agent. Consequently the relative capacities of the contending agencies (perhaps even the same agencies) will vary in different arenas.

Hough provides ample evidence which could be used to support such an analysis of Soviet politics. For example, he argues that the system is an authoritarian one in terms of political freedom (particularly for the individual), but points to the development of restraints on government that have developed in recent decades, including increased formal political controls over the police, and the development of informal constraints such as greater freedom of criticism.[44] Hough argues that power in the Soviet Union varies with the policy area:

> In the spheres of foreign and defense policy, one gains the impression of deep leadership involvement and of participation limited to specialists . . . In the transportation realm, on the other hand, one has the sense of little leadership involvement, fairly wide debate in the media, and domination by the major interest group, the railroads. In the realm of wages, it is unclear who is making policy, but one gains the sense of real responsiveness to workers and peasants.[45]

He regards this variation of power with the policy area as the safest generalisation about the distribution of power in the Soviet Union. He goes on to argue, as a second generalisation, that the strongest political actors below the leadership level are 'vertical' or branch, not regional, officials:

> Whether one wants to emphasise the role of the ministries, the Secretariat and departments of the Central Committee, or a specialised complex cutting across these and other institutions, one is talking about a type of politics that is different from, say, Yugoslavia, where bargaining among republics seems to dominate.[46]

His third generalisation is that among the specialised branch interests those associated with industrial growth have been in a position of special power. His fourth generalisation ('the most difficult judgement of all') is that the distribution of income, which has shifted in an egalitarian manner in favour of workers and peasants, may well be a response to the power of these occupational groups.

On the basis of such conclusions it seems that the concern of this book with the political conditions of the relations of production (that is, struggles between state and party agencies) touches on what are in any case the most important arenas of struggle in Soviet politics. However, the analysis of such struggles, particularly struggles over attempts by the party leadership to regulate the Ministries, will not be concerned with which agent 'has the power', since power is not a capacity to act which is inherent in an agent occupying a particular social location. Rather, the analysis will simply be concerned to elucidate the political relations operative between the top-level party and state agencies, since if power can be said to be located anywhere it is located in the arenas of struggle, i.e. in the political relations between agents, not in the agents themselves. This is not to deny that agencies can extend their capabilities by improving their internal organisation and their means of calculation, and increasing their resources, but such improvements themselves are conditioned by relations with other agents.

State and Party agencies and economic policy

Constitutionally the Supreme Soviet is the supreme authority of the state, with two chambers (the Council of the Union and the Council of Nationalities), but Hough's analysis makes it clear that it is not the most important political arena in the Soviet Union. While not treating the Supreme Soviet simply as an ornamental figurehead, Hough argues that its role in the policy process is less than that of other major institutions.[47] Its Standing Committees have increased their activity in recent years, which must have affected the process of policy formation to some extent, and its Praesidium does have legislative powers in between meetings of the Supreme Soviet itself. Nevertheless, a great deal more legislative work is done by the Council of Ministers, sometimes together with the Party Central Committee. Consequently, although the Supreme Soviet is a legislative body, and Soviet government is parliamentary in form, the parliament is not the only legislative body, and the legislative power of extra-parliamentary organs such as the Central Committee constitutes a major restriction on the role of the

Supreme Soviet. The Communist Party predominates over the state, though this is not the same thing as party apparatus domination over the state apparatus.[48]

Apart from the Supreme Soviet, and its associated arenas of Praesidium and Standing Committees, the Council of Ministers is, as Hough says, a vital institution in the Soviet political system, though its associated Praesidium is much more important since it is a smaller body composed of senior members of the Council, meeting more frequently, and is termed 'the working organ of the Council of Ministers', empowered to decide 'urgent questions' and to 'speak in the name of the government of the USSR'.[49] The division of labour between the Praesidium of the Council of Ministers and the Central Committee Secretariat is obscure, according to Hough.[50] It appears to handle economic questions just below the level of significance required for Politburo consideration. The functions of the various interdepartmental committees or commissions attached to the Council of Ministers are a mystery, since they are rarely even mentioned in Soviet sources. A little more is known about the departments of the apparatus attached to the Council of Ministers. For our purposes, the main point to remember is that the Council of Ministers must examine the economic plan as a whole, and confirm the material balance of the most important economic items worked out by Gosplan.

Apart from the regulation of individual Ministries conducted by the Council of Ministers itself, or its associated agencies, the main regulatory agents are the top-level party agencies themselves: the Central Committee, its Secretariat (with its own apparatus) and the Politburo of the Central Committee. Their interrelationships and their relations to the Ministries are discussed by Hough.[51] This discussion will rely heavily on that material. The predominance of party over government is most clearly shown by the formal obligation (which is adhered to in practice) on party members working in government agencies to carry out the decrees of the extra-parliamentary party committees, particularly the Central Committee. The only decisions which are unconditionally obligatory on the government are those emanating from the collective party organs, and except for a period in the 1940s and early 1950s these have been the scene of the most crucial policy-making decisions. However, the relationship between party agencies and state agencies is much more complicated than simply one apparatus subordinating the other, and it is in analysing these relationships that a concept like 'articulation of arenas of struggle' shows its uses. Many of the agencies themselves can be considered arenas of struggle, since the concept does not imply that the struggle need take a particular form or be conducted overtly or with a particular intensity. The arenas themselves must consequently be discussed in order to clarify the effectiveness with which activities within some agencies can be regulated by other agencies.

Many Western analyses (such as elite or totalitarian ones) treat the Party Congress as effectively regulated by the Central Committee or the Politburo, despite the fact that Party rules designate it as the ultimate authority within the Party. Yet Hough argues quite effectively that, despite its tame appearance, speeches there are attempts to influence future policy, and that they may even affect current policy if a strong current of opinion is seen to be running among the delegates. Certainly, the speeches at the Twenty-Fifth Congress advocating that certain rivers be diverted to flow into Central Asia seem to have had an effect, since that is now official policy, despite lobbying to locate industry in Siberia and the Far East (where the raw materials are), rather than Central Asia (where the population is rising quickly). Certainly, however, the Congress does not have democratic control of the Central Committee in the sense of a free vote to elect the Central Committee. It is not clear how the 'slate' of candidates to be elected is compiled, but it may be that the size of the 'slate' is manipulated so that the Central Committee generates a balance of forces inside the Politburo. If Congress members crossed off the names of Central Committee nominees (which they have not apparently done in recent years) they could at least prevent some nominees from being elected to the Central Committee. As a remote possibility, this could affect the balance of forces inside the Politburo, since the long average tenure of Central Committee members following the removal of Khrushchev may enhance their position in relation to the General Secretary, so the balance of forces in the Central Committee may affect the line-up inside the Politburo.

Pre-Congress meetings may indicate the balance of forces and this may affect the drawing up of the 'slate' for the Central Committee.

However, election to the Central Committee seems to depend more on the post held than on personal characteristics and loyalties (which is an argument against the 'personalistic factions' approach of the 'conflict school'). It is institutions rather than individuals who are represented, according to Hough, which suggests that the 'slate' is compiled partly as an administrative device to ensure adequate information flows, and is partly an attempt to create a more unified agency of decision. This is also suggested by the fact that 88 per cent of 1976 voting members of the Central Committee had already been selected as Supreme Soviet deputies, though the Central Committee has a narrower social base than the Supreme Soviet and has, on average, an older membership. Unfortunately there is little information on the work of the Central Committee, as opposed to its membership. It meets comparatively rarely; it does not feature the kind of debate between party leaders which it did in the 1920s. Judging by Brezhnev's published replies, many of the speeches seemed to be requests for more resources. Thus it might seem that the Central Committee played a relatively minor role in politics in the Brezhnev period. Yet both the low turnover of members since 1965 and the policies emerging suggest that the Central Committee may be an arena of institutional bargaining, and members do, it seems, receive Politburo papers on policy issues, which means they have a political role outside the actual Central Committee meeting. This provision of information suggests the possibility that the Politburo leadership makes a real effort to elicit Central Committee members' views informally and to respond to them. Even if the General Secretary simply gathers information in an informal fashion and avoids antagonising too much of the Central Committee, then, as Hough says:

> the Central Committee still is a crucial body in the political system. Since the Central Committee encompasses representatives from all types of ministries and all regions of the country, a policy that is responsive to a consensus or to the

centre of opinion in it is going to be responsive to a wide range of interests in the country. In addition, of course, the Central Committee's potential role in any succession crisis always makes it of even more crucial interest in the long run.[52]

It seems to me that this point must be made a little more strongly than Hough does: the Central Committee, even when not in session, must be an arena of informal struggle between various state agencies, and only those struggles that cannot be resolved by informal accommodation must go on to the Politburo.

This implies that the Politburo is run on the basis of 'consensus' committee politics, with the General Secretary of the Party operating in many respects as 'chairman of the board' on the Politburo, arbitrating between conflicting institutional objectives to reach a workable consensus. Certainly Hough's analysis suggests such a conclusion for the Brezhnev period.[53] He argues that the Politburo has been the real cabinet of the Soviet system. The Politburo discusses the annual economic plan. In the past, different variants of the plan have been discussed and the plan has been returned to Gosplan for reworking. On another occasion, discussion was detailed enough to lead to an increase in the number of grain elevators. The Politburo discussions most frequently referred to are economic ones, though foreign policy questions occupy what is officially described as 'a large place' in the work of the Politburo. Other issues are mentioned less frequently. The preparation of questions to be discussed is assigned to officials of the Central Committee Secretariat apparatus, though Ministries also prepare reports for it and the Minister may stay for that discussion. Apparently (although this semi-official account should not be taken at face-value) decisions are reached on the basis of arriving at a consensus, rather than votes, in a manner similar to many Western committees. Thus, although the Constitution designates the Council of Ministers as the supreme *state* executive body, the Politburo is effectively the most important executive body in the Soviet political system, and it is clear from what is known about the matters which it decides upon that it is the most important agency regulating the

activities of the planning and plan-implementing agencies
(particularly the economic Ministries).

However, the detailed regulation of the Ministries by the
party (as opposed to regulation by the Council of Ministers and
its Praesidium) is left to the departments attached to the
Secretariat of the Central Committee. Crudely, the Secretariat
consists of politicians (such as the General Secretary), while the
attached apparatus consists of officials. The various departments are formed along branch lines and supervise Ministries
and other similar institutions such as State Committees.
However, the complex and subtle relations between the
Secretariat apparatus and the Ministries make it impossible to
discuss this supervision and regulation in terms of the dominance of one apparatus over another (party over state).

To understand this, it is necessary to review Hough's
evidence on the structure of the Secretariat apparatus and the
career patterns of its staff before going on to examine the relations operating between Secretariat and the Ministries. The
Secretariat departments are formed along branch lines, i.e.
they supervise Ministries or other similar institutions. These
departments are headed by the Secretariat itself, with most of
the secretaries responsible for more than one department.
These secretaries have a general political background, but the
officials in the departments have much more specialised
backgrounds, which makes them highly qualified specialists in
the policy area which they oversee. The career patterns of these
Central Committee staff are as differentiated as the structure of
the apparatus itself, which is to say highly differentiated, with
at least twenty-one departments, divided into a total of 150 to
175 sections. The basic staff members of departments are called
'instructors', but there are also a number of high-level
'inspectors' for special assignments, and a fairly large number
of departments also have a 'group of consultants' attached to
them. The latter seem to be involved in the task of preparing
major decisions, on leading a year-long study on a problem,
and so on. Hough argues that these departments and sections
do not direct the activities of the Ministries which they oversee,
but serve more as a 'White House staff' to the General Secretary
and the Politburo, so they do not require an enormous staff.[54]

One has the picture of a Secretariat apparatus which confirms some important *nomenklatura*[55] appointments and elections (although this is sometimes a formality), which supervises fulfilment of party and state decisions (but cannot on its own do so in a comprehensive or systematic way) and which prepares draft decisions for consideration by the most senior party agencies (but does so with the help of and in consultation with other interested parties).[56] This is hardly a picture of a very powerful regulatory body ensuring close party control over the state apparatus. It certainly does not support a conception of a totalitarian monolith or elite domination (unless the elite is defined as much wider than the Politburo and Central Committee).

In trying to assess the relation between the Secretariat apparatus and the senior government agencies, one is forced to acknowledge that these relations are complicated by the fact that the Secretariat is structured like a mini-government, not only in its division into branches, but also in its hierarchy of offices. Relations between the apparatus and various state agencies are thus affected by the relative standing of the official concerned. This clearly means that on an interpersonal level relations between the officials of the Secretariat and those of the Ministry they oversee can be ambiguous, but it does not tell us about the relative strengths of these agencies in the case of conflicting objectives.

As Hough says, this duplication of offices in the Secretariat apparatus and the Ministries is intended to give the leadership access to more than one source of advice and information, but the extent to which it does so is by no means obvious, as will become apparent. What is important is not the precise rankings of each official, but that the differences are subtle ones, so the Secretariat and its apparatus cannot pre-empt the policy-making role, with the government simply executing policy. At least short of the point of final decision, policy-making must involve the sort of committee politics familiar in the West. It is in these ambiguous relations that one finds the basic explanation of why the Ministries are effectively subordinated to the CP in certain respects, but manage to escape regulation in other respects, as became evident in Chapter 3.

Hough analyses the apparatus–Ministry relationship as a relationship which is not purely an adversary one.[57] This dovetails very well with my previous remark that arenas of struggle may well involve co-operation as well as conflict between the various agencies engaged in the arena. Central Committee Secretariat officials, Hough argues, must be pushed into representing the interests of those whom they are supervising. That is, at times they must convey the objectives of the various Ministries to the Central Committee, or Politburo (or 'temporary commission'), and support these objectives themselves. In other words, the supervisory process at times leads to an advocacy role for the specialised Secretariat officials. The relevant department and the Ministry often seem to work together for 'their' branch in the appropriations process. Hough argues that the crucial question is whether to emphasise the conflict or the co-operation between the Ministries and the Secretariat departments. There is little information on this, but it obviously varies with the type of question involved.

On questions involving the performance of that branch, relations depend on whether it is an intra-branch or inter-branch question. An intra-branch question will involve tension or struggle between the Secretariat department and the Ministry (usually, I imagine, the senior levels of the Ministry since they appear to protect their own sub-agents such as enterprises from outside supervision). Where it is an inter-branch question (as in competition for, say, investment resources – in other words, what Hough calls 'the appropriations process') there are likely to be alliances between the department and the Ministry. This is most evident in the budgetary and planning processes.

If the department and Ministry are in agreement, then I presume that the struggle then moves on to the next arena, for example where the Politburo considers the annual plan of the Council of Ministers (assuming the dispute has not been resolved in the Council of Ministers itself or in its Praesidium). Quite what the 'next arena' is could of course itself be a matter of struggle, since one Ministry might feel it has a better chance of winning in the Council of Ministers, while another may prefer the matter to go straight to the Politburo.

Hough argues that Western scholars have been absorbed with the regime's policy towards the intelligentsia, and have access to liberal intellectuals who have formed a strong impression of the role of Central Committee officials in enforcing this policy. Thus these officials have become familiar in an intra-branch, adversary role (ensuring compliance by the relevant Ministries, with consequent losses by liberal intellectuals in various cultural and overtly political struggles). Yet Hough argues, 'westerners clearly should be giving more attention to the cooperative side of the ambivalent relationship between supervisors and supervised'.[58] The co-operative side is particu-larly evident in the budgetary process, including the way funds are acquired in the cultural realm, in which (according to Hough) neither Westerners nor liberal intellectuals are par-ticularly interested.

To the extent that co-operation rather than overt conflict is operative in these relations, the supervisory or regulatory role of the Secretariat officials may be ineffective, from the view-point of the leadership. Thus although, as Hough puts it, 'the leadership evidently hoped to obtain independent advisers with sufficient expertise to judge the ministerial reports and pro-posals and hence to give themselves the ability to judge perfor-mance accurately and to decide policy for each branch on the basis of a real freedom of choice',[59] this need not be the case. Hough wonders whether the use of specialised personnel in this way has not meant the penetration of the values of the specialised elite into the political leadership as much as or more than the enhancement of control over the policy process, giving rise to the familiar pattern of the regulated coming to dominate the regulators. Certainly, as was seen in Chapter 3 in the area of economic policy, the Ministries have been able to escape regu-lation in important respects, at least prior to the 1979 reform. However, this is not to be explained in terms of the 'values' of the officials concerned, for this sociological concept of 'values' treats them as the primary determinants of the 'goals' of the actors. Rather, the formation of objectives by agents must be seen, not in terms of values which are thought to be somewhat passively internalised, but in terms of the available concepts which form the basis on which the agent calculates objectives in the light of current circumstances. This calculation involves both which objectives are to be pursued and also the ways of achieving them. It is not a matter of values 'penetrating' an arena, i.e. being imported by agents who are carriers of a set of values which they have internalised like germs, but rather of the means of calculation to which the agents have recourse. Often included in part of any struggle is an attempt to provide alternative means of calculating objectives, coupled with an attempt to win over the adversary to using the alternative means. As was clear from Chapter 3, part of the reason why various aspects of economic performance in the Soviet Union are inadequately regulated is the fact that only one means of calculating and thus monitoring performance was being used. Regardless of the 'values' or desires of various agents, this has meant that the activities of various sub-agents have been inadequately regulated. In this case, the lack of a serious attempt by the Secretariat officials or the central planning agencies to improve the 'accounting indices' measuring plan implementation has made it relatively easy for the Ministries to escape regulation or to struggle successfully against forms of regulation which were disagreeable to them.

Conclusion

Discussion of these issues in this way avoids the reduction of political analysis to a 'personalistic' level at which some analysts (but by no means all) seem content to leave it. The concern here with these central political institutions has been to appraise them in terms of their capacity to regulate, despite struggles, the activities of the Ministries and thus to change the relations of production (including relations of distribution). This capacity is determined by the state of play in the various arenas of struggle, including the possibilities to have recourse to other arenas to affect the outcome in the initial arena.

One of the striking features to arise from the examination of the party machinery designed to help regulate the state agencies is the considerable specialisation of the Secretariat officials. Although Hough draws attention to this, and provides evidence of it, he does not appear to relate it to the problems of co-ordination of inter-Ministerial relations. It seems that only the most senior politicians (and perhaps those aspiring to senior posts) have acquired a broad range of experience and expertise. This lack of generalised expertise must be an additional factor in the difficulties of the Secretariat in supervising the Ministries (apart from the small size of the Secretariat apparatus in comparison with the rest of the party and state hierarchies). Any inter-Ministerial struggle will probably involve inter-departmental communication among the Secretariat officials who may have difficulty in resolving their differences because of a lack of sufficiently common means of calculation. This may be part of the reason why the common complaint is heard that 'too many questions are dragged before the Central Committee'.

Certainly such practices may be partly for the desired lobbying effect of taking the dispute into a more powerful arena with a wider audience, or may be due to a reluctance to take responsibility for the resolution of the dispute, but the relatively narrow expertise and experience of the officials may genuinely create difficulties in deciding the best way to resolve the disputes, whatever agreement there may be on 'values' (ultimate objectives).

The major conclusion to be drawn from the political relations between party and state agencies, which is perhaps most clearly illustrated in the case of the relations between the Central Committee Secretariat and the Ministries, is that despite effective party control over state agencies, such state agencies as the Ministries do have a political basis for alliances with sections of the central party agencies. Individual Ministries can at times use their relations with the section of the Central Committee Secretariat which supervises them to influence policy formation or policy implementation (the latter is probably easier to influence). This means that the capacities of Ministries and other subordinate state agencies to influence policy formation and implementation place definite political limits on the central agencies' regulation of the economy. Furthermore, the 'supreme' party and state agencies suffer additional limitations on their capacities to regulate the economy and to form economic policy because of the inherent difficulties of the overall co-ordination of relations between the state agencies.

Such difficulties are not primarily the result of the narrow specialisation of the Secretariat officials, which has just been mentioned, but rather of the sheer volume of information which has to be dealt with in forming policy. This is probably the main cause, for example, of the involvement of Ministries and other agencies in the working of Gossnab, which is supposed to plan and supervise material technical supplies, but which functions ponderously precisely because of the difficulties of centrally designating the allocation of supplies with sufficient precision. Hence the planning of supply becomes entangled in the actual process of distribution of supplies by Ministries, which allows the latter considerable scope to escape regulation in certain respects, but only on condition that they engage in struggle and negotiation within Gossnab over supplies. This ensures that they are regulated to at least the minimal degree necessary to secure the broadly defined fulfilment of the overall plan. To take another example, Hough points out that while the Politburo has the final say in determining wages or social policy (such as welfare measures), Gosplan has to balance the various concrete demands with the available resources.[60] This involves the participation of the Ministry of Finance. However, the sheer volume of information which threatens to inundate Gosplan means that it is not the main state agency dealing with wages and social policy. The process of policy formation in this respect devolves in large measure on to the State Committee for Labour and Social Questions, though it must co-ordinate its decisions with a non-state agency, the All-Union Central Council of Trade Unions, as well as various other state and party agencies.

It is such difficulties (both of co-ordinating relations between various state and party agencies and of co-ordinating the information necessary to form a policy which can be effectively implemented) which give the subordinate agencies the capacity to influence policy formation and implementation. Rather than a totalitarian party or an elite co-ordinating the overall division of labour, by means of the regulation of plan implementation, what we seem to be dealing with is a series of agencies whose activities are indeed regulated, but whose capacities derive partly from the very difficulties of effective regulation. This means that various aspects of the process of policy formation are delegated to the very agencies which are supposed to implement policy; this is apparently also the case with legal policy,[61] but our concern at the moment is with economic and social policy.

The effects of such political relations between party and state agencies on the relations of production could be summed up by saying that there is sufficiently effective central regulation of the economy to prevent the various subordinate state agencies (such as enterprises or Ministries) from pursuing entirely autonomous objectives. In other words, it is reasonable to talk of a co-ordination of the division of labour at the level of the overall social formation. Yet such regulation does not preclude the various subordinate state agencies from pursuing their 'own' objectives within this regulatory framework, both by influencing policy formation and by using their partial autonomy to influence policy implementation. Thus inter-Ministerial disputes over resources, adjustments and mutual accommodations between various agencies, and a mutual dependence on regular flows of information, are important features of Soviet politics. Legal regulation of the economy has only a limited effect, because legal specifications of relations between agents are secondary to political determinants of those relations. Rather than indicating that there is an elite or even a ruling class able to control the political conditions of access to the means of production, the analysis of the evidence presented in this chapter suggests that party 'dominance' over the 'state machine' largely takes the form of effective but limited co-ordination of relations between agencies and of adjudication of disputes between state, party and trade-union agencies. While particular agencies may be excluded on particular issues, it seems to be the case that on economic and social policy issues (rather than, say, defence or foreign policy) all the relevant agencies appear to have access to some kind to policy formation and implementation. In other words, all relevant agencies seem on the evidence available to have some effect on the co-ordination of the division of labour, which means that the processes of formation and implementation of economic policy give a multiplicity of agents access to the means of production, in a form which makes it difficult for a particular group of agents to set the terms of other agents' access. Nevertheless, the central party agencies and the central planning agencies do predominate in determining other agents' access.

It is for this reason that disputes and elaborate processes of consultation and negotiation between the various party and state agencies appear to be endemic features of Soviet politics. They are the corollary of what might be called 'multiple access to the means of production', since if one set of agents does not very clearly predominate in regulating the economy, and hence in fixing the terms of access to the means of production by other agents, then the terms of access must be an object of constant struggle and negotiation. In such a situation regular flows of information are vital if the means of production are to be used effectively, but this raises the problem of the handling of that information, which will be qualitatively diverse and in some respects quite esoteric. The difficulties of co-ordinating and interpreting such information in the process of policy-making are formidable, and this is one of the reasons why subordinate agencies are involved in what at first sight seems a highly centralised mode of policy formation. The genuine difficulties of handling information may be related to the conservatism which is apparent both in plan construction and other policy areas: where the ramifications and inter-connections between decisions cannot be calculated in advance, then past 'experience' becomes the best guide to the way to integrate diverse objectives into a reasonably coherent whole.

The conditions are thus present for what I called towards the beginning of this chapter an 'admixture of adjustment, regular flows of information and struggles over resources'. This does indeed seem to be what much of Soviet politics is like. However, the apparent difficulty in resolving inter-Ministerial disputes can be guessed at from what Hough calls the 'incrementalism' of the budgetary process, and other policy processes. The apparent atrophy which developed in Soviet politics from the mid-1970s cannot be due solely to the ageing of the leadership. The continual pumping in of increased resources for the same objectives with apparently little change in the relative priorities as to the allocation of resources between Ministries suggests a stalemate. This apparent stalemate can hardly be a genuine consensus unless Ministries are willing to accept their budgetary allocation because they all feel sure it will be greater the next year. Yet it cannot be said that this apparent stalemate can be resolved by, say, broadening the expertise of departmental and Ministerial officials, or by a better legal specification of relations between the top-level state and party agencies, for not enough is known to be able to analyse these political struggles in such detail. On the face of it, it does seem unlikely that such changes by themselves would have a great impact on the conduct of Soviet politics.

However, despite the lack of detailed evidence on the political struggles which are the condition of the transformation of the relations of production, one need not despair of analysing the effects of such struggles on the class structure. This is because the outcomes of those struggles are observable in terms of the actual policies. Thus the 1979 economic reform may have been an attempt to break the apparent stalemate over economic priorities. The priorities which are of concern in this book are not simply economic ones, in the narrow sense of the production and physical distribution of goods and services, but also social priorities, in the sense of policies which affect the development of the relations of production. Of particular concern are the 'welfare' policies which affect the distribution of income, since this is an important component of any analysis of the class structure. For this reason, the next chapter will be concerned with public policy in the area designated loosely by what are termed 'social consumption funds'. These cover, for example, health, education, housing, pensions and various kinds of recreation, though not all aspects of the areas covered by the 'social consumption funds' will be dealt with. The examination of such policies may well further elucidate the state of play in and between the various arenas and agencies discussed in this chapter, but more importantly it should provide the means for analysing the forces at work on the contemporary class structure of the Soviet Union.

Notes

1. P. Hirst, *On Law and Ideology*, Macmillan, London, 1979, ch. 5.
2. Ibid, p. 96.
3. E. B. Pashukanis, *Law and Marxism: A General Theory*, Ink Links, London, 1978. Hirst's critique of Pashukanis in his chapter 5 extends to his appendix 1, and he also discusses the work of the Austro-Marxist Karl Renner in some detail in chapter 5.
4. Hirst, *On Law and Ideology*, p. 101. This position is attributed by Hirst not only to Renner, but also to 'an Althusserian theorist like Bernard Edelman'. Edelman is a French lawyer whose book on French photographic copyright law was translated by E. Kingdom with an introduction by P. Hirst: B. Edelman, *Ownership of the Image: Elements for a Marxist Theory of Law*, Routledge & Kegan Paul, London, 1979.

5. This forms chapter 4 of P. Carlen and M. Collinson (eds), *Radical Issues in Criminology*, Martin Robertson, London, 1980.
6. Pierre Lavigne and Marie Lavigne, *Regards sur la Constitution Soviétique de 1977*, Economica, Paris, 1979.
7. For a brief account of the Lavignes' work, see G. Littlejohn, 'The Soviet Constitution', *Economy and Society*, vol. 9, no. 3, August 1980.
8. For an English-language version of both the draft and final versions of the 1977 Constitution, see W. Butler, *The Soviet Legal System: Selected Contemporary Legislation and Documents*, Parker School of Foreign and Comparative Law, Columbia University, New York, 1978.
9. J. Hazard, W. Butler and P. Maggs, *The Soviet Legal System*, 3rd edn, Parker School of Foreign and Comparative Law, Columbia University, New York, 1977. Each chapter consists of a brief commentary on an area of Soviet law, followed by a series of extracts from Soviet sources giving parts of a statute or decree, reports of court cases, and sometimes comments on the area by Soviet legal theorists.
10. J. F. Hough and M. Fainsod, *How the Soviet Union is Governed*, Harvard University Press, 1979, ch. 10 'The Institutional Actors'.
11. The adequacy of such approaches have been challenged in P. Hirst, 'Economic Classes and Politics', in A. Hunt (ed.), *Class and Class Structure*, Lawrence & Wishart, London, 1978; and in B. Hindess, 'Classes and Politics in Marxist Theory', in G. Littlejohn, B. Smart, J. Wakeford and N. Yuval-Davis (eds), *Power and the State*, Croom Helm, London, 1978.
12. For an account and critique of such approaches, see B. Hindess, 'Marxism and Parliamentary Democracy', in A. Hunt (ed.), *Marxism and Democracy*, Lawrence & Wishart, London, 1981.
13. J. F. Hough, *The Soviet Union and Social Science Theory*, Harvard University Press, 1977, p. 112. Lavigne and Lavigne, *Regards sur la Constitution Soviétique*, do not draw attention to Burlatskii in the same way as Hough does, though they do refer to him. The concept of an 'advanced socialist society' is also discussed by M. Lavigne, 'Advanced Socialist Society', *Economy and Society*, vol. 7, no. 4, November 1978.
14. The implications of this in the case of 'national' constituencies for any nation-state theory can be deduced from S. Zubaida, 'Theories of Nationalism', in Littlejohn *et al.* (eds), *Power and the State*.
15. B. Hindess, 'Democracy and the Limitations of Parliamentary Democracy in Britain', in *Politics and Power 1*, Routledge & Kegan Paul, London, 1980. Hindess in effect proposes an alternative conception of democracy in terms of the mechanism for selecting personnel and for reaching decisions, a position which is elaborated from his 'Marxism and Parliamentary Democracy'.
16. S. White, *Political Culture and Soviet Politics*, Macmillan, London, 1979, ch. 8. This book elaborates the argument which can be found in S. White, 'The USSR: Patterns of Autocracy and Industrialism', in A. Brown and J. Gray (eds), *Political Culture and Political Change in Communist States*, 2nd edn, Macmillan, London, 1979.
17. A. Brown, 'Political Developments: Some Conclusions and an Interpreta-

tion', in A. Brown and M. Kaser (eds), *The Soviet Union since the Fall of Khrushchev*, Macmillan, London, 1975, p. 248.

18. Hough, *The Soviet Union*, pp. 10–12, 22–4. There is also a discussion of the concept in Hough and Fainsod, *How the Soviet Union is Governed*, ch. 14 *passim*, esp. pp. 547–8.

19. A. H. Brown, *Soviet Politics and Political Science*, Macmillan, London, 1974. This is an excellent introduction to Soviet politics which surveys the field and then concentrates on three approaches: (i) political institutions, (ii) groups, interests and policy process, (iii) political culture. As White, *Political Culture and Soviet Politics*, acknowledges, Brown was instrumental in setting White's work on Soviet political culture in progress.

20. Brown, *Soviet Politics*, pp. 40–1. While Brown defends the use of the concept, it does not form one of the main approaches to be used, in his view. The *main* approaches are as indicated in the previous note.

21. In the first place, Weber did not use the concept of ideal type in the same way in all his writings: see J. Rex, 'Typology and Objectivity: A Comment on Weber's Four Sociological Methods', in A. Sahay (ed.), *Max Weber and Modern Sociology*, Routledge & Kegan Paul, London, 1971. Second, the main assumptions embodied in Weber's concept of ideal type are highly questionable: see, for example, P. Q. Hirst, *Social Evolution and Sociological Categories*, Allen & Unwin, London, 1976. Third, his use of the concept in his analysis of politics has been subjected to serious criticism: see, for example, A. Weights, 'Weber and "Legitimate Domination" ', *Economy and Society*, vol. 7, no. 1, February 1978. The critical literature on Weber is too vast to be discussed seriously here, yet it seems to have done little to diminish Weber's impact on contemporary political science, perhaps because the use of Weberian concepts therein is largely unacknowledged. I am indebted to Professor J. Beetham for the insight that the contemporary concept of an elite as constituted by the heads of different bureaucracies owes more to Weber than to, say, Pareto.

22. C. J. Friedrich and Z. K. Brzezinski, *Totalitarian Dictatorship and Autocracy*, Oxford University Press, 1965.

23. See Hough, *The Soviet Union*, chs 4–6; and Hough and Fainsod, *How the Soviet Union is Governed*, chs 8, 9, and *passim*.

24. White, *Political Culture*, ch. 5. White argues for the continuity in many important respects between contemporary Soviet political culture and the pre-revolutionary political culture. This implies that any undemocratic features of Soviet politics result from a failure to change the political culture more thoroughly than has in fact been the case. The possible changes to which he draws attention in his chapter 8 are hardly indicative of the kind of effectiveness of ideological means of control which is required to sustain seriously the totalitarian approach.

25. Hough and Fainsod, *How the Soviet Union is Governed*, pp. 520–1.

26. Ibid, pp. 523–4. The use of the concept is retained in an eclectic manner on pp. 527–8.

27. See G. Parry, *Political Elites*, Allen & Unwin, London, 1969; and P. Thoenes, *The Elite in the Welfare State*, Faber, London, 1966.

28. Hough, *The Soviet Union*, pp. 210–11.
29. Ibid, p. 204.
30. The problems of such a position are more fully analysed in Hindess's review of Steven Lukes, *Power: A Radical View*, Macmillan, London, 1974: see B. Hindess, 'On Three-Dimensional Power', *Political Studies*, vol. 24, no. 3, 1976.
31. Although I call this approach Weberian since Weber was one of the earliest to formulate such a position, similar conceptualisations can also be found in Marxist analyses of politics: see, for example, Ralph Miliband, *The State in Capitalist Society*, Weidenfeld & Nicolson, London, 1969. The unifying element, in Miliband's argument, is the common educational and social background and resulting social inter-action between the heads of the various bureaucracies.
32. For example, in Hough and Fainsod, *How the Soviet Union is Governed*, p. 527, we find that 'A high-level or even middle-level administrator clearly has a greater impact on decision-making than an average worker or peasant.' This is typical of the vagueness in defining the elite which arises when its social location is thought to be an effect of the presence of bureaucracies, a view which is extremely widespread.
33. Ibid, p. 531.
34. Ibid, p. 532.
35. Ibid, p. 534.
36. Ibid, p. 543.
37. Ibid, p. 547.
38. Brown, *Soviet Politics*, ch. 3, esp. pp. 72–4. However, Brown by no means completely rejects the 'interest-group' approach, and indicates the types of group which would repay further study.
39. Hough and Fainsod, *How the Soviet Union is Governed*, p. 548.
40. I have already used the concept in G. Littlejohn, 'State, Plan and Market in the Transition to Socialism: The Legacy of Bukharin', *Economy and Society*, vol. 8, no. 2, May 1979.
41. Brown, *Soviet Politics*; White, 'The USSR' and *Political Culture*.
42. White, *Political Culture*, ch. 6, 'The Impact of Marxism-Leninism', p. 142, points out that it seems 'clear that the Soviet authorities have failed to bring about that total transformation of socio-political values to which (unlike Western governments) they have for more than two genera-tions been committed'. However, he also cautions (p. 141) against 'judg-ing the performance of the Soviet propaganda agencies by altogether unrealistic criteria', and towards the end of his last chapter he does pro-vide evidence of a generational change in political attitudes among émigrés; the attitudes of younger émigrés appear to combine acceptance of extensive public ownership and the comprehensive provision of welfare with a commitment to a thorough democratisation of Soviet polit-ical life and institutions. Such attitudes would not be too surprising in the light of Hough's analysis (*How the Soviet Union is Governed*, ch. 8) of public participation in policy formation. However, the evidence avail-able is too meagre to reach firm conclusions about the distribution of forms of political calculation among the general population in the Soviet

Union. Supporters of the concept of 'political culture' could claim with some justice that lack of available evidence is the main reason why this form of analysis is not more developed. However, unless the relation is established between the deployment of concepts in a struggle, on the one hand, and the conditions and outcome of that struggle, on the other, it will remain extremely difficult to establish why some 'cultural traits' persist and others change, and in these circumstances the 'political culture' approach will be left simply *registering* the changes taking place (where the evidence is available), rather than successfully analysing them.

43. Hough, *The Soviet Union*, p. 204.
44. Hough and Fainsod, *How the Soviet Union is Governed*, ch. 14, section on 'The Distribution of Power'.
45. Ibid, pp. 550–1.
46. Ibid, p. 551.
47. Ibid, p. 368.
48. Ibid, p. 449.
49. Ibid, p. 380.
50. Ibid, pp. 381–3.
51. Ibid, chs 11, 12.
52. Ibid, p. 466.
53. Ibid, pp. 466, 473–9.
54. Ibid, p. 423.
55. Ibid, p. 430. *Nomenklature* is a system of lists of important posts and of the people who are candidates for them. Its existence is one of the most important bases of Western critiques of Soviet elections as undemocratic.
56. Ibid, p. 438.
57. Ibid, p. 444.
58. Ibid, p. 446.
59. Ibid, p. 447.
60. J. F. Hough, 'Policy-making and the Worker', in A. Kahan and B. Ruble (eds), *Industrial Labor in the USSR*, Pergamon, New York, 1979.
61. G. B. Smith, 'Socialist Legality and Legal Policy in the Soviet Union', in G. B. Smith (ed.), *Public Policy and Administration in the Soviet Union*, Praeger, New York, 1980.

5
Welfare and Consumption: Relations of Distribution

Introduction

It is impossible in one chapter to cover all aspects of welfare and forms of income. The education system, for example, will not be dealt with here, despite the fact that consumption of education resources could be considered a part of the real income of the Soviet population, and certainly constitutes a part of the social consumption funds for the purposes of the Soviet state budget. The areas which will be covered here will be housing, health and social security, all of which affect family budgets. These aspects of welfare and income are useful indications of living standards and show the effects of social policies. As indicated in the previous chapter, while there is very little direct evidence available on the course of political struggles, the operation of social policies can be treated as an outcome of struggle, indicating to some extent the 'state of play'. In addition, the operation of social policies can be considered as part of the process of struggle, since the implementation of policy can itself be thought of as a 'strategy of power', a means of affecting the balance of forces within the social formation.

Thus social policies on welfare and consumption illuminate the political process and, since they form an important component of relations of distribution, they are also vital to any understanding of relations of production and hence the nature of class relations in the Soviet Union. Furthermore, social policies on welfare and the associated patterns of consumption are important because, if socialist planning is *not* a matter of direct consciousness by society of its own needs and the willing of the means to meet those needs, then a policy of 'to each according to his needs' requires a specification of needs.[1] The expenditure patterns of social consumption funds can only be effectively appraised in terms of the specification of needs and of the adequacy of the means employed to satisfy those needs. The specification of needs could take the forms of measurement of needs and/or the articulation of 'perceived' needs by the agents 'experiencing' the needs. Thus the specification of needs is partly a political process in the sense of a struggle by competing agencies to have their needs registered and hopefully satisfied (fully or partially).

Any specification of needs, and thus of socially defined standards, immediately runs into the problem of the diversity of criteria of need. This is a problem which is likely to grow as both knowledge of social relations and the capacity to meet basic criteria grow.[2] The diversity of criteria for the satisfaction of needs also generates the problem of the interrelations between various social and economic policies. Thus, for example, in the Soviet Union improved housing may reduce the demand for certain kinds of health care, particularly for hospitalisation of certain medical cases.

Consequently, while the main aim of this chapter is to appraise the impact of the areas of social policy examined upon the real income of the Soviet population, it is necessary to examine the way in which the implementation of the various social policies is organised, and to treat the process of implementation as itself a political process. Nowhere is this clearer, perhaps, than in the first policy area to be discussed, namely, housing.

Housing

The diversity of criteria which can be pertinent to the appraisal of an area of social policy is clearly apparent to George and Manning:

> the development of housing under socialism involves issues which touch on the very core of the new society: the nature of the city and the country, and the relationship between them;

the nature of the family, property relations, architecture and the creative arts; and the pattern of economic investment.[3]

After a brief review of classical Marxist and early Bolshevik views on housing, they discuss historical developments which show the enormous difficulties faced by Soviet housing policy from its inception to the present day.

The pre-revolutionary housing situation was appalling; even in Moscow and St Petersburg well over half the housing was wooden, and the average dwelling space for the urban population (around 7 square metres *per capita*) was so badly distributed that 70 per cent of single workers and nearly 50 per cent of married workers had only a corner of a room. Such conditions may well have been a vital factor in the demise of the Tsarist empire.[4] Much of this housing was burned for fuel during the civil war, with the result that when the population started to return to the cities in the 1920s overcrowding remained acute, since building was outstripped by migration to the cities. Unplanned urbanisation between 1926 and 1939 set a world record: 'Rural to urban migration totalled 40 million: equivalent to the total for Europe between 1800 and 1940.'[5] It is in this context that the Soviet internal passport system and the 'infamously close liaison between house managers and police'[6] should be understood.

To these difficulties should be added the damage caused by the 1941–5 war: 1710 cities and towns were destroyed, amounting to 6 million dwellings which had housed 25 million people.[7] Reconstruction began where possible during the war, and the fourth Five Year Plan (1946–50), while only 77 per cent fulfilled for housing, improved the average *per capita* space by half a metre over the 1940 level. Yet it must be remembered that around 20 million people had died in the war and that even then specifically urban space at this time was scarcer than before the war. Housing construction was boosted during the 1950s, when it exceeded planned levels for the first and only time in Soviet history. This is partly because plans suddenly became more ambitious in 1957, when a decree ordered an immediate increase of 100 per cent in the volume of new housing to be built during the Five Year Plan period 1956–60.[8] This was more than fulfilled, and the amount of new housing has continued to rise.

However, while this represented a substantial increase in the house-building programme, housing has since steadily slipped back as a proportion of total investment, from about 20 per cent in the mid-1950s to about 15 per cent in the early 1970s.

Furthermore, the quality of building workmanship has often been shoddy, and the planning of housing poor. The inadequacies in planning, particularly the poor co-ordination of industrial and urban growth, were officially recognised as early as 1960.[9] The main problems in housing still seem to stem from the fact that 'planning and finance spring primarily from different sources',[10] in other words financing housing through industrial Ministries does not aid the local co-ordination of local services which the city soviet must attempt; in addition, as was noted in Chapter 3, it contributes to a rapid turnover in the labour force as people change jobs in order to get better housing. How far the latter problem will be alleviated by the measures (associated with the 1979 economic reform) to improve housing and reduce labour turnover remains to be seen.

Political aspects of housing provision
It seems appropriate to turn now to the issue of the politics of Soviet housing, before discussing housing outcomes (the distribution of housing among the population) and their implications. According to George and Manning, as a result of conflicts between economic and social criteria, the supply of and access to housing is determined by two competing criteria – need and economic incentive.[11] Yet they structure their examination of the contemporary housing situation into three aspects – demand, supply and finance – thus creating a distinction between need and demand. The distinction between (legitimate) need and demand *seems* to rest on a conception of need as emanating from the population, which is presumably structured in some way, giving rise to a variety of needs. Allocation on the basis of legitimate need would then amount to the self-recognition by society of these needs and the supplying of the means to satisfy them. Where this process is blocked in some way, for example by competing government economic priorities, then they argue that it is 'more accurate to talk of demand rather than need as the general determinant of

supply'.[12] The reservation of need to a non-conflictual situation (as in a socialist utopia?) amounts to an effective denial of any relationship between a definition of need and a political process of struggle and accommodation between various agencies. Yet the analysis by George and Manning shows that demand and supply (of which finance is itself an aspect) are not purely technical or economic matters in the present-day Soviet Union. What they do not seem to appreciate is that neither can need be a purely technical or economic matter, and if that is so, then the distinction which they make between need and demand is pointless.

The reason for my insisting on denying that George and Manning make any effective distinction between the concepts of need and demand (which is a comparatively minor problem in their otherwise highly useful discussion) is to prevent needs from being relegated to a non-conflictual (non-political) utopia and to subject the concept to a certain amount of critical scrutiny. Needs do not simply emanate from a population whose structure is transparent to observation but are always discursively registered. Thus there are no unproblematic 'objective needs' since the 'recognition' of needs is a theoretical and political process. We have already seen that George and Manning also juxtapose need and economic incentive as two quite distinct criteria. However, the registration of need by a state agency depends not only on the expressed wants of other agents and on the specification of need (for example, so many square metres of housing space *per capita*) but on the aims of the registering state agency or of some higher agency. Thus what is registered as a need will be the outcome of a struggle in which various technical and overtly political arguments will be deployed. Thus, rather than treating incentives (whether material or moral) and need as distinct and competing criteria determining the supply of a social service such as housing, the analysis of the provision of social services should concentrate on the interrelation of need and incentive. That is, the analysis of need should not be conducted in terms of a depoliticised expression of the inherent characteristics of the population, but as the outcome of a process of reconciliation (however achieved) of diverse aims of various agencies, including the use of incentives to mobilise either the population at large or various agencies within the social formation towards the achievement of 'national' objectives.

With these considerations in mind, it is possible to return to George and Manning's discussion of 'demand, supply and finance' of housing for information on the political processes involved in housing provision. They argue that 'ever since housing owned by industries was nationalised rather than municipalised after the Revolution, there has been conflict between industries and Soviets over the provision and control of housing and associated services'.[13] This conflict is built into the organisational and budgetary control which Ministries have over many city agencies, even those which are also subject to control by the city soviet: hence the problem is one of the predominance of industrial Ministries in a system of 'dual subordination'. The result is a failure of official attempts to control and predict the growth of large cities. The reasons for this conflict are as follows:

> First, city and non-city enterprises are only coordinated at a very high level. Second, at that level state planning responsible for city affairs continues to be divided between the State Planning Commission (Gosplan) for industrial production and the State Construction Committee (Gosstroi) for housing construction. Third, since industrial growth has been a major aim, this arrangement has enabled industrial Ministries to dominate urban development, particularly in newer industrial or smaller cities where soviets are dependent on one industry, or are administratively remote from the Republic level where major decisions can be made. In effect the demand for housing space where industries need workers tends to be met by industries themselves. However, the proper standard of such housing in terms of adequate space, services, location (particularly with respect to pollution) and maintenance cannot be easily enforced by the soviets. They are by comparison to industry financially weak, do not own the houses, and are politically weak with respect to controlling location.[14]

While preoccupied with different theoretical concerns than

George and Manning, Sternheimer provides evidence to support their argument at many points.[15] For example, in discussing the control by Gosplan and the Ministries over decisions made at local level, he points to examples such as that of Volgograd, where thirty-nine new enterprises were constructed in violation of the city's *genplan* (general municipal plan for a city's physical and economic development), a state of affairs directly attributable to Ministerial pressure.[16] The most significant result of this preponderance of Ministerial power has been for the pattern of location of housing and in particular the growth of large cities. In matters of budgetary allocations, the rich and powerful are consistently the most well rewarded.[17] The reasons probably concern external economies of scale: in larger cities the infrastructure already exists, labour is more skilled, supply routes are shorter, and so on.

Clearly, then, the provision of housing involves political processes which at least partially undercut official housing policy aims, and it is worth examining some of these processes in more detail, the better to understand the outcomes in terms of actual housing provision. Leaving aside the private and co-operative housing sectors, which will be dealt with later, state housing is allocated on the basis of a waiting-list, rather like British council housing. According to George and Manning:

> an applicant to get on the waiting list must demonstrate sufficient need in terms of existing space, amenities, state of health and so on. Subsequently, people are actually housed from the waiting list in order of original acceptance. However, this system is modified in several important ways... In general these advantaged groups include either those with exceptional needs (the ill, large families, and so on) or those politically favoured (specialists, the military, those who do 'socially useful activity').[18]

Yet they accept the argument that too much should not be made of these housing privileges, which are in many cases small. The conclusion that one can draw is that the political distribution of means of consumption can and usually does leave scope for those with greater political influence to affect the distribution process. For this reason, rationing is not necessarily better than a market distribution of means of consumption in terms of its economic and political effects, unless, say, the distribution is subject to public participation which closes off or diminishes such scope for political influence. It should be borne in mind, however, that such public participation may be as technically easy to effect in the case of supervised (planned and monitored) market distribution of the means of consumption. If, as I have argued elsewhere,[19] the conditions of commodity exchange have an important influence on its social effects, then there is no *a priori* reason to treat 'the commodity form' as having certain essential effects, and in certain circumstances it may well be politically preferable to rationing or some other administrative means of 'distribution according to need'.

The specific administrative framework for 'distribution according to needs' (as modified by criteria of economic incentive) has important effects on the outcome of the various conflicting pressures, though these effects are not unitary throughout the social formation, precisely because the housing decisions are the outcome of struggle, and the various agencies involved in this arena have diverse relations with one another in different localities. This is a point noted by Sternheimer[20] and by George and Manning, who point to the willingness of the leadership to engage in organisational 'experiments' and to the lack of clear specification of the relationships between various agencies.[21] The result is

> that their relative strength varies considerably from one area to another and confused jurisdiction is common: a decision may have to meet the interests of the local soviet, the housing office, the house committee, the party, a trade union and so on. There is 'widespread dependence on personal relations' and in many respects the outcome is the same as for higher level conflicts between soviets and enterprises – political ideals are compromised.[22]

Some housing agencies are not subject to dual subordination, and are therefore the ones most likely to enhance local control and public participation in the implementation of housing policy. However, their effectiveness is seriously diminished for a variety of reasons. The key body in the local housing arena is the housing office, within which the technical inspector is the most important single agent. He is broadly responsible for managing the housing stock, access, and so on. However, the general level of training and efficiency at this level is poor, according to George and Manning, and since Khrushchev's time voluntary administrative bodies have been encouraged both to improve housing management and to generate greater public participation in government: 'In the event they came to be used far more as free labour than as a form of political representation.'[23] Attempts have been made to get the House Committee (*Domkom*) to control the housing office but, like attempts to strengthen the city soviet itself, they have made little headway.

The weak position of the city soviets and of public partici-pation is clear from the following points drawn from Sternheimer, and from George and Manning. There is no local fiscal control, since city and county budgets combined are only a small proportion of the total state budget (around 14 per cent in 1970, at a time when the urban population was around 56 per cent), and local taxes cannot be levied (since 1959 when the enterprise building tax was abolished). The mechanisms for ensuring local responsiveness do not work very well: there is a high turnover of deputies on local soviets, which militates against the development of expertise in dealing with the various agencies; the duties of local administrators exceed their powers; the attitudes of local administrators can be seen from the finding that 82 per cent of them believed that they took account of public opinion in reaching their decisions (and surprisingly in view of complaints about housing, 62 per cent of the population agreed with them); the administrative mechanisms for ensuring accountability of officials work poorly.[24] If housing were really controlled locally, then it would be difficult to explain the chronic under-investment in services associated with housing, particularly sewerage. Yet there is a degree of local co-ordination, as Sternheimer points out, with the party playing a fairly rational urban management role[25] without which Soviet urban administration would not work as well as it has through what has been and will continue to be a very rapid process of urbanisation. However, to say that there is some local co-ordination of decisions which has mitigated the effects of some of the Ministerial agencies' pursuit of their own specific aims is not to say that the current situation of the city soviets is satisfactory. There is a clear need in my view to incorporate cities in a more politically effective way than hitherto. The removal of housing from the control of Ministries and enterprises would make public participation in the implementation of housing policy a much more effective affair. As it is, George and Manning are probably correct when they argue that 'the existence of a private sector in housing including individual, collective farms and cooperative building, and a small market in subletting, has provided the most direct form of "participation" in housing for many Soviet citizens'.[26] It therefore seems appropriate to turn to these sectors of housing provision.

Bearing in mind earlier remarks about the effects of administrative and commodity distribution of means of consumption, it should be pointed out that current forms of non-state housing provisions are varied: 'Housing in the Soviet Union stands apart from the other social services in that around 50 per cent of existing stock is privately owned (including a small proportion of cooperative flats which are effectively owned on mortgage from the state), and one-third of new housing built is private or cooperative.'[27] However, the private and co-operative sectors should not be treated exclusively as 'bastions of privilege'. It is certainly true that in the early 1970s a co-operative flat cost about six times the average wage to buy, and a 40 per cent deposit was required. However, this is not the most privileged sector of housing provision, since official provision of housing at low rent for the politically privileged is the most favourable form of access to housing, and, as we shall see later, the co-operative sector faces considerable planning obstacles which reduce its attractiveness as an option. Furthermore, with regard to other private forms of housing, rural private housing is often the only form available and frequently lacks basic amenities. State housing is generally of better quality and is heavily subsidised.

The inadequacies in housing provision are to some extent made good by the private and co-operative sectors. It is perhaps easy to argue that it would be preferable if these inadequacies were rather eradicated by increased investment, better planning and by the dissociation of housing from industrial Ministries, so that city soviets were directly responsible for urban housing. However, this is easier said than done, since, as George and Manning point out:

> the determinants of the supply of housing are divided amongst different (and in some respects competing) bodies. In general, there has been a close shaping of housing policy by economic policy, although the detailed realisation of this is in fact a quite complex political process. Consequently, political initiatives to affect the organisation and supply of housing have often been frustrated, or at least distorted in their implementation.[28]

Thus the political processes involved in providing access to a major means of consumption (that is, the political processes involved in some of the relations of distribution) have their own effectivity which, among other things, reduces their amenability to any democratic pressure for greater public participation. This raises the question which will be the main concern of the next section: namely, what are the effects of these processes in terms of actual housing outcomes and their social consequences?

The social distribution of housing

Perhaps the most striking outcome of the competition between Ministries to build their 'own' housing, and their consequent refusal to be constrained by the existing plans of city soviets, has been the inordinately high proportion of housing investment (around half the annual housing investment) which is 'spent on repairing old buildings and constructing new buildings to replace habitable space demolished in redevelopment schemes'.[29] While Jacobs does not mention it, the repair problems (and internal decoration problems) lead to a flourishing black market, or rather 'grey' market, to use Katsenelinboigen's terms.[30] Jacobs gives an excellent account of the reasons for the poor state of repair of Soviet housing:

The emphasis on quantity of housing and the planner's obsession with cutting production costs are partially responsible for the low quality of Soviet housing. By trying to cut costs on capital repairs (during the period 1966 to 1969, 115 million roubles allocated for capital repairs was not used), the local authorities are actually shortening the life of their housing. Poor construction, followed by poor maintenance and repair, leads to premature decay of the buildings and might help explain the high rate of attrition of Soviet urban housing.[31]

The effects on quality of rushing to fulfil the plan by the end of the annual plan period, so well known in industry, are also evident in the housing sector.

In the light of these phenomena, one can appraise the quality of Soviet housing. Between 1961 and 1971, 10 per cent of the living area *constructed* lacked the three basic amenities of running water, sewerage and central heating: 'In 1970, only 77 per cent of Soviet urban dwellings in the public sector had running water, while only 74 per cent had sewerage and 72 per cent had central heating.'[32] These figures take no account of privately owned housing, which in 1970 accounted for about 30 per cent of the urban housing stock, and in which standards of amenities fall very far below public-sector standards. The expense of installing the amenities is probably the limiting factor here, since most of this housing is on a city's outskirts, which anyway tend to be less well provided with amenities. In small towns the standard of amenities in public housing is appreciably worse than in larger cities, and since there is proportionately more private housing in small towns presumably the standard of amenities there is abysmally low. Jacobs claims that in the public sector the list of building and design faults, and problems of planning and management, resulting in the poor quality of Soviet housing and the low standards of amenities, could go on for pages.[33] Thus, while recent improvements in design and construction have substantially improved the quality of Soviet housing, particularly compared with the late 1950s, there is in Jacobs's view no other industrial country with housing conditions as bad as in the USSR.

Apart from regional and rural–urban differences in housing,

the major difference in the social distribution of housing is between the state, private and co-operative sectors. It has already been argued that the private and co-operative sectors are not necessarily 'bastions of privilege', and it should be clear from the above discussion on the quality of housing why this is the case with most private housing, which is either rural, located in small towns or located on the outskirts of larger cities. However, the co-operative sector is clearly an option for higher income groups, and while amenities are clearly better than in much private housing, various obstacles are placed in the way of prospective co-operative members, 'seemingly in an attempt to avoid a scramble for places on waiting lists, which can sometimes have backlogs of six years or more'.[34] In terms of various indices (absolute space or the percentage of public-sector construction) co-operative construction has gone down since the mid-1960s to the early 1970s.

Thus official enthusiasm for co-operatives seems to be waning, according to Jacobs, which is in contrast to the impression given by George and Manning. One reason may be that some housing co-operatives are fairly privileged, and in catering for middle and upper income groups, housing co-operatives threaten the homogeneity of Soviet society. Certainly planners seem to have been at pains to mix the co-operatives in with state housing and to limit the extent of co-operative housing, and while the personal expenditure involved did limit the purchasing power of the upper income groups Jacobs suggests that 'it may be that the availability of cars has now been able to do the same thing, at less cost in effort and materials of the state'.[35]

Private housebuilding in cities is discouraged, and in the capitals of the various constituent Republics and in most major cities no land or credits have been granted since 1962. Just as in the state and co-operative sectors, there are relatively privileged housing groups, so there are such groups in the private sector, mostly in the case of *dachas* owned by city-dwellers, but the general picture is that shortages of material and finance, coupled with a lack of official sympathy for private housebuilding, account for the poor condition of private housing.

Effects on the distribution of income

The average Soviet family (as opposed to the poorer than average family) spends 4 or 5 per cent of total family income on rent alone, compared with around 11 per cent in the USA or 7 per cent in the United Kingdom. While it is possible to sublet in the USSR, this cannot be done systematically in a way that creates a source of unearned income. Consequently the subsidised nature of Soviet state housing, which is paid for from taxation (mostly turnover tax, i.e. in the form of higher prices for consumer goods and services), means that the effect of Soviet housing policy on the distribution of income is probably on the whole fairly egalitarian.[36]

Health

As in the case of housing, it is difficult to understand the Soviet health service without an appreciation of its historical development, and this will be briefly discussed here.[37] In July 1918, the world's first health ministry was established, preceding the UK Ministry of Health (established in 1919): this was the People's Commissariat of Health of the RSFSR. A Medical Workers' Union (for *all* medical workers including doctors) was set up in 1919. For rural health services, despite initial unwillingness to use 'second-class doctors', the Bolsheviks relied to some extent on 'feldshers' (from the German for 'army surgeon') who were (and are) not as highly qualified as doctors. However, even today feldshers do not 'fill the gaps' generated by lack of doctors. While there are still considerable problems in persuading doctors to live in rural areas, the feldshers do not predominate in areas where doctors are lacking. Rather, there is a 'positive association' between the distribution of rural doctors and feldshers, suggesting that the latter at times function as medical auxiliaries to the doctors.

Once the epidemics associated with the civil war were overcome, prophylaxis (preventive medicine) re-emerged as a key concern in 1924. With the introduction of the New Economic Policy, there was a limited resurgence of private practice, doctors having to choose complete public or private work. Despite 'penal' taxation of private practice, there are still a few private polyclinics in the Soviet Union, but no private hospitals and no system of 'pay-beds.' Related to the First Five Year Plan, the health services were explicitly directed to give priority to the industrial health service. The use of health posts in industrial enterprises now became the first priority, and with the increase in women at work a special health service section was developed for women and children. There was also a branch set up to plan and organise the sanitation of the rapidly growing urban areas, and medical training was taken out of the universities, the number of years of study being reduced to four, in conjunction with the rapid growth of medical research institutes.

Collective farms were made largely responsible for their own health care, though there were medical 'flying squads' to deal with epidemics, and the number of rural hospital beds doubled during the First Five Year Plan. However, the general result of the emphasis on industry was the neglect of rural health. At the same time, women were encouraged to become doctors, and 75 per cent of doctors were women by 1934. The 1936 Constitution included the right to free health care and established an All-Union Ministry of Health. This completed the development of the central administration of medicine and the process of political subordination of the medical profession. The tripartite division into industrial health, women and children, and urban sanitation, coupled with the absence of effective worker or public participation, led to the way being opened to increasing academic and technical dominance, and to the influencce of the hospital. According to George and Manning,[38] this trend was confirmed when in 1947 polyclinics and in 1956 sanitary-epidemiological (public health) stations came under hospital control. One might add that, related to this academic and technical predominance, as in the West, is the absence of women doctors from senior administrative and research posts. It is noticeable that now, as the prestige and pay of the medical profession is being increased, half of those studying to become doctors are men, though this has not yet worked its way through into the profession itself, where women still form 70 per cent of practising doctors.

The rapid pre-war expansion and modernisation of the health services made a substantial contribution to the war effort, and in many ways this seemed to confirm the general Soviet approach to health. In 1954 for the first time since collectivisation the farmer benefited from occupational priority.[39] Since then the trends have been towards greater rural–urban equality in provision (to the point where rural areas have more pharmacies per head than urban areas), greater emphasis on hospitals (especially bigger ones, where economies of scale and greater medical specialisation are possible) and a deliberate emphasis on 'professionalising' the medical profession. The latter includes a professional oath on graduation and limitations on the practice of medicine by those without special training.

The general effect of these developments and the expansion of the Soviet health service has been to alter the patterns of morbidity to those more typical of high-income countries with low infant mortality, with the emphasis shifting towards diseases of middle and old age, particularly lung cancer, cardio-vascular disease and mental ill health.[40] The demographic trends are towards an ageing population, with the size of the cohorts entering old age rising rapidly after 1980. While exact figures on morbidity and mortality are rather scarce, it does seem as if there is a greater problem than in Britain with some infectious diseases, particularly in the warmer southern parts of the USSR. There also seems to be greater provision for the treatment of tuberculosis than is the case in Britain.

Health politics: administration, finance and policy

As Kaser points out, 'The absence of extensive morbidity series precludes judgement on the appropriateness of the Soviet medical service to meet the demands on it.'[41] The development of medical personnel differs markedly from that in the West and, being labour-intensive, may appear wasteful, but this may not be the case given Soviet standards of nutrition and housing. The process of planning the deployment of personnel and equipment is related to the medical statistics coming in to the Ministry of Health from hospitals, dispensaries and mass screening, with the latter giving an indication of the extent of otherwise undiagnosed illness. Thus registered needs are partly generated by the administrative practices of the health service.[42] For this reason it is important to understand the administrative structure of the health service. While the Soviet health service is often described as highly centralised, it is less so than it might at first appear. Certainly, in December 1969, a new Public Health Act was passed by the Supreme Soviet, aiming at eliminating variations in medical practice and in the interpretation of regulations,[43] but it did not eliminate the departmental structure of the health service. Other Ministries and corresponding organisations can run their 'own' health services, with permission from the Council of Ministers, the most substantial being provided by the Ministries of Transport, Civil Aviation, Defence and Internal Affairs.[44] The USSR Ministry of Health is given the function of co-ordinating their services.

Institutions directly responsible for the delivery of health care are divided into three sectors: namely, general clinical and industrial medicine, maternity and child care, and public health. Despite the reduced emphasis on 'the industrial principle' since 1957, such a division of labour seems clearly designed to meet industrial needs: the first sector for maintaining a productive labour force, the second for reproducing the labour force efficiently, and the third to prevent illness from reducing the labour supply. Thus there is still scope for strong conflicting pressures on the doctor to meet both the needs of the patient and those of industry. A high degree of specialisation, so frequently reported in discussions of the division of labour in the Soviet Union, seems evident in the health services as well. Thus there is a variety of health institutions whose activities overlap, with poor co-ordination.

At the district level, the chief physician, as head of the district hospital, co-ordinates polyclinics, dispensaries and public and industrial health services. At the regional level, the chief medical officer is responsible for all medical services. The result is often that many primary-level physicians feel that they are merely referral agents for a hospital-dominated set of institutions at the district level. At the regional level, the dominance of academic medicine continues, with a proliferation of specialities that promote excessively compartmentalised activity and a blinkered perception of the patient. These complaints are also familiar in Britain. Thus 'the articulation and impact of popular demand has been weak in the face of political constraints on resource allocation and the planning process'.[45] It therefore seems appropriate to examine, first, the planning process, and second, the methods of financing the health service.

Health planning

While the agencies involved in the process of elaborating the annual health plan (and integrating it to the annual economic plan) are clear from Popov's account,[46] it is not clear which techniques or methods of planning predominate. It seems that the balance method, the method of ratios and proportions, and the establishment of norms and standards, are the main planning methods. That is, the material and labour balance methods are used, as in the rest of the economic plan, while ratios and proportions, and norms and standards, are used to establish targets for the plan. Thus 'a standard ratio of medical facilities to population size is of great importance in planning the development of the health services'.[47] Presumably this technique of ratios and proportions is used to relate the growth of facilities to demographic trends, and in that sense to fit services to expected medical need, but on the whole it seems to be the 'supply side' which is emphasised. In other words, it seems to be the delivery of services that is the main criterion in the establishment of requirements.

However, while there may be a certain amount of over-emphasis in the planning process on increasing the *delivery* of health care, it would be misleading to imply that there was no attempt to relate health-care provision to need. Popov distinguishes between 'health norms' and 'health standards'.[48] He defines the former as 'scientifically established indices of environmental conditions and of the medical care required by the community or by various population groups, as well as of the utilisation of facilities', whereas the latter are defined as 'indices relating to the resources required to meet the needs specified by the norms, i.e. indices relating to the public health facilities and the availability of medical care'. To put it crudely, 'norms' refer to needs (including needs as indicated by use of existing facilities) whereas 'standards' refer to the resources required to meet those needs. There are 300 such indices, and a substantial proportion of them could be counted as 'norms'. This sophistication of the Ministry of Health's definition and registering of need cannot be discounted in any serious appraisal of the social effects of the health service.

Health finance

The implementation of the health plans is of course dependent on adequate finance, which comes mainly from the social consumption funds, of which they form nearly 20 per cent (or 4 per cent of the net material product). In addition, a further 1 per cent of the net material product (NMP) is spent by state enterprises, trade unions and collective farms, with a small contribution from social insurance funds and private payments. Soviet data on the composition of health finance are scarce, according to Kaser.[49] Government finance is predominantly channelled through the Ministry of Health, and apart from social insurance the other main source of finance is from the socialised enterprises' operating budgets or profits. In the case of collective farm hospitals, for example, the collective farm provides the building, heating, cleaning, etc., while the Ministry of Health supplies the medically qualified personnel. Roughly one-sixth of health care is provided in this way. Profits can be used for resort stays at spas, or in holiday areas, with an enterprise or trade union sometimes building its own facilities in such areas. Such practices resulted partly from the takeover of spas after the Revolution, and partly from the housing problems of the cities.[50]

At the level of regional health facilities, salaries take over 50 per cent of the budget, food about 10 per cent and medicines about 8 per cent. Medicines are charged for, except when provided in hospital. Free medicines constitute around 70 per cent of all medicine, but there is no sign of implementing the official policy of phasing out such charges. In addition, there is private payment for care (both legal and illegal payment). There are a few 'paying polyclinics', and those which exist are administered and financed by the local authority like any free facility. The payments which are not legally sanctioned are the unofficial fees for 'tipping' ordinary medical staff, but this is so general that a scale of rates has been set out by various commentators on Soviet health.[51]

One result of the forms of organisation and finance of the Soviet health service has been that it has been provided in a remarkably inexpensive manner. This has continued to be the case despite the fact that the number of doctors increased by 85 per cent between 1960 and 1974, so that the Soviet Union provides over twice as many doctors per head of the population as Britain, and despite the fact that, administratively speaking, hospitals predominate. One reason for this is that since the late 1920s real incomes in general have doubled, whereas the incomes of health staff have only increased by half. In addition, there has been a 'sparing use of capital'[52] both in terms of ancillary equipment and in terms of hospital construction; part of the saving in terms of hospital construction has been achieved by standardising hospital buildings over very long periods, so that those built recently are generally indistinguishable from those which are much older. Furthermore, careful planning seems to have increased the occupancy rates for hospital beds, i.e. it has decreased the time during which beds are empty, thereby making further use of available facilities. This may partly account for the increase in treatment of rural patients in urban hospitals. Finally, some 80 per cent of patients receive their entire treatment in out-patient establishments.[53] Such considerations should not be forgotten when claims are made that Soviet health care is wasteful.

Soviet health policy

Following this discussion of the administration and finance of Soviet health, it is now possible to assess the priorities of Soviet health provision and their relation to need, despite the lack of evidence on patterns of morbidity. In other words, it is now possible to assess Soviet health policy. While it is clear that in the past industrial provision took precedence over other aspects, and urban provision took precedence over rural provision, this now happens despite rather than because of official policy. The attempts to reduce overlap in provision by different institutions (especially primary-care institutions as opposed to hospitals) and the attempts to equalise urban–rural provision have had the effect of reducing such stark differences in priority as previously existed. Priorities are now of course partly related to demographic and morbidity trends. While the

USSR has had a low dependency ratio – the ratio of (i) – those too young or old to work to (ii) – the economically active population – this is now disappearing. As indicated earlier, the morbidity patterns are similar to Western Europe or the USA, with a residual problem of infectious disease. However, these determinants of medical priority are affected by others: the provision of doctors has generated a demand for home visits (despite the official preference for hospitalisation), the provision of polyclinics and dispensaries has generated a demand for specialist hospital services, and the provision of mass screening has generated need in the form of otherwise undetected illness.[54] It is intended to extend this screening to the entire population. One effect of this would be to equalise to some extent the relative emphasis on prevention and on cure. Despite the official aim of keeping prevention as a high priority, it has tended to take second place to cure as a form of health care.

Apart from prevention, the other early Bolshevik ideals for the health service were that it should be comprehensive, involving workers' participation, universal, free, and state-provided.[55] These form convenient headings for the discussion of contemporary Soviet health policy. As George and Manning point out, the notion of comprehensive health care is difficult to circumscribe, since it depends on the current state of knowledge. For that reason it tends to be left to professional judgement, which is powerfully influenced by economic and political constraints. The encouragement by the Ministry of Health of autonomous specialisation and technical develop-ment, and the increasing 'professionalisation' of the medical personnel (despite the lack of independent political status of the medical profession) have led to an emphasis on high-technology medicine concerned with acute life-threatening disorders such as cancer and heart disease.

Health and democracy
Although these diseases are of growing importance in an ageing population, this emphasis *may* not correspond very closely to the main patterns of morbidity (mental illness, bronchitis, influenza and back injuries), which suggests that the impact of workers' participation, or indeed of any public participation, is

weak. The mechanisms of participation are, first, the public health commissions, which exist at all levels from the Supreme Soviet to the district soviets. These seem to defer to technical expertise. Second, trade unions monitor industrial safety, but the effectiveness of this varies with the enterprise. They do, however, encourage physical exercise and the use of health resorts. Third, patients and the CP can use the press for quite severe criticisms of aspects of health care or even of individual doctors.[56] Fourth, there are popular movements, as well as organisations such as the Red Cross and Red Crescent societies, with 80 million members. Despite these mechanisms of participation, George and Manning argue that they are outweighed by the specialisation of medicine and the centralisation of management, which is difficult to reconcile with real popular and mass participation.

Without wishing to contradict totally arguments for a deemphasis of professionalism and expertise, such arguments in favour of a more democratic health service need to be made very carefully. It is by no means easy to democratise a largely state-provided health service and prevent the individual from becoming a passive recipient and consumer of health care. The reason is the obvious one that state provision of health care requires the establishment of standards of health care for the population if there is to be any attempt at uniformity and universality of provision. Among other things, this requires the certification of various kinds of medical personnel as competent to deploy certain health-care skills, since otherwise there would be no way of ascertaining whether provision was uniform or universal, or how far short of these aims the health service was. In the absence of market pressure by the consumers on the medical practitioners (although, as we have seen, this is by no means completely absent in the Soviet Union), democratic pressure by the laity on those certified as competent requires a considerable cultural improvement (acquisition of skills) by the population at large and the dissemination of knowledge about the changing social distribution of health needs and health provision. It must be remembered that knowledge about the social distribution of health needs and provision largely depends on the collection of statistics by the very medical personnel or agencies who are going to be subject to democratic scrutiny. While there does appear to be an overemphasis on high prestige, high-technology medicine in some parts of the Soviet health service, the de-emphasis of professional expertise cannot be carried to the point where treatment cannot be competently undertaken or where adequate statistics cannot be compiled. Soviet doctors currently spend a great deal of time on paperwork, but presumably at least some of this is necessary for adequate health planning. Consequently democratisation would probably involve changing medical training to promote the encouragement by medical personnel of the active involvement of lay personnel, a greater dissemination of medical knowledge among the population, and a greater emphasis on prevention.

Access to health care

To return to the discussion of the early Bolshevik ideals for the health service, three ideals have not yet been mentioned: namely, that it should be universal, state-provided and free. The concern with universal coverage of the population clearly concerns the problem of the distribution of services and of access to health care (access to an important means of consumption). There are various different categories of the population which could form the basis of differential criteria of access. Those discussed by George and Manning are social class, geographical location, age, sex and illness type.[57] With regard to social class, the 'closed-access' facilities available to personnel in certain Ministries, certain occupational groups or to certain party members could be regarded as associated with the process of class formation. More clearly the small private market and the much more widespread practice of 'tipping' must disadvantage the poor, though George and Manning do not point out that most of this 'tipping' is connected to hospital, home, dental or other specialist treatment, whereas 80 per cent of patients are treated entirely as out-patients. However, this merely enables one to gauge the extent of the advantage associated with monetary payments, it does not eliminate the fact of such advantage. To some extent, this may be offset by the additional health care which workers (including women workers) receive at their place of work – a service which is sometimes markedly superior to general medicine. As indicated earlier, geographical inequality is a more serious matter, and is not helped by the distribution of feldshers, but is mitigated by urban treatment of rural patients. With regard to age, all children are regularly screened and are dealt with under the specialist maternity and child-care services, whereas the old lose access to industrial polyclinics, so are thus disadvantaged. This disadvantage of the old is partly offset by measures to re-employ pensioners,[58] which both maintains their eligibility for industrial health care and reduces the incidence of ill-health among pensioners. It will be further offset, probably, by the increased attention to geriatric care as the proportion of the population beyond normal retirement age increases. The relative advantage of children is partly offset by the higher birth rate in rural areas, where health-care facilities are scarcer. The influence of sex is less likely to disadvantage Soviet women, since so many doctors (especially in primary care) are themselves women. The influence of type of illness on access to health care is hard to determine. George and Manning argue that its assessment requires some measure of equivalence between qualitatively different needs such that one can decide that, for example, mental-illness needs are as well served as heart-disease needs. This example is interesting since, in their criticism of excessive technical and academic orientations in the Soviet health service policy, they appeared to be arguing as if they had some such measure of equivalence. At least some such claim is implicit in their arguments as to what kind of medical care to develop, though to be fair, they realise that this is not an easy issue, and they are merely advocating a change in emphasis among the various priorities (a change which I support, despite my remarks about the need for great care in this area). The priorities they regard as compromising the ideal of universal coverage are those in favour of certain 'elite' members, workers, the young, and acute life-threatening illnesses, such as heart disease or cancer.

The ideal that the service should be uniform and state-provided has effectively been covered when discussing democratisation and participation. The main limitations on this ideal are almost the same as those concerning whether the service should be free, namely the formal and informal private sectors, which have also already been discussed. The fact that the health service is predominantly state-provided and free guarantees a minimum level of professional care, on which minimum level the lower income groups are more dependent than the higher ones,[59] so the overall effect of the Soviet health service on the distribution of income is probably to redistribute it to the lower income groups of the population, despite the privileged sectors of the health service.

Soviet health: conclusion

To conclude this discussion of the Soviet health service, one could say that the early Bolshevik ideals have only been partially realised, and that there are various grounds for criticism, such as the provision of private health care or 'closed-access' facilities for the privileged, and the political use of psychiatric hospitals. Whether one criticises the academic production of high-technology medicine with little public participation in policy decisions[60] or praises the strategic role of the physician in directing and administering the health service[61] must remain a matter of continuing debate. Other short-comings include lack of choice of 'polyclinic facilities, bureau-cratic rigidities, overlapping of services and their fragmentation for the care of different members of a family, and the time wastage by physicians on routine clerical duties which could be performed by others'.[62] These must be balanced against such positive features as general availability and accessibility of the health services, 'planning towards definite goals, very high ratios of medical personnel and hospital beds per 10 000 of the population, the provision of an educational ladder from para-medical to medical education, refresher courses for doctors [and] excellent mid-wifery'.[63] Overall, one must agree with George and Manning that the Soviet health service is one of the most technically adequate in the world (from what they consider to be a narrow perspective) and one of the most justly organised.[64]

Social Security

In the case of health it is clear that whatever the problems of lack of participation, health care does work to some extent on a basis of need (admittedly defined in a way that reflects the concerns of the medical profession itself, as well as the party and Ministry pressures which are responsible for a small privileged health-care sector). It is thus possible to appraise health planning in terms of health outcomes (patterns of morbidity) despite the limitations due to the scarcity of published morbidity data. The use of mass screening, poly-clinics, dispensaries and health posts means that, despite an emphasis on the quantitative 'supply side' in medical services (so many hospital beds, etc.), the provision of health care is related to need. It is not so clear that this is the case with social security because, as we shall see, for some forms of social security there is no set of mechanisms for the registration of need equivalent to the health-screening and recording procedures just mentioned. Rather, it seems to be assumed that the workings of other policies in the Soviet Union simply eradicate certain kinds of social security need (for example, the need for unemployment benefits).

To see why this is the case, a brief historical review of social security in the Soviet Union is necessary. Because the Bolsheviks had used the inadequate social security provision before the Revolution as a major target for their criticisms of Tsarism, they had little alternative but to attempt a compre-hensive system of social insurance afterwards. However, despite various modifications, the policy was too ambitious to be properly implemented until economic conditions improved under the NEP.[65] State insurance coverage for wage-earners increased from 5.5 million people in 1924 to 10.8 million in 1928. Old-age pensions were also introduced in 1928, for men aged 60 and women aged 55. Life expectancy in 1928 was 44, whereas it is 70 today, but retirement ages remain the same. The result is that old age and disability pensions combined were around 73 per cent of all social security expenditures in the period 1960–72.[66]

Following the First Five Year Plan, social insurance benefits became subservient to the drive towards industrialisation. Social insurance was consequently designed, first, to increase the supply of labour; second, to increase labour discipline; and third, to give more favourable treatment to workers in high-priority industries. Included in the measures to increase the labour supply was the abolition of unemployment benefit in 1930, but in 1938 the length of maternity benefits was reduced from sixteen to nine weeks. Pensioners were encouraged to stay on at work, by allowing them to keep part (and, from 1938, all) of their pension in addition to their earnings from work. Labour discipline was favoured by gradually making benefits dependent on length of uninterrupted employment. Industrial priorities were reinforced by ease of qualification for benefits, or by higher benefits and more generally favourable treatment for workers in industries central to plan fulfilment or in hazardous or underground employment. Such priorities were easier to implement when the administration of these funds were transferred in the early 1930s from government departments to the trade unions. Trade-union members were paid higher sickness benefits than other workers. Apart from changes concerning maternity benefits and the employment of pensioners, the social security system has not changed a great deal since the 1930s, and its administrative structure has remained the same.

The main change in the 1930s was an increase in the number of people covered, from 10.8 million in 1928 to 31.2 million in 1940, a small part of which was the provision of old-age pensions for salaried workers as well as manual workers. Collective farmers were still forced to rely on inadequate mutual aid societies, but the industrial social security system was now quite effective, in contrast to the early 1920s, which saw a progressive ideology combined with a lack of resources to implement the progressive ideas. In the 1940s the main change was the 1944 extension of family allowances, originally introduced in 1936. Family allowances have not changed much since then, and seem to set rather strict conditions of eligibility by contemporary Western standards, being designed to increase the birth rate yet not discourage women from working.

Following the death of Stalin, there was a substantial improvement in social security provision with the State Pension Law of 1956. Although collective farmers and other self-employed people were still excluded, it meant that henceforth social security was less dominated by the demands of the labour market and the drive for industrialisation. The four main changes of the 1956 Act, which was promoted by Khrushchev, were, according to George and Manning:

> First, the coverage was extended to cover most workers and employees and their dependants. Second, the rates of benefits were substantially increased . . . Only family allowances were not increased. Third, benefits were made more egalitarian as between the low paid and the highly paid. The minimum pension was raised far more than the maximum pension. Fourth, the regulations concerning the coverage of the various risks in the scheme were streamlined to reduce anomalies. Thus the new Soviet social security became comprehensive both in terms of people in the industrial sector and risks. Government funds were to be used to supplement contributions from employers.[67]

The situation of the collective farmers was improved considerably under the legislation of 1964, which helped to stem rural migration to towns. Old-age, sickness, disability and maternity benefits were provided to all collective farmers. The scheme was financed on a national basis by contributions from each farm which were to be supplemented by state grants (thereby presumably forcing the richer farms to pay more in contributions). The level of benefits was lower than for workers, partly because of lower wages and partly because of regulations.

It may be the case that the slowing down of the process of converting collective farms to state farms is partly related to the extra social security costs which would be incurred, though the differential will have been diminished since 1964 because wage differentials between collective farmers and workers are now less, and because other social security provisions are now equal between the two groups.[68]

There have been no major statutory reforms since 1964, but there have been a series of measures designed to improve the position of collective farmers and the low paid, as well as to emphasise the welfare rather than the economic aspects of social security. Thus, while the contemporary social security system still bears the marks of its effective origins in the 1930s, a series of measures during the 1970s show an increasing awareness that individuals and families are still falling through the social security net. Probably the biggest changes have been the successive improvements in the minimum amount of pension, the 1974 introduction of an income-tested family allowance scheme designed to deal with poverty, and the improvements in the minimum wage in relation to the average wage, which affects pensions since they are earnings-related. The lot of collective farmers has also been improved: in 1967 their retirement age was reduced by five years, to make it the same as for workers; in 1970 the rules for payment of sickness benefit became almost the same as for workers; and in 1971 the same happened for rules regarding pension payments. With regard to the shift of emphasis from labour discipline to welfare, length of employment was abolished as a condition for maternity benefit in 1973, though there is only one sign of this being extended to other benefits: in 1975 there was a change in the qualifying conditions for sickness benefit, so that those with three or more children can now receive their full earnings regardless of length of employment.

Following this brief historical sketch, which emphasises how recent is some of the social security provision, it is possible to proceed to an analysis of the present social security situation, and some of its effects.

Social security administration, finance and policy
The most striking features of the (i) finance, and (ii) administration of social security are (a) the absence of employees', workers' and collective farmers' contributions (instead the state enterprises, collective farms and social organisations contribute, supplemented by the state budget), and (b) the role of the trade unions in administering the social security provisions. To deal with the administration first, the involvement of the trade unions in social security could be seen as part of the development of non-state forms of administration (part of 'the withering away of the state'), and as fulfilling one of Lenin's objectives for the development of social security, namely that workers should play a full part in its management.[69] It should be clear from the discussion of law and the state in Chapter 4 that this is not necessarily the beginning of (or an aspect of) any process of 'the withering away of the state'. Such a conclusion is reinforced if one examines the precise

nature of trade-union involvement in social security.

Clearly the State Committee on Labour and Social Questions is the most important agency, in the sense of co-ordinating social security policy. Trade-union control of the most important state agencies involved in administration and policy formation on social security is, however, more nominal than real.[70] While there is direct trade-union involvement in the State Committee on Labour and Social Questions, most commentators feel that its greatest effect is on wages. This has a subsequent effect on pensions and other benefits, but this situation suggests that the trade unions are placing social security as a poor second compared with wages. In any case, the State Committee seems to function largely as an inter-preter of decisions emanating elsewhere, rather than as a policy initiator. In interpreting and co-ordinating decisions, it issues directives to the fifteen constituent Republican Ministries of Social Security, which in turn operate through regional, district and local offices. The trade unions are particularly involved at the local level, with elected members doing unpaid work over and above their normal working hours to administer social security.

Pensions for the old and disabled are determined and paid out by the Ministry of Social Welfare, with trade unions at the local level limited to producing the necessary documents and helping applicants to fill in the relevant forms. They also take part in decisions on eligibility for pensions. However, trade unions are entirely responsible for the administration of sickness and maternity benefits. As we saw in the discussion of the health service, sickness benefits are related to attempts to maintain labour discipline. The separate system of social security for collective farmers is run on similar lines. Thus the involvement of trade unions lowers the costs of administering social security, and identifies the trade unions with measures which are at least partly designed to enhance labour discipline, while bringing very little return to the trade unions or their members in the form of capacity to exert democratic pressure on social security policy or its implementation (except decisions on individual eligibility). If this is taken to be the beginning of non-state democratic forms of administration, then it is not a very auspicious beginning.

In the light of this picture of the predominance of state forms of administration of social security, administrative structures which at least have the merit of being fairly straightforward, it is difficult to understand the reasons for the budgetary organisation of the sources of finance for social security. As mentioned earlier, social security is non-contributory[71] in the Soviet Union, i.e. the beneficiaries do not contribute directly to the building up of the funds from which they draw benefits. Thus the principle propounded by Lenin that employers contribute to social insurance, rather than deducting the contributions from employees' wages (directly or through income tax), has been met. Yet, while there might be some residual justification for separating the funding and administration of social security for *kolkhoz* workers, there seems little point in now insisting on separate contributions from state enterprises.

The fact that state enterprises contribute to the social security funds rests on the budgetary position of state enterprises which is supposedly distinct from that of other state agencies (including the Ministries to which they are subordinated). As Lavigne points out,[72] this argument is weak and was in any case effectively ignored for budgetary purposes prior to the 1965 economic reform. Furthermore, the 1979 reform tended to diminish again the distinction between state revenues and state enterprise revenues, since it envisaged a stable rate of taxation on enterprise 'profits', with the rates being differentiated by Ministries. Thus the economic distinctiveness of state enterprises from the state, and hence the *fiscal* nature (levy on an economically distinct agent) of these budgetary operations, is by no means clear. Consequently there seems to be no great merit in insisting on employers' contributions as distinct from state contributions (either directly or through the state social insurance scheme funds). The system of administration of social security is complex in its procedures, but the organisational structure is fairly straightforward. Since the payment of these benefits is not related to the 'profit' of the enterprise concerned (but is determined by other criteria such as length of employment), it seems pointless to retain a budgetary category which does not act as an economic incentive and does not (despite local trade-union involvement) promote serious democratic involvement in the administration of social security.

Social security policy

Having dealt with the administration and finance of social security, it is now possible to turn to policy. One of the classical Marxist criteria for the appraisal of an area of social policy such as social security is the extent to which it contributes to the transformation of 'bourgeois right'. In the case of social security, as with other aspects of social policy such as health and housing, the extent to which 'bourgeois right' has been transformed can be gauged in terms of the extent to which criteria of 'need' predominate in the provision of benefits, rather than criteria related to wages. Failing that, the extent to which income inequalities are mitigated by the provision indicates how far the social effects of wages are undercut or neutralised. It is therefore necessary to discuss the criteria for eligibility for the various social security benefits, as well as the scale of resources devoted to them.

The social policy clearly implicit in all the criteria of eligibility for social security is quite evident: rather than promoting forms of income that are independent of wages (and in that sense defined in terms of the needs of the recipient) the social security system is on the whole defined in a way that sustains wage labour as a form of income. In other words, social security can hardly be considered to be undercutting the wage form. This connection of social security payments with the labour market means that, while the system is comprehensive, it definitely does leave a variety of groups either partially covered or not covered at all, and there is no comprehensive public assistance scheme to act as a 'safety-net' against poverty in these circumstances. Families are legally required to support those of their members who are in financial need. There are forms of public assistance, but these are the responsibility of constituent republics or individual collective farms. Consequently such public assistance is neither uniform nor comprehensive, and provides only residual amounts to meet exceptional cases. Of course, social security payments need not be the only means of 'transforming bourgeois right', i.e. undercutting the wage form of income and promoting social forms of consumption. Health and education within the state budgetary heading of 'social consumption funds' and state housing (which is technically outside the 'social consumption funds') are all potential means of doing so. Hence an appraisal of the social policy implicit in social security must include a consideration of the scale of resources devoted to it, in comparison with other forms of social consumption.

The state budget represents over 60 per cent of national income in the Soviet Union, and within that budget social and culture expenditures represent about 35 per cent of the total. Of these expenditures, education constitutes about half, while one-sixth goes on public health and sports and the rest (about one-third) goes on social security.[73] Social security expenditure has been growing faster than health care, and the two of them combined have been rising generally faster than education within the social consumption funds. The result is that social security and health combined have been showing slowly rising percentages in relation to the state budget and national income (the net material product, which is calculated on a somewhat different basis from the Western index of gross national product).[74] As is fairly well known, this pattern of expenditure has largely been determined by demographic patterns, i.e. the growing number of old-age pensioners. Consequently, since the dependency ratio worsened after 1980, due mainly to a fairly rapid increase in the population living beyond retirement age, the prospects seem remote for the further use of social consumption funds to undercut wages as a form of income.

The effects of social security
To complete the assessment of social security, it is necessary to consider the likely effects of its organisation and its various provisions. The first social effect to be considered is that of its organisation and finance. The administrative structure of social security means that it is a potentially readily accessible arena of popular participation in social administration, but this is hardly the case today, despite trade-union involvement and the budgetary insistence on employers' contributions, which somewhat spuriously suggests workers' control of the profits of industry.

The state budget directly finances about half of all social

security expenditures, a proportion which is likely to grow as the retired population grows more rapidly than the social insurance fund. Thus social security is a form of redistribution of the social product which is largely effected through the state budget: in other words, it is a transfer payment, one of whose sources of funds (in the form of employers' contributions) does not form a tax in the usual sense. Since there is no strong reason in the state sector for sources of finance to coincide with the agencies making expenditure decisions, there seems to be a clear case for simplifying the budgetary arrangements by abolishing employers' contributions. These contributions form part of the cost price of industrial profits, but this accounting problem could be overcome by increasing turnover tax by the amount of the 'lost' contribution from state enterprises.

The redistributional effects of social security are difficult to assess in the absence of systematic data. Since the social security system does not use many qualifying conditions which are unrelated to wage labour, thereby undercutting the wage form, it might at least be expected by socialists that it would mitigate the effects of wage-induced income inequalities. To some extent it may seem that this does happen, since (as we have seen) workers on low wages benefit relatively more from various forms of social security provision. In addition, workers on low wages are also exempted from paying income tax, and various basic consumption items (transport, some kinds of food) are subsidised to keep prices down, which must help lower income groups more. On the other hand, income tax is not particularly onerous for any Soviet income group, and these price subsidies were already taken into account in the calculation of the socially acceptable minimum subsistence level of 50 roubles per month *per capita* (as at 1983). It is evident that many pensioners and families with young children fall below this 'poverty line'. What is not clear is how many, but the findings of social scientists that many do fall through the social security net was probably largely responsible for the introduction in 1974 of child allowances (or family allowances, as they are sometimes called). This scheme, which has already been mentioned, provides a supplement of 12 roubles per month per child until the age of 8 for families with a *per capita* income below 50 roubles per month. George and Manning quote a source which claimed that this scheme virtually doubled the number of children covered, which now became 37 per cent of *all* children under the age of 8, and involved a five-fold increase in total expenditure.[75] Thus social security may now have some redistributional effect in favour of low-income families with young children. The overall redistributional effect of social security is not easy to assess, however, and some commentators feel that the redistributive impact of such monetary transfers will be small.

The attempt to reach completely full employment rather than provide unemployment benefit seems to be related to the lack of a systematic public assistance programme and the use of equalisation of wages as the main policy instrument to equalise benefits (and hence real income). Rather than a systematic monitoring of the conditions under which people are not adequately covered by social security (coupled with the provision of specific benefits to 'fill the gaps' in the system), the Soviet approach to these problems is simply to try to ensure that everyone has a wage and to increase those wages regularly in a manner which reduces wage inequality. While this approach is admirable in so far as it works, it has at least to the mid-1970s left many families in need of income maintenance. It has also generated inflationary pressures which could force price rises which reduce the purchasing power of the social security monetary transfers, thereby reducing any equalising effect they may have.

Hence the effects of social security cannot be properly assessed without an appraisal of wages policy, which is more the concern of the next chapter than this one. For the moment, it is sufficient to note that there has been a steady policy of reducing wage inequality which has had some effect.[76] Yet it is difficult to see how an overall policy on wages will help the 10 per cent of Soviet families which are one-parent families, who presumably depend on only one wage plus either divorce maintenance payments, survivor's benefits or an unmarried mother's allowance. This is precisely the sort of case where the issue of detecting gaps in the social security net becomes relevant. However, it must be admitted that there is no reason why the social security system alone should be expected to bear the burden of attempts to equalise real income in the Soviet

Union. The other aspects of social consumption need to be considered together with social security.

Conclusion: An Assessment of Welfare and Consumption

Wages, housing and the various components of the social consumption fund all affect the distribution of income, and the connection is even closer than that because of the earnings-related nature of many social security monetary transfers. Some estimate of the interrelation between these various aspects of the distribution of income needs to be made. Evidently such considerations are already taken into account in Soviet social policy, though, according to Rzhanitsyna,[77] some accounting problems have still to be solved; the effects of the social consumption funds on family incomes are at the moment only assessed on the basis of aggregated estimates. According to these, payments and benefits from the social funds markedly reduce the differentials in living standards, averaging 30–40 per cent of the families' aggregate income in the lower-income groups, and 15–20 per cent among high-income groups. One might think that the cumulative effect of policy is clear when Rzhanitsyna says that between 1966 and 1975 the number of inhabitants in families living below the 50-rouble minimum declined by almost 70 per cent. Yet it is not clear how far this is due to wage increases, and how far it is due to expenditures on social consumption funds. It is a reasonable guess that the child allowances introduced in 1974 made a substantial contribution to reducing the number of inhabitants who are below the 50-rouble minimum. However, it can be no more than a guess, in the absence of detailed data.

Even if some of this income equalisation is due to the social consumption funds and housing subsidies, rather than wages policy, is it redistributive in favour of the lower-income groups when one takes account of the sources of such expenditure? In other words, is public finance generally redistributive in the USSR? It has already been indicated that some commentators are doubtful about this. Wiles is also doubtful.[78] Although Wiles is correct in saying that only vast research could extract an answer to the question, progressive or regressive, we do have the aggregate estimates mentioned by Rzhanitsyna to go on. Furthermore, the argument put forward by George and Manning that the social security system is regressive or neutral has its weaknesses, particularly in their analysis of the state budget. They base their analysis of the state budget on 1965 figures provided in the English edition of Lavigne's *Les Economies Socialistes*.[79] Their claim that indirect taxation is regressive is probably misleading, though, as Bush points out,[80] no comprehensive and systematic data are published on rates of turnover tax. Wiles is willing to hazard the opinion that it is slightly progressive.[81] Furthermore, it is clear that the composition of the state budget has changed since 1965.[82] Thus, even if turnover tax were regressive, it only constitutes 32 per cent of budgetary receipts and is offset by the very mildly progressive income tax (9 per cent) and revenues of various kinds from state enterprises (54.2 per cent). The effect of the remaining 4.8 per cent, which is mostly personal taxation, is probably progressive. While George and Manning point out that regressivity must also be judged in terms of benefits, and while they are arguing at this point only with respect to social security, it is likely that both health and housing have progressive redistributive effects. Thus Wiles puts a strong case for house rents being progressive: '*kolkhozniki* build, own and inherit their own dwellings tax free, the urban poor enjoy a vast subsidy, the upper middle class must join co-operatives and pay full cost (but can resell for a capital gain)'.[83] Similarly, unless one is going to put a very high price on the privileged sector of health care (the so-called 'fourth directorate'), then health-care benefits probably are progressive, with low-income families benefiting disproportionately from the care of non-life-threatening morbidity which is dealt with mainly through out-patient care. Thus the aggregate estimates referred to above mentioned by Rzhanitsyna do not seem to be inconsistent with what is known about the provision of housing, health and possibly even social security.

In addition to the lack of systematic evidence on the effects of each of these forms of welfare, the effects of the interrelation between them is even more obscure. The kinds of complex inter-relation between the various aspects of social policy are virtually impossible to discuss seriously in the face of the lack of systematic evidence in the fields of housing, health and social security. While such evidence may be available within the relevant Ministries, it is not at all clear how much of it is co-ordinated with a view to producing an overall set of inter-related social policies. Such collation of information as does take place within the State Committee on Labour and Social Questions seems to be largely concerned with the distribution of income, though as the example of Rzhanitsyna makes clear it is never published in sufficiently detailed form for it to be subjected to really serious scrutiny.

While it is clear that maintenance of production and of a stable, disciplined labour force are not the only concerns of social policy, they still remain the predominant concern to a degree which is more appropriate to an industrialising society than to one which has already largely succeeded in creating an industrial base. While other instruments of social policy are actually and potentially available, the adjustment of wages and the quantitative provision of facilities (in housing, health care, etc.) seem to be the main instruments used. The development of a sophisticated system capable of registering diverse needs, making its information available to public scrutiny and allowing substantial public participation in both policy formation and the administration of social policy – these are features of Soviet welfare provision which must remain a hope for the future. Many of the effects of these policies are opaque, even it seems to those concerned with implementing them and monitoring their effects. Unfortunately such criticisms are easier to make than to rectify. It could well be that the rising proportion of old-age pensioners, whose pensions will register the 'knock-on' effects of large wage increases during the 1970s, will generate its own inflationary pressures, as well as reducing the scope for expanding other forms of social consumption. The rising birth rate among comparatively low-income (often rural) families of Central Asia will generate further demographic demands on social consumption, again further reducing the room for manoeuvre. This demographic 'squeeze' from both ends of the age spectrum, producing a deteriorating depend-ency ratio, can only be offset by rising productivity, which is an area where the Soviet economy was experiencing difficulties in the late 1970s.

However, although many social welfare provisions are

evidently still designed to increase production, it is not at all clear that they do so. For example, the connection of some of the housing stock to particular Ministries and thus to particular state enterprises is now partly responsible for the loss of productivity due to high labour turnover, since people change jobs in order to improve their housing. That is why I argued in the section on housing for a dislocation of housing from industrial Ministries and for the politically more effective incorporation of city soviets. This would also make it possible to persuade workers in good housing to agree to redeployment in situations where changes in work procedures or investment would make workers redundant (even if they kept their jobs). So it would make it easier to shed labour where this was appropriate and where alternative employment was available, thereby increasing productivity in a different manner.

This suggestion is not proposed as a remedy to the problems of the Soviet economy, but merely to indicate that a more detailed analysis of the interrelation of various social and economic policies than is possible at the moment could well yield proposals that both meet the kind of criticisms made in this chapter and improve Soviet economic performance. Without some such analysis based on detailed evidence, the 'incrementalism' which various commentators have suggested characterised policy formation during the Brezhnev era could come to look more and more like the 'ossification' which some critics claimed to discern towards the end of the Brezhnev period.

Notes

1. See G. Littlejohn, 'State, Plan and Market in the Transition to Socialism: The Legacy of Bukharin', *Economy and Society*, vol. 8, no. 2, May 1979, where it is argued that among the 'needs' which have to be specified are the conditions of existence of agents of plan implementation, and that such agents could be organisations rather than human individuals.
2. For a discussion of these and other problems confronting socialist attempts to specify 'appropriate' social policies, see N. Rose, 'Socialism and Social Policy: The Problems of Inequality', in *Politics and Power 2*, Routledge & Kegan Paul, London, 1980, pp. 111–35.
3. V. George and N. Manning, *Socialism, Social Welfare and the Soviet Union*, Routledge & Kegan Paul, London, 1980, p.133.
4. Ibid, p.135.

5. Ibid, p.139.
6. Ibid, p.141.
7. Ibid, p.142.
8. E. M. Jacobs, 'Urban Housing in the Soviet Union', in *Economic Aspects of Life in the USSR,* NATO Directorate of Economic Affairs, Brussels, 1975, pp.65–90.
9. George and Manning, *Socialism and the Soviet Union*, p. 144.
10. Ibid, p.145.
11. Ibid, p.145.
12. Ibid, p.146.
13. Ibid, p.147.
14. Ibid.
15. S. Sternheimer, 'Running Soviet Cities: Bureaucratic Degeneration, Bureaucratic Politics, or Urban Management?', in G. B. Smith (ed.), *Public Policy and Administration in the Soviet Union,* Praeger, New York, 1980, pp.79–108.
16. Ibid, p.94.
17. Ibid, p.97.
18. George and Manning, *Socialism and the Soviet Union,* p.150. See also Jacobs, 'Urban Housing in the Soviet Union', pp.70,71, for a more detailed discussion of the administration of housing waiting-lists.
19. Littlejohn, 'State, Plan and Market in the Transition to Socialism'.
20. Sternheimer, 'Running Soviet Cities', pp.83–4.
21. George and Manning, *Socialism and the Soviet Union,* p.152.
22. Ibid.
23. Ibid, p.157.
24. See Sternheimer, 'Running Soviet Cities', pp.87–91, for a more detailed account of these administrative mechanisms of accountability.
25. Ibid, pp.99–102.
26. George and Manning, *Socialism and the Soviet Union,* p.157.
27. Ibid, pp.153, 154.
28. Ibid, p.153. Similarly, they point out (on p.155) that 'Generally the finance of housing and associated services is a very complicated affair influenced broadly by several interlocking "markets" for housing, and several interlocking "interest groups", for local services.'
29. Jacobs, 'Urban Housing in the Soviet Union', p.73. Jacobs continues: 'While such repair work and redevelopment work may be beneficial, or even necessary, they absorb so great a proportion of housing investments that the volume of additional housing available each year must suffer as a result.'
30. A. Katsenelinboigen, 'Coloured Markets in the Soviet Union', *Soviet Studies,* vol. XXIX, no. 1, January 1977, pp.62–85. Presumably raw materials are frequently stolen from construction projects to effect the repairs.
31. Jacobs, 'Urban Housing in the Soviet Union', p.76. However, Jacobs suggests that improvements in design and the increasing use of industrially produced prefabricated building components may reduce some of those repair problems, and the (later) remarks by George and Manning,

Socialism and the Soviet Union, p. 151, on the quality of housing to some extent vindicate Jacobs's prediction.

32. Jacobs, 'Urban Housing in the Soviet Union', p.74.
33. Ibid, pp.75, 76.
34. Ibid, p.82.
35. Ibid, p.84.
36. This remark is necessarily conjectural, in view of the paucity of evidence on the distribution of income in the Soviet Union. A. McAuley, *Economic Welfare in the Soviet Union*, Allen & Unwin, London, 1979, p.93, provides evidence on housing subsidies. Evidence (on p.94) suggests that in 1960 there was a negative association between education, medical care and housing subsidies on the one hand, and income on the other. Yet over all, he suggests (on p.97) that non-cash social consumption expenditures were regressive. So the position with respect to the effect of housing subsidies alone on the distribution of income is unclear, because the evidence is so meagre.
37. For an extensive (roughly half the book) and sympathetic examination of the history of the Soviet health service, see G. Hyde, *The Soviet Health Service: A Historical and Comparative Study*, Lawrence & Wishart, London, 1974. This book is particularly helpful to the British reader because of its comparisons with the British NHS. Historical accounts can also be found in George and Manning, *Socialism and the Soviet Union*, pp.106–11; and M. Kaser, *Health Care in the Soviet Union and Eastern Europe*, Croom Helm, London. 1976, pp.36–44.
38. George and Manning, *Socialism and the Soviet Union*, p.111.
39. Kaser, *Health Care in the Soviet Union*, p.42.
40. Hyde, *The Soviet Health Service*, p.288. The growth in mental ill-health is almost certainly more apparent than real, and is the result of a greater willingness to diagnose and treat it, following the lapsing in the 1950s of claims that mental ill-health was dying out under socialism.
41. Kaser, *Health Care in the Soviet Union*, p.49.
42. The role of mass screening is made clear by G. A. Popov, *Principles of Health Planning in the USSR*, World Health Organisation, Geneva, 1971, pp.38–44.
43. Hyde, *The Soviet Health Service*, p.245.
44. Kaser, *Health Care in the Soviet Union*, p.44. This is doubtless related to the privileged 'fourth directorate' of the health service described by George and Manning, *Socialism and the Soviet Union*, p.122, a range of closed facilities provided for privileged government and party members.
45. George and Manning, *Socialism and the Soviet Union*, p.115.
46. Popov, *Principles of Health Planning*, ch. 1, esp. pp. 25–6.
47. Ibid, p.22.
48. Ibid, p.130.
49. Kaser, *Health Care in the Soviet Union*, p.62.
50. Ibid, p.63. Hyde, *The Soviet Health Service*, devotes a chapter to the emphasis on recuperative holidays in Soviet medicine. While the system is sometimes abused, they do seem to have some value.
51. Kaser, *Health Care in the Soviet Union*, pp.64–6, as well as other

sources referred to by George and Manning, *Socialism and the Soviet Union*, p.122.

52. Kaser, *Health Care in the Soviet Union*, pp.67–8. This lack of equipment may be why hospitals are considered rather poor by Western standards. There are problems of poor food, hospital-spread infection (perhaps related to the wearing of everyday clothes under surgical gowns), and so on.

53. Popov, *Principles of Health Planning*, p.133.

54. George and Manning, *Socialism and the Soviet Union*, p.114. Thus, unlike their discussion of housing, George and Manning appreciate here that technical and administrative practices affect the registration and even the articulation of demand. Similarly, they recognise the political determinants of medical need which stem from the Ministry of Health and the medical profession itself. Thus many of my criticisms of their remarks on housing demand do not apply to their analysis of medical need.

55. Ibid, pp.122–3.

56. Ibid, pp.125–6; Hyde, *The Soviet Health Service*, pp.290–1.

57. George and Manning, *Socialism and the Soviet Union*, p.124.

58. M. E. Ruben, 'The Soviet Pensioner: An Element in the Labour Supply', in *Economic Aspects of Life in the USSR*, NATO Directorate of Economic Affairs, Brussels, 1975, pp.197–205.

59. H. Vogel, 'Social Security and Medicare', in *Economic Aspects of Life in the USSR*, NATO Directorate of Economic Affairs, Brussels, 1975, pp. 207–33; this argument appears on p.215.

60. George and Manning, *Socialism and the Soviet Union*, p.127.

61. Hyde, *The Soviet Health Service*, pp.289–90.

62. Ibid, p.290.

63. Ibid, p.289.

64. George and Manning, *Socialism and the Soviet Union*, pp.127–8.

65. Ibid, p.38.

66. Ibid, p.44, gives figures from an International Labour Organisation report which differ slightly from those given by Vogel, 'Social Security and Medicare', table 4, p.227. However, these differences are not serious for old-age and disability pensions. In 1974, 28 million drew old-age pensions, 12 million disability pensions and 4 million service pensions, so around two-thirds of these expenditures are on old-age pensions. See K. Bush, 'Soviet Living Standards: Some Salient Data', in *Economic Aspects of Life in the USSR*, NATO Directorate of Economic Affairs, Brussels, 1975, p.59. If two-thirds of these pensions are old-age pensions, then this means that around 50 per cent of social security expenditure is on old-age pensions.

67. George and Manning, *Socialism and the Soviet Union*, p.42.

68. The details of the measures to equalise provision for the two groups are given below. However, this does not mean that the situation is now equal. M. Lavigne, *Les Economies Socialistes: Soviétique et Européennes*, Armand Colin, Paris, 1979, points out (on p.307) that despite a tendency in this area to an equalisation between town and country, the state only

covers 80 per cent of the social needs of the collective farmers as against 90 per cent of workers and employees.

69. See George and Manning, *Socialism and the Soviet Union*, p.33.

70. While Gosplan is admittedly involved in many other aspects of planning, one can gain an indication of the relative administrative capabilities of Gosplan and the All-Union Council of Trade Unions by comparing the respective size of their buildings, which stand next to each other in Moscow. The trade-union building seems rather small by comparison. More importantly, the very fact that Gosplan is integrating social security planning with other aspects of the economic plan must give it a considerable say in the outcome of discussions in the State Committee on Labour and Social Questions.

71. Vogel, 'Social Security and Medicare', pp.207–8.

72. Lavigne, *Les Economies Socialistes*, pp.334–5.

73. Ibid, pp.332–3.

74. See the statistical discussion and appendix to Vogel, 'Social Security and Medicare'. Vogel's figures only go up to 1972, but the more general figures on the budget provided by Lavigne, *Les Economies Socialistes*, for 1979 suggest that this trend has continued.

75. George and Manning, *Socialism and the Soviet Union*, p.54.

76. Thus M. Matthews, *Class and Society in Soviet Russia*, Allen Lane, The Penguin Press, London, 1972, p.75, figure 6, notes a substantial equalisation of wages between 1946 and 1966. In 1968 the minimum wage was fixed at 60 roubles a month (he states on p.66). L. Rzhanitsyna, *Soviet Family Budgets*, Progress Publishers, Moscow, 1977, p.129, table 24, suggests that the minimum wage since then has gone up to 70 roubles in many occupations. Bush, 'Soviet Living Standards', p.53, suggests that this minimum wage was going to be extended to the entire public-sector work-force, other than *kolkozniki* and domestic servants, by the end of 1975. According to Lavigne, *Les Economies Socialistes*, p.337, income tax is not payable on wages below 70 roubles, and income-tax rates are reduced for wages from 71–90 roubles.

77. Rzhanitsyna, *Soviet Family Budgets*, p.136.

78. P. Wiles, 'Recent Data on Soviet Income Distribution', in *Economic Aspects of Life in the USSR*, NATO Directorate of Economic Affairs, Brussels, 1975, p.125. The arguments by Vogel, and by George and Manning, on this issue are on pp.224 and 60 of their respective texts.

79. M. Lavigne, *The Socialist Economies of the Soviet Union and Europe*, Martin Robertson, London, 1974, p.284. The figures are quoted on p.60 of George and Manning, *Socialism and the Soviet Union*.

80. Bush, 'Soviet Living Standards', p.55.

81. Wiles, 'Recent Data on Soviet Income Distribution', p.125.

82. The following figures are derived from Lavigne, *Les Economies Socialistes*, pp.334–7.

83. Wiles, 'Recent Data on Soviet Income Distribution', p.125. This position differs from that of McAuley, *Economic Welfare in the Soviet Union*: see note 36.

6

The Analysis of the Class Structure of the Soviet Union

Introduction

It was argued in Chapter 1 that one could not designate state-socialist societies as 'transitional social formations' on the grounds that they exhibited certain features which approximated to an ideal state of affairs. Rather than adhere to such a teleological definition of socialism, which would imply that a socialist society was tending in a certain direction, the argument implied that a society could be considered socialist if it could be demonstrated that class relations had been seriously weakened or were non-existent. The purpose of this chapter is to investigate whether (and if so, to what extent) class relations are operative in the Soviet Union. It will be remembered that it was argued that if class relations were weak or non-existent, the relatively open access to the means of production would mean that the differential forms of access of various agents would be subject to constant challenge by other agents, and would thus be an object of struggle and negotiation. One could add now that such struggles might well be subject to adjudication by certain legal or political agencies. Such a situation would not preclude differentiation of economic agents; indeed, this is inevitable in any division of labour, and would include a differentiated occupational structure for individuals, but such differentiation would not entail a fairly systematic enhancement or restriction of agents' capacity for action deriving from differential access to the means of production. This does not mean that there could be no systematic differences in the capacities of agents deriving from some other determinants of the division of labour, such as demarcations between individuals on the grounds of gender, ethnic group or age.

This chapter begins with a fairly general discussion of the relation between occupational structure and class structure, followed by an examination of Lane's analysis of the Soviet occupational structure. This introduces the official Soviet view of the class structure (which Lane criticises) and shows the broad changes in occupational structure since the late 1920s. The view that there is increasing similarity between the Soviet and capitalist occupational structures is criticised. To illustrate the Soviet occupational structure in more detail, various aspects are examined: the position of women in the occupational structure, collective farm workers, the concept of 'the intelligentsia', and the related issue of the connection between education and the occupational structure. Following on from this, the relationship between the Soviet occupational structure, collective agents and the class structure is discussed. To substantiate the conclusion of this section that class relations do not seem to operate within the state sector of the economy, but do operate between the state and collective farm sector, the next section deals with the distribution of wages and income. The concluding section of the chapter, which also draws on the analysis of Chapters 3, 4 and 5, is on the presence (and extent) of class relations in the Soviet Union.

Occupational Structure and Class Structure

The acceptance of the possibility of a change in location of economic agents, or of groups of agents, has led some theorists to define class boundaries in terms of the lack of movement of agents. Thus classes are sometimes said to coalesce or crystallise around some set of economic locations whose membership is fairly static. However, the specification of a class boundary should not be confused with the issue of whether an agent (or group of agents) can move across it. The concept of 'class' does not refer to the openness or closure of the division of labour to the movement of agents between locations, but to the differential capacities of agents *deriving from* their occupying different economic locations (having different forms of access to the means of production). Without such a specification of a class boundary, it is impossible to decide whether the movement of agents in question should be considered simply as occupational mobility of individuals, a change of class position by individuals or groups, or a structural change in the relations of production. The difficulty of specifying the nature of boundaries, and the related difficulty of deciding on the nature of changes in the division of labour, have had important effects on the study of occupational or social mobility. It is in some ways fairly easy to study the occupational mobility of individuals, given that the payment of wages usually entails a specification of the tasks to be performed and the skills required. This is often already recorded or fairly easily obtainable from an interview. However, the study of 'group mobility' is generally defined less clearly. It may refer to a group of individuals from a common origin crossing a boundary, or a group of individuals constituting a collective agent whose location is changing (either by crossing a boundary, or because the structure of the division of labour is itself changing). The concept of 'social mobility', as it is usually deployed, does not readily distinguish between the mechanisms generating economic locations (structural conditions of action of agents which are subject to alteration in the course of struggle) and the mechanisms distributing individuals or even collective agents to those locations. Consequently it does not make it easy to analyse the changing occupational structure as recorded in official statistics or in social surveys.

The most common confusion which arises from this state of affairs is the identification or confusion of the occupational structure (which can only refer to the economic location of individuals) with the class structure. Yet the class structure can also refer to the economic location of collective agents. If one refuses to identify the occupational structure with the class structure, this raises two separate problems. The first is how to decide on the class position of collective agents who do not appear directly in the occupational structure, for example joint-stock companies or state enterprises. The second is that while individuals may be located in occupational positions within such collective agents (positions which cannot be equated with the positions of the collective agents themselves), individuals may also be simultaneously located in several other collective agents. For example, individuals may simultaneously be members of a state enterprise, a trade union, and the Communist Party. All these agents have some impact on the division of labour, though their importance as determinants of the division of labour varies. Both these problems raise in a new form a question which has already come up: namely, which boundaries in the division of labour are to be considered as class boundaries? This time the question arises in the form: what is the unit of analysis of the class structure? The answer must be that there is no single unit, in the sense of an agent of a particular kind. In the past various sociologists have attempted to treat individuals in occupational positions as *the* unit of analysis of the class structure, but this has tended to mean that other agents have been treated as identical to (or entirely derivative of) this 'prime' unit of analysis.[1]

It is now possible to specify more clearly the relationship between the occupational structure and the class structure, assuming that class relations are a feature of the social formation in question. In a sense the occupational structure is both less than and more than the class structure. It is less than the class structure, because it does not coincide with collective economic agents which may be part of the class structure. It is more than the class structure, because it is determined not only by the class structure but also by other non-economic determinants of the division of labour such as gender attribution, nationality, state and party policy, and even the organisation of the state itself. To put it another way, the occupational structure does not directly register the presence of collective agents, though it does so indirectly because such agents have their own internal organisation and hence an associated occupational structure. On the other hand, the occupational structure may well register the effects of other, non-economic determinants of the division of labour. Consequently the occupational structure is only a partial indicator of the effects of the relations of production, since it only shows the distribution of individuals within the division of labour. This distribution does not show directly the economic location of collective agents, or the relative capacities of any economic agents. Furthermore, it does not directly distinguish between mechanisms allocating individuals to economic locations (which may be affected by a variety of determinants) and mechanisms generating those locations themselves (which may be affected by the same or other determinants). Finally, since it does not indicate the relative capacities of the different economic agents, it cannot show how far these capacities enable some agents to predominate in co-ordinating the division of labour, thereby to some extent determining their own conditions of existence, and securing for themselves a disproportionate share in the distribution of income.[2] In other words, it cannot *directly* show whether the relations of production involve class relations.

Nevertheless, the occupational structure is a good starting-point to try to elicit the presence or extent of class relations, since it should indicate some of the effects of class relations on the division of labour. It should indicate at least some of the effects of class relations on individual economic agents, who are frequently used as the unit of analysis in official statistics or social surveys. Consequently there may be empirical evidence of such effects, and bearing in mind the above reservations about the somewhat opaque relation between the occupational structure and the class structure it should be possible to appraise this evidence in terms of the extent to which it indicates any systematic effects of differential access to the means of production, as opposed to other, non-economic determinants of the division of labour.

The Soviet Occupational Structure: Lane's Analysis

As is fairly well known, the official Soviet view of the class structure refers to the existence of two classes and one stratum, the workers, peasants and employees (some of the latter are sometimes called the 'intelligentsia'), whose interrelation is structured by non-antagonistic contradictions. As Lane points out: 'A non-antagonistic contradiction is one which may be resolved by quantitative change, whereas an antagonistic contradiction can only be resolved by a qualitative one.'[3] Lane takes the view that the dialectical concept of contradiction entails antagonism and its resolution by qualitative change, so the term 'non-antagonistic contradiction' is in his view confusing and inappropriate. What the official theory seems to be attempting in using such a term is to distinguish contradictions which can be resolved 'within the parameters of a given social system',[4] rather than ones which can only be resolved by changing the social system itself. So a classless society can be achieved by a guided growing together of the classes.

In contrast to the official Soviet position, Lane and O'Dell define the working class 'to include in the Soviet Union all manual and non-manual labour occupied in publicly owned institutions concerned with production, distribution and exchange'.[5] They elaborate this a little later:

> In our view, non-manual workers in production enterprises are not, as assumed by Stalin and others, part of a separate stratum outside . . . the working class; they become an integral part of it. This is because in a Marxist sense their relationship to the means of production is the same as that of manual workers: all are wage-earners employed in state-owned enterprises; all contribute directly to production in the national economy; all to some degree share a similar political ideology.[6]

This is consistent with the view expressed elsewhere by Lane that state-socialist societies are not classless, but are not antagonistic class societies either: they are single-class societies or workers' states.[7] According to Lane, 'the cultural formation and political arrangements characteristic of the superstructure of society are not yet at the socialist level'. These superstructural determinants generate forms of inequality which are not epiphenomena but are contradictions built into the system as long as the level of production leaves some socially determined wants unfulfilled: in other words, as long as the level of productive forces is too low. This is not the place to rehearse arguments about the adequacy of the base–superstructure metaphor or the 'problematic of the productive forces'. Such arguments were referred to in Chapter 1.[8]

All that will be noted here is that Lane seems in these later works to have dropped his earlier objection to the use of the concept of non-antagonistic contradictions, since he is arguing here that in the Soviet Union we face a non-antagonistic class society which *is* a class society precisely because the low level of the productive forces produces superstructural features whose contradictions apparently give rise to forms of inequality. Without these forms of inequality, it is clearly implied that the Soviet Union would be a classless rather than a single-class society. For my own part, I cannot conceive of a single-class society, since (as I have repeatedly stated) the concept of class relations refers to significantly differential access to the means of production. If all agents are in a 'single class' then relations between them are classless.

However, despite my not sharing this view on the difference between class and classless society, Lane's works (as well as that of Lane and O'Dell) are of considerable interest to an investigation of the Soviet occupational structure, because of their recognition of forms of inequality within the 'single-class' society. For example, Lane points out that the Soviet literature on the subject of the intelligentsia and employees is highly ambiguous, with different sociologists dividing non-manual workers into different numbers of groups, even within the categories of employee and intelligentsia.[9] Similarly, various numbers of strata are distinguished within the manual working class (although usually the three strata are considered to be unskilled, semi-skilled and skilled manual workers), and within the 'peasantry' (although again three strata are often distinguished: namely, the unskilled, the mechanisers and administrative personnel). Yet Lane is not content simply to note Soviet attempts to analyse these forms of inequality, as can most clearly be seen in the work of Lane and O'Dell, where it is argued that 'the simple categorisation of manual and non-manual workers in terms of the quality of their labour input becomes increasingly less relevant . . . [but that] other distinctions between various strata of the working class have more salience'.[10] These distinctions are based on occupational differentiation (itself based on the character of work performed and the place a worker has in the system of social production), educational background, financial rewards and culture. Unfortunately, Lane and O'Dell do not explicitly theorise the concepts of character of work performed and place in the system of social production. Nevertheless, one can provide an account of the historical changes in the occupational structure, using the work of Lane and O'Dell and that of Amvrosov.[11] See Table 6.1. As Lane and O'Dell put it: 'These facts serve to illustrate the rapid structural change that has taken place: a swift population growth, a movement of population from village to town, the creation of an urban working class with a recent peasant background.'[12]

Table 6.1   **Percentage changes in the overall Soviet occupational structure**

	1928	1939	1959	1974	1977
Industry					
Manual	12.4	33.2	49.5	60.6	61.6
Non-manual	5.2	17.0	18.8	21.6	22.7
Sub-total	17.6	50.2	68.3	82.2	84.3
Agriculture	82.4	49.8	31.7	17.8	15.7
Total	100.0	100.0	100.0	100.0	100.0

Sources: D. Lane and F. O'Dell, *The Soviet Industrial Worker*, Martin Robertson, London, 1978, pp. 7–8 (derived and corrected); and A. A. Amvrosov, *Sotsial'naya Struktura Sovetskogo Obshchestva*, Politizdat, Moscow, 1975, p. 20.

Lane and O'Dell believe that the evidence supports the view

> that the Soviet *occupational* pattern substantially follows that of Western capitalist counties . . . The more industrialised a society becomes, (i) the smaller the proportion of the labour force engaged in agriculture, and (ii) the higher the ratio of non-manual workers in the non-agricultural labour force.[13]

In view of the growth in non-manual occupations, it is perhaps surprising that 'public administration' has declined as a percentage of the labour force since 1959. This is clearly related to the use of voluntary workers among the trade unions and social organisations, which is considered as enhancing popular participation in 'the administration of things'. We saw in Chapter 5 that George and Manning did not consider that this was very effective as a form of participation, and from the arguments of Hirst discussed in Chapter 4 we might expect that it may not be very effective as a form of administration either. Such a view is supported by Hough,[14] who argues that both the State Committee for Labour and Social Questions and Gosplan face a real danger of inundation by the incredible level of detail on which they and the trade unions must work. The use of trade unions (in addition to state agencies) must solve some of these problems by spreading the work-load, but Hough argues that 'the deep involvement of the trade unions in Soviet labour and wage policy creates a serious administrative problem for the Soviet system because trade unions are subordinated to no governmental agency'.[15] The party organs, as in so many similar situations, serve as the common superior which co-ordinates activities and adjudicates disputes. However, the Politburo has little time to deal with the details of wages policy, so the co-ordination of policy in this area remains a trouble-some problem. More important, however, from the point of view of policy implementation, is the lack of training in administration and the high turnover of voluntary trade-union workers involved in social security administration. It is this lack of expertise and the problems associated with it which support Hirst's argument to the effect that state administration can be preferable to voluntary forms of provision of various services, since it can secure certain defined minimal standards of performance.[16] For such reasons, the lack of growth of the 'public administration' sector of occupations may be less desirable than proponents of democratic administration might imagine.

With regard to manual occupations, Lane and O'Dell argue that the general level of skill has increased between 1961 and 1972.[17] While this is doubtless true, they themselves point out that part of the recorded increase in skill is due possibly to the use of regrading as a disguised form of wage increase. Further-more, there is a heavy use of ancillary workers to supply raw materials from within the same factory, using artisan labour. Lane and O'Dell argue that the continuing demand for manual labour is due to the relatively lower technological level of the USSR, which means that extensive and intensive growth are taking place in parallel rather than in sequence.[18] This is almost certainly still correct, but they then argue that the actual *structure* of the labour force is largely determined by the kind and level of technology, and the socially accepted ways of manning (or staffing, as I prefer to call it). They refer to Braverman in arguing that it is in the context of similarities in the division of labour that the organisation of the work process in the USSR has parallels with the capitalist West. Yet it is not clear that the structure of the labour force is all that similar to the capitalist West (unless one is contrasting industrialised societies with, say, agrarian ones). Certainly in the USSR there has been the familiar tendency within industry for the proportion of the work-force engaged in 'material production' to fall, from 88.3 per cent in 1940 to 75.4 per cent in 1976.[19] It is also true that, using Western definitions of primary, secondary and tertiary sectors of the economy, the USSR in 1976 resembled Italy and Austria of 1960, rather than the USA of 1960,[20] so that it might be possible to attribute most of the differences within the secondary sector (manufacturing and construction) to a technological lag between the capitalist societies and the USSR. However, this would be courting the danger of attributing too great an effectivity to technological determinants in structuring manual occupations in the labour force.

Lane and O'Dell are quite willing, it seems, to concede that the *non-manual* labour force is not occupationally structured to neatly fit in with the needs of technology. Thus they note the growing numbers of engineering and technical employees (ITRs),[21] and the smaller share than in the West of the labour force constituted by lower-grade white-collar workers.[22] They quote a Soviet source to the effect that this smaller share of 'administrative' workers (office staff) is largely a consequence of the artificial limitation of the number of salaried workers *when their functions were handed over to the ITRs*. The Soviet source argues that ITRs should be completely relieved of office work.[23] It is somewhat surprising that they do not seriously consider whether analogous 'artificial' limitations are placed on the *manual* labour force. It would be hard to deny that changing levels of technology are an important determinant of the occupational structure of the labour force, but if both intensive and extensive growth are taking place it is not immediately clear that changes in technology are the main determinant, rather than, say, another determinant which they mention, socially accepted ways of staffing. In any case, changes in technology are themselves partly determined by the central planning agencies and the socially accepted ways of staffing. The last point is illustrated by Lee, who argues that 'rationalisation' of technology by the workers themselves is symbiotically related to engineering failures, to badly designed equipment which has to be accepted in a situation of supply difficulties.[24] It is an activity which declines as any new technology introduced gets older (that is, as the problems of its introduction are overcome). So the labour force is not only being restructured by technology but is itself constantly adapting technology to existing practices. While the introduction of automation does affect the educational profile of the worker and the content of labour, and consequently does lead to a restructuring of the labour force in favour of more skilled manual occupations, the continuing difficulties of technological innovation should not be ignored. The 'parallels with the capitalist West' are mainly evident at the macro-social level (that is, with very broad classifications of the occupational structure, such as manual/non-manual) and over fairly long time periods which indicate trends which it is *presumed* will continue to eradicate the differences in Soviet and capitalist occupational structures. Lane and O'Dell argue that the small service sector and the low proportion of employees in clerical occupations should not be allowed to obscure the similarities between the Soviet occupational structure and that of capitalist societies,[25] but the former results from specifically Soviet forms of organisation of the economy. One can quite accept their argument that greater attention should be paid to forms of socialisation and patterns of recruitment, and to the political context in which the Soviet worker is situated,[26] while still devoting greater attention than they seem to consider necessary to the occupational structure itself.

The extent to which the Soviet occupational structure continues its past trend of increasing similarity to that of the West cannot be simply taken for granted, when, as Feshbach among others indicates,[27] current practices may well slow down the rate of technological change which is supposed to bring about the restructuring of the labour force along lines similar to the capitalist countries. For example, to return to the issue of auxiliary workers, Feshbach points out that there are 85 of them for every 100 basic wage-workers in the USSR, compared with 38 per 100 in the USA. Furthermore, very little progress has been made in reducing their share in the work-force. There are various obstacles to the redeployment of this section of the labour force. First, there is the difficulty of firing an incompetent worker. Second, much of the secondary output in a given plant consists of work done to compensate for the vagaries of the supply system. Third, the size of the work-force in a given factory is of prime importance in determining the basic wage levels for the manager, his assistants and the enterprise workers, which is a clear disincentive to the efficient use of labour. On top of this is the often-noted problem of labour turnover, which has remained at around 20 per cent per annum from 1959 to 1974. This reported rate understates the actual rate of turnover, because it excludes by definition certain 'acceptable' reasons for departure such as being drafted into the armed forces, becoming disabled, retirement, or ending temporary work. Feshbach estimates that inclusion of these cases would raise the annual turnover rate in industry to 30 per cent. And 40 per cent of those who leave one job for another change their trade or speciality. Given these factors, Feshbach argues that it is no wonder that industrial labour productivity in the USSR is about half that in the USA. He concludes thus:

> In view of the inexorable decline in the size of new additions to the labor force, the projected reduction in capital investment in the current Five Year Plan, and the limited prospects for sustaining high gains in productivity among Soviet workers, the impact of labor force structure and composition on economic growth in the USSR is likely to be of major importance in the next two decades.[28]

If such a conclusion is accepted, then any argument about the technological determination of the occupational structure must be qualified by a recognition of the reciprocal effect of the Soviet occupational structure on technological change (within the current institutional context of economic planning).

The issue of the similarity of the Soviet industrial occupational structure with that of the West can be further illuminated by examining the distribution of the industrial labour force among different branches of industry in 1960 and 1975, as Feshbach has done (see Table 6.2).

Table 6.2

Branch of industry	1960	1975
Total	22 620 000	34 054 000
Electric power	397 000	686 000
Coal	1 196 000	1 009 000
Chemical and petrochemical	792 000	1 753 000
Ferrous metallurgy	1 047 000	1 369 000
Machine-building and metal-working	7 206 000	13 816 000
Construction materials	1 575 000	2 151 000
Timber, woodworking, and pulp and paper	2 698 000	2 795 000
Light industry	3 860 000	5 109 000
Food industry	2 164 000	3 015 000

Source: M. Feshbach, 'The Structure and Composition of the Industrial Labor Force', in A. Kahan and B. Ruble (eds), *Industrial Labor in the USSR*, Pergamon, New York, 1979, p. 17.

The most striking features of Table 6.2 are the rapid growth in industrial employment between 1960 and 1975[29] and the 'disproportionate' growth in the machine-building and metal-working branch of industry. This is the most important branch in terms of numbers of workers, amount of investment and significance for defence. It accounted in 1975 for more than 40 per cent of the total employment in industry, being more than two and a half times as big as the next largest branch, the so-called 'light' industry sector. After the chemical and petro-chemical branch, it is the fastest-growing branch in industry. Can it really be said that this pre-eminence of one branch, with its associated skilled work-force, is similar to the occupational structure of a capitalist economy? It is clearly a result of state economic policy, as are many other features of the Soviet occupational structure, whether directly or indirectly. This is evident from an analysis of mechanisms of allocation[30] and from an examination of changes in the overall Soviet economy which affect the occupational structure in various ways. To illustrate this, various aspects of the Soviet occupational structure will be discussed, beginning with the position of women.

The Occupational Structure of Soviet Women

It may come as something of a surprise to find that Feshbach notes that 'the educational attainment of women, especially in the younger ages, is higher than that of men'.[31] This is stated with respect to industrial wage-workers, rather than the whole population, a view which is corroborated by Lapidus.[32] Lane and O'Dell provide evidence to suggest that it may soon be true of the whole population.[33] However, even if educational provision were perfectly dovetailed with the occupational structure, the improving educational position of women is something which would only show up in the future, since it is too recent a phenomenon to affect the current distribution of women in the occupational structure.

If we turn to the current occupational structure, the most striking feature is that women constituted 51 per cent of the labour force in 1978, and have done so since 1970. For historical reasons, women comprise over half the population, so that not all of them are yet employed in wage labour, but over 87 per cent of them are now either employed or studying full time.[34] This participation rate is supported by official ideology, as well as by economic pressure (with aspirations probably outrunning incomes), but it

> has not obliterated many features which, in the USSR as elsewhere, distinguish male and female employment. Indeed the sharpest line of differentiation among Soviet industrial workers today is that of sex. In the occupational structure as in the family, sex remains a significant basis for the allocation of social roles, with the result that male and female workers differ in the distribution of income, skill, status, power and even time.[35]

Women are concentrated in particular sectors of the economy and in particular occupations. Of the roughly 68 million women employed in 1975, 20 million were in agriculture, 24 million were in services, 16 million in industry and roughly 7 million were in other sectors (construction, transport, forestry and communications).

Three industrial branches (machine-building and metal-working, textile, and food) account for 70 per cent of all female *industrial* employment.[36] 'Moreover, in industrial employment, as in the professions, women are concentrated at lower levels of the pyramid, in low-level, unmechanised and unskilled jobs.'[37] In the 1960s newly mechanised and automated work went primarily to the males, and women still account for 80 per cent of the auxiliary workers in industry. This is an important point for any future attempts to raise productivity, because it will be difficult to retrain women by evening or correspondence courses if they continue to do most of the domestic labour. For similar reasons, women are less engaged in technical innovation by rationalisation,[38] and have lower levels of socio-political participation than their male counterparts.[39] While women are better represented among technical specialists than among skilled workers in industry, they are largely absent from positions of managerial authority. Although the percentage of female enterprise directors rose from 1 per cent in 1956 to 9 per cent in 1975, they have not moved into management to the extent that their training, experience and proportion of the relevant age cohort.[40] Women are frequently over-qualified for the job they hold, so their lower earnings are not exclusively the result of lower qualifications or productivity. The gap between male and female earnings is around 30 to 35 per cent. This is narrower than the 40 per cent gap in the USA and several West European countries, but wider than the 27 per cent gap in Scandinavia.[41]

The reasons for these differences in wages do not simply lie in the distinctive characteristics of the female labour force (whose occupational and educational distribution is clearly recorded)[42] but in certain features of Soviet economic organisation and policy, which are highlighted in a particularly clear manner by Lapidus, who is well aware of the interconnections between economic and social policy. Indeed, she points out that since the mid-1960s the Soviet leadership has become increasingly sensitive to the unexpectedly complex interaction between social and economic problems, which is one of the reasons for the recent growth in social science research.[43] The reasons Lapidus adduces for the wage differences between men and women are, first, that those sectors which have high wage levels and high wage differentials are precisely the ones where women are underrepresented, and second, that blue-collar jobs are better paid, even when white-collar employees have a higher level of educational attainment. Finally, she argues that the possibility of direct wage discrimination cannot be ruled out. Thus 'equality of economic opportunity for women has not followed automatically from higher levels of educational attainment and labor-force participation'.[44]

Turning from differential wages to other aspects of the disadvantageous position of women, Lapidus refers to three main features affecting the allocation of women to occupations: the sexual stereotyping of occupations (based on biological and psychological stereotypes), the continuing identification by both men and women of authority with men (which is now recognised as a problem in political circles), and the official treatment of household and family responsibilities as primarily and properly the domain of women, leading to a reinforcement of cultural norms by legislation. Only women are assigned dual roles in the occupational structure and the family.

While women do seem to be starting to reject this attribution of a primary role in the family combined with a high labour-force participation rate (for example, there is an increasing tendency for women to initiate divorce, which used to be fairly unusual when men were demographically 'in short supply'), it is still the case that housewives have more children than working women, that time-budget studies show that 75 per cent of domestic duties are done by women and that women effectively advance the occupational mobility of males by freeing them for study. Yet there is now a positive relationship between female employment outside the home and male help within it, so perhaps this link is now beginning to be broken. In the meantime, family roles continue to be assigned priority and so define the nature and rhythms of female employment. According to Lapidus, 'Soviet family responsibilities intrude into the workplace to a degree unprecedented in contemporary industrial societies.'[45] Provisions officially made for pregnancy leave and so on are predicated on the view that child-rearing and other family responsibilities must take a certain priority which work arrangements can only accommodate. This is why women are so underrepresented in enterprise activities requiring additional time and energy, as well as in volunteer movements, sport and in public affairs generally. As Lapidus puts it, the boundaries between occupational and family systems are permeable, but in opposite directions for men and women. For women, home intrudes into work, while for men work intrudes into the home.

The sexual division of labour both on the job and at home, combined with the differential permeability of the work–family boundary for males and females, may have acted as buffers to cushion the strains created by changing female roles, as Lapidus argues.[46] Yet she is surely correct to point to the continuing sources of strain. The first is that, since the massive participation of women in full-time paid employment has eroded the traditional rationale for a sexual division of labour within the family, it has increased the level of conflict between men and women over the division of domestic tasks. This is a source of marital instability. The second source of strain is the extreme tension which has been created between female work and family roles as currently defined. The pressure to reduce family commitments entails the deliberate limitation of family size. Lapidus considers this as the most threatening manifestation of female resistance to the combined pressures of work and family roles. By impinging on a wide range of economic, political and military concerns, it has compelled a fundamental reconsideration of the whole spectrum of policies involving female work and the family role.

Social Policy and Female Waged Labour

This brings us to the point that the family is often treated both as an object and as an agent of implementation of social policy. Soviet policy has encouraged women to acquire new skills and aspirations that compete with their traditional domestic roles. As Lapidus points out, this sort of policy contradicts the high value attached to the family, the critical social roles attached to it, and the large investments of time and energy needed to sustain it. It is for this reason, and because the resulting tensions may be exacerbated by economic and demographic trends, that there has been a growing urgency in attempts to confront the social conditions and consequences of female waged labour. Without reforms in the system of vocational training and placement, women are likely to find it increasingly difficult to get into highly skilled technical employment. They will tend to be absorbed into routine white-collar and service occupations. If the low level of office technology is borne in mind, the routine nature of such tasks are likely to be trying for the increasingly well-educated women who come to fill them.

Lapidus gives a succinct review of the debates in which attempts have been made to grapple with these issues.[47] One group of proposals aims at changing the labour market by reforming vocational education to give the highest priority to upgrading the skills of women workers, as well as increased incentives to enrol in such programmes, which should be adapted to the schedules and responsibilities of working mothers. A second group of proposals aims at improving working conditions, partly by including domestic responsibilities in the definition of work. A third group of recommendations would increase the supply of consumer and everyday services to reduce the strain of women's dual roles. This group of recommendations is associated with studies which show the social and economic costs of inadequate services and child-care facilities, and the slow progress in these spheres has encouraged calls for a greater reliance on co-operative and even private arrangements (nannies and governesses). As Lapidus points out, none of these proposals call for the eradication of the distinction between *men's* and *women's* work, with the associated changes in the structure of family or work.

According to Lapidus, these issues now occupy a major place on the political agenda, as can be seen from the 1976 Party Congress, the 1977 Constitution, the reorganisation of the State Committee on Labour and Wages into the State Committee on Labour and Social Questions,[48] and the setting up in October 1976 of Standing Commissions to address the problems of women workers and mothers.

It is now clear that the social situation of women, in

particular their occupational distribution, is partly an effect of a series of state policies (whose effects are themselves not unitary) and partly an effect of gender attribution. The official ideology favours the easing of the dual burden of home and production, and has led to policies whose implementation is leading to some improvement in the position of women *vis-à-vis* men. In addition to the measures mentioned above by Lapidus, the educational position of women is clearly improving, male help in the household has improved to some extent, and general measures to improve housing, the production of consumer durables and the retail trade network must have eased the burden of domestic work somewhat (thereby further removing grounds for male resistance to participating in it, which of course by itself will not end such resistance). Those state policies that maintain gender differences in the occupational structure are clearly being increasingly questioned (although equally clearly the debate is not over yet),[49] and they are partially mitigated by the effects of other policies.

The evidence examined appears to support the view that the occupational distribution of women is an effect of mechanisms of allocation of individuals, rather than an effect of class relations between men and women. These mechanisms have clearly themselves become an object of debate, with struggles over them beginning to take place in various arenas (not only in individual families, but in the trade unions and even in the State Committee on Labour and Social Questions). Consequently prospects for changes in these mechanisms are opening up, and although such prospects are by no means overwhelming the fact that the current operation of these mechanisms places certain obstacles in the path of a strategy of intensive economic growth gives one hope that they may be changed in a way which furthers the equalisation of the social situation of men and women.

Collective Farm Workers

According to Lane and O'Dell,[50] there is little sign of collective farms 'withering away' at present, so it would seem that the class of collective farmers will be with us for some time to come.

This ignores an important component of Soviet views: namely, the so-called 'industrialisation of the countryside' and the associated development of inter-*kolkhoz* associations and agro–industrial complexes.[51] When one takes these developments into account, it is not so clear that there is no sign of the eventual elimination of collective ownership, and hence of collective farmers as a class.

Despite rural–urban differences in educational level, housing and to a lesser extent in health care and social security, there does seem to be some justification for Soviet claims that the differences between collective and state property are being steadily eroded. These differences can be summarised as those relating to their respective juridical statuses, their internal organisation, their relation to external agencies and the forms and levels of distribution of income among their personnel. Dealing first with the juridical status of *kolkhozy* compared with *sovkhozy*, it is clear that it does have some effectivity, though this does not really stretch to election of *kolkhoz* chairman. The extent of this autonomy, and its effects on investment and on the incomes of *kolkhoz* members (making both more dependent on financial results than in the case of *sovkhozy*), were discussed in Chapter 3. The autonomy of *kolkhozy* is being eroded by state control of certain infra-structural investment, by 'directive planning' of *kolkhoz* sales, and by the inter-*kolkhoz* associations and the agro-industrial complexes. In other words, the juridical autonomy is being increasingly eroded by the relations with external economic agencies whose impact on the decisions of the *kolkhozy* is considerable. To this process of erosion of autonomy can be added the various bodies set up by the state to encourage standardisation of practices, such as the Federal Council of *Kolkhozy*.

The change in the internal organisation of the *kolkhozy* has altered their occupational structure, though the precise changes are not clear from the evidence available. One can deduce from Lane and O'Dell that non-manual rural labour must be around 7 per cent of the total Soviet population in the mid-1970s.[52] A figure of similar magnitude is given by Lane for the mid-1960s for the *kolkhoz* population.[53] This suggests their occupational structure may be quite similar to that on state farms. However, he adds that mechanisers (tractor and machine–harvester drivers and operators) were around 10–13 per cent of the *kolkhoz* labour force, which means that between 78 and 84 per cent of the *kolkhoz* labour force was probably fairly unskilled. This contrasts with *sovkhozy*, where only 41 per cent of the labour was unskilled in the mid-1960s. However, the massive investment in agriculture since the mid-1960s must have affected the occupational structure of manual collective farmers, by creating more skilled manual operations. This trend has probably continued with the 1979–80 reforms, which have also affected agriculture, giving further encouragement to agro–industrial units, and to the personal plots (with their associated livestock).[54]

This recent encouragement of personal plots should not be taken as increasing the differences between the class position of the collective farmers and that of *sovkhoz* agricultural workers, who are counted as an agricultural working class and whose numbers grew from 1.6 million in 1940 to 8.4 million in 1973.[55] As was indicated in Chapter 3, the personal plots within larger agricultural units such as *kolkhozy* and *sovkhozy* are very inter-dependent with these larger units (in contrast to urban personal plots). The difference in their economic function in the two sorts of farms is related to their different size, the greater size of personal plots on the *kolkhozy* serving to cushion members against the effects of their lower (and somewhat more variable) level of income. The importance of 'private activity' (which is presumably largely concerned with the sale of produce from the personal plots) on the incomes of *kolkhozniki* and state employees can be seen from the work of McAuley (see Table 6.3).[56]

Table 6.3 refers to *all* state employees, and so it does not give a clear indication of the relative importance of 'private activity' on state farms. What the table does show, however, is that the proportion of total income which the *kolkhozniki* derive from their personal plots declined from over half their income in 1960 to less than one-third in 1974. This decline was a relative, not an absolute one.

Yet despite the relative decline in the proportion of income derived from the personal plots, and despite the increasing similarities between *kolkhozniki* and state employees,

Table 6.3   The structure of personal income: state employees and
kolkhozniki, **USSR, 1960–74 (roubles per year)**

Source of income	State employees				Kolkhozniki			
	1960	1965	1970	1974	1960	1965	1970	1974
Earnings from								
state	376.1	473.8	623.8	742.3	34.1	36.9	48.0	70.4
kolkhoz	—	—	—	—	110.3	204.0	310.3	398.2
Private activity	24.2	29.8	41.4	41.3	171.7	194.6	227.2	239.8
Transfers	90.6	111.1	152.5	187.0	4.9	16.2	66.0	69.6
Other	8.8	9.6	16.2	13.7	7.9	8.3	7.6	13.5
Personal income	499.7	624.3	833.9	984.3	328.9	460.0	659.1	791.5

Source: A. McAuley, *Economic Welfare in the Soviet Union*, Allen & Unwin,
London, 1979, p. 35.

McAuley is right to point out that there are still significant
differences between the two groups. The differences in the
sources of income will be maintained, but income differentials
may narrow, if output from personal plots is increased
substantially as a result of the decree of January 1981.[57] In any
case, the decree also applies to local authorities and may lead to
a similar rise in the use of personal plots among state
employees, both urban and rural. This decree will certainly
increase the land available for use as personal plots, but it is too
soon to say whether this encouragement of personal plots and
private livestock will reverse the relative decline in the share of
total *kolkhoznik* income derived from 'private activity'. It may
not do so, because improved transfer payments, such as the
child allowance introduced in 1974, may offset any absolute
increase in income from 'private activities', thereby further
reducing the differences in forms and levels of income between
state employees and *kolkhozniki.*

The impact of transfer payments so far, however, has not
been sufficient to equalise incomes between *kolkhozniki* and
sovkhoz workers. Rzhanitsyna shows that while the trend has
been towards equalising transfer payments, full equalisation
has not yet taken place.[58] First, *kolkhozniki* only received about
three-quarters the wage in 1975 that state farm workers
received (and only about two-thirds the average wage for the

whole economy). Second, the lower average wages are not offset by higher payments from the social consumption funds (SCF). The reverse is the case.

Thus the impression to be gained from Rzhanitsyna confirms the stress laid by McAuley on the continuing differences in income level and composition between *kolkhozniki* and state farm workers. Consequently, while the juridical autonomy and internal organisation of *kolkhozy* may be changing, with resulting changes in their internal occupational structure, it is not at all clear that such changes will result in an elimination of differences between state farm and collective farm workers' incomes. For example, the 1975 establishment of a 70-rouble minimum wage for state employees may have made the *kolkhozniki* relatively worse off.[59] Nevertheless, despite these continuing differences, current agricultural policies mean that the elimination of collective farms is still on the political agenda. Whether it will be completed without prior substantial improvements in agricultural performance remains to be seen.

The 'Intelligentsia'

There are difficulties in defining the 'intelligentsia' as a single, separate stratum. The varying definitions of the intelligentsia make it somewhat difficult to examine the concept within a brief space, however. For example, if we take Churchward's definition,[60] in which the intelligentsia consists of 'persons with a tertiary education (whether employed or not), tertiary students, and persons lacking formal tertiary qualification but who are professionally employed in jobs which normally require a tertiary qualification', then we are faced with a stipulative definition which by itself is quite compatible with the claim that the intelligentsia includes state and party functionaries. This contrasts with the position of Lampert,[61] who draws a distinction between the intelligentsia and the functionaries of the state or the political apparatus. A position which might be considered as somewhere between that of Churchward and that of Lampert is taken by Hirszowicz with respect to Poland.[62] She argues that the nineteenth century concept of the intelligentsia has been revived, securing the preservation of a myth deeply embedded in the national tradition of many East European countries. The components of this old concept, though not included in sociological definitions, affect contemporary understanding of the concept and explain the disparity between purely structural distinctions and the cultural meanings attached to them.[63]

Thus she treats the 'intelligentsia' as in a sense a myth, a part of the political culture, with its origins in the past, rather than as a distinct occupational group:

The three main components of the nineteenth-century intelligentsia were (1) social status marked by social conduct inculcated by breeding and training; (2) qualifications for carrying out certain professional activities; and (3) social functions, especially ideological and political leadership. The difficulties of dealing with the problem of the intelligentsia in modern East European societies stem from the dissociation of these characteristics . . . The dissociation of status characteristics makes of the educated strata a mixture of different occupational and professional groups with different norms, aspirations and attitudes . . . It follows that what could be regarded as broad generalisations about *the intelligentsia* have to be replaced with detailed studies of various institutions, professional groups and occupational communities including *apparatchiki*, technical intelligentsia, creative intelligentsia, higher and middle management, teachers and research workers.[64]

Without endorsing Hirszowicz's general approach,[65] it seems to me that her refusal to treat the intelligentsia as a single distinct occupational group (a stratum) is correct.

However, if the intelligentsia is not defined as a single occupational group, then it can only be defined in terms of its educational level or of its political role. Defining it in terms of its educational level entails a stipulative definition, as already

indicated in the case of Churchward.[66] Such an approach
certainly avoids many problems, since educational certification
establishes fairly clear demarcation criteria, but it leaves open
the theoretical question of the social significance of the group
being demarcated.[67] As Churchward himself points out,[68] such
a group which on his definition numbers 'almost eleven million
is not likely to have any high degree of homogeneity'. He goes
on to argue that the intelligentsia is neither a 'ruling class' nor a
'managerial class'. In that case, the only basis for treating them
as an object of analysis is their educational qualifications. To
define them as distinct on educational grounds amounts either
to confusing mechanisms of allocation with economic location,
or to claiming that mechanisms of allocation are the main
determinants of location, or else are very closely linked with the
main determinants of economic location. That is to say, an
educational definition of the intelligentsia amounts to saying
that the process of allocation of individuals to occupations is (at
least for the highly educated) intimately connected with the
process of creation of occupations. While I have indicated
earlier that I am critical of such a position, such criticism will be
left till later.

Turning to a definition of the intelligentsia in terms of its
political role or position, it must be clear that such a definition
depends upon one's analysis of Soviet politics. If the various
central state and party agencies engaged in the process of major
national policy formulation are dependent on information
which has to come either from enterprise managers, Ministry
officials or technical experts of various kinds, then it is possible
that one, or a combination, or all of such groups could act in
concert to control effectively the decisions regarding the
disposition and use of the means of production. In other words,
their political position could be used to secure privileged access
to the means of production, thereby securing a better income
for themselves. This is quite a common sort of argument with
regard to the Soviet Union, and would amount to grounds for
treating them not simply as a single occupational group (a
stratum) but as a class. The analysis of the concept of class
developed in Chapter 1 did allow that the relation between
various agents might be such as to enable them effectively to
'dictate their own terms' for the access by other agents to the

means of production. In other words, even if agents (including collective agents) did not by themselves possess the means of production, the relations between a group of different kinds of agents might enable them collectively to establish favourable terms of access to the means of production, in a manner similar to the relations between, say, a landowning company, a bank and an industrial company.

However, while not denying that there is a substantial concentration of political power in the arenas of struggle constituted by relations between the central state and party agencies, the analysis in Chapter 4 suggested that no single group within the 'intelligentsia', or combination of groups (associated with different agencies), would be able to act in concert at all times in a situation of institutional struggle over various issues. While the analysis provided by Andrle, and more especially Tartarin (among others),[69] indicated that it is entirely possible to use one's occupational position to divert illicitly some real income to oneself, due to the inability of the state to scrutinise closely many activities in a detailed way, the very fact that such practices are widespread, and by no means exclusively confined to white-collar occupations, suggests that the 'intelligentsia' is not in a very privileged situation. It is certainly not able to secure for itself a very high income, if one accepts Churchward's definition of 'intelligentsia'.[70]

Perhaps Matthews is the most forceful proponent of the view that privilege and an associated highly unequal distribution of real income are important features of the social structure of the Soviet Union.[71] Yet by international standards, he concludes, the Soviet 'elite' is poor and lacking in independence, though it is a long way from the egalitarian ideals proclaimed by the Soviet state. Furthermore, his claim that the differences in income may be no less than the USA is effectively undermined in a note by Wiles,[72] who calculates that the United Kingdom (not the USA) has almost exactly the same ratio of top to average income as the USSR, if income is defined as wages plus fringe benefits including orthodox state social services. The ratio for both countries is 5.5 to 1. However, if all UK income (including 'capitalist' incomes) is taken into account, Wiles calculates that the United Kingdom is 'considerably more unequal than the USSR'. The evidence on the USA will be discussed later. The case for a ruling class or elite able to secure a substantially unequal share of national income for itself thus seems weaker than Matthews would argue, even accepting Matthews's own evidence, which ignores the effect of the informal sector on the incomes of the rest of the population,[73] and which probably overestimates the real income effect of better housing, health care and holidays.

With the possible exception of the personnel of the central state and party agencies, the 'intelligentsia' cannot be considered a distinct class from the manual working class.[74] Furthermore, no good reason has been provided in any of the analyses discussed for treating the 'intelligentsia' as a single occupational group or stratum. In this respect I agree with the position of Lane and O'Dell, though they do not address themselves directly to the other question of whether the 'intelligentsia' are a separate stratum inside the working class. They simply argue, as quoted earlier, that non-manual workers *in production enterprises* (my emphasis) are not a separate *stratum*, on the grounds that in a Marxist sense they are in the same *class* position and share a similar political ideology. This is a rather oblique answer, since various Soviet and Western analyses quite happily treat the 'intelligentsia' as a distinct stratum within the class of those employed by the state, and since the 'intelligentsia' is not usually considered as being confined to production enterprises.

This critique of the usefulness of the concept of 'intelligentsia' for analysing either the occupational structure or class relations has raised the question of the role of education as a supposed mechanism of allocation of individuals to occupational positions. It is to this question that we must now address ourselves.

Education

It has already been indicated with respect to women that educational level is not all that neatly dovetailed with occupational position in the Soviet Union. This is the case despite the existence of manpower (*sic*) planning and attempts at occupational placement.[75] Claims that education is functionally integrated with the occupational structure are common with respect to capitalist societies, even among Marxists,[76] so it is not surprising to find educational level used to define the 'intelligentsia' in some cases, or to see Lane and O'Dell in effect adapting Hopper's functionalist analysis of educational systems to the Soviet Union.[77] Lane and O'Dell's analysis of the relation between education and occupation will therefore be treated as an example of this sort of analysis which closely associates mechanisms of allocation of individuals with determinants of economic location.

In analysing the education system, Lane and O'Dell make use of Turner's concepts of 'sponsored' and 'contest' mobility, as well as the concept of 'cooling out', which form the basis of Hopper's work.[78] The Soviet Union is treated as a contest education system[79] in which high levels of occupational aspirations are 'cooled out' by the educational system to achieve a better match between ambition and the occupational structure. This system is modified by a degree of sponsorship in the case of women, who are channelled into lower-status occupations.[80] However, Lane and O'Dell do not argue that ambition or educational level are exactly matched to occupation. They point out that 'dissatisfied' manual workers tend to have a higher level of education than 'satisfied' ones, and they agree with arguments that manual workers are paid higher wages to compensate for the monotony of the work, drawing attention to the disjunction between the 'pyramid of preferences' of school-children and the 'pyramid of requirements' of the nation.[81] However, this simply leads them to conclude that there will be further functional adjustment by the education system, which will probably further develop its 'cooling-out' processes so that high morale and work-force stability will be promoted by the reduction of the aspirations of school-leavers.[82]

The two mechanisms by which the 'cooling-out' process is thought to be developing in the Soviet Union are 'the provision of an infinite number of channels for advancement (the alternative route)' and 'forms of tempering ambition in the school system' such as vocational guidance.[83] Yet they recognise that many school-leavers want, and many students receive, an education for reasons of personal satisfaction, rather than as training for a job. They also argue that, despite overt socialisation and explicit vocational guidance, the authorities have not been able to develop a general desire for a career in manual as opposed to non-manual jobs. Furthermore, they point out that people who end up as administrative workers receive their education in engineering and the applied sciences.[84] These latter points suggest the following: that the 'alternative routes' have the effect of legitimating and perhaps even reinforcing educational aspirations as much as cooling out these aspirations; that vocational guidance and other cooling-out mechanisms have a limited effect; and that in any case the education system does not have to fit all that closely with the occupational structure (even though it is intended that it should) because occupational positions are filled anyway, either by *praktiki* ('practicals') who have learned on the job as they have been promoted within the enterprise, or by people with an appropriate *level* of education, the content of which may not be very relevant to their occupational position.

If the latter points are correct, then educational selection and certification are not as intrinsically important for occupational placement as Lane and O'Dell seem to believe. They are certainly correct to point to the rapid secular decline in the proportion of *praktiki*,[85] but this simply means that the expansion of education provision provides a socially acceptable criterion for occupational selection, namely an educational certificate. As they apparently realise, it does not mean that determinants of change or stability in the occupational structure itself are unimportant, nor does it mean that the educational qualifications that are administratively used as a criterion of occupational selection bear any very close relationship to the tasks and skills of the various occupations, any more than it does in capitalist societies. It would be surprising if, in the Soviet Union as in other countries, the education system did not have a 'life of its own' in the sense that pedagogical concerns have their own impact on curriculum content and teaching methods, and that these concerns, as well as the ambiguities in what Lane and O'Dell call 'the different values that the elites seek to inculcate',[86] have the effect of insulating the content of educational provision from the 'requirements' of the occupational structure which are in any case poorly understood by the central planning agencies. It is by no means clear that any planning to establish a closer fit between education and occupation will be all that successful, partly because the skills of an occupation often change even if the occupation itself retains the same designation, partly because the occupational structure itself changes (for various reasons including changes in state policy), and partly because the education system is not amenable to rapid change, especially if the curriculum is specialised rather than general. For this reason, educational level is a poor basis for defining different occupational groups, such as the 'intelligentsia', though it might be a useful research indicator of occupational boundaries whose determinants would then have to be theorised.

The Soviet Occupational Structure, Collective Agents and Class Relations

It is now possible to discuss whether class relations operate between occupational categories of agents. It was argued earlier in this chapter, however, that class relations may well be operative between collective agents and that, while the internal organisation of such agents would mean that they each had their own internal occupational structure, the class position of the individuals within such an agent should not necessarily be equated with the class position of the agent itself. Hence relations between occupations need not exhaust the possibilities for the existence of class relations in a social formation. Soviet theorists themselves take membership of a collective agency, such as a *kolkhoz* or state enterprise, as an important index of the class position of an occupation, yet they weaken this by their treatment of the 'intelligentsia' as a stratum.[87] So the rejection of the idea that the 'intelligentsia' can be treated as a stratum at least clears out of the way an important obstacle to the analysis of class relations in the Soviet Union, since the treatment of the 'intelligentsia' as a stratum glosses over what may be important differences between collective agents within the state sector.

The relative capacities of different economic agents are not immediately apparent from tables on the occupational structure. All that can be directly concluded from such evidence is that there have been rapid changes in the occupational structure, changes which are now slowing down. Yet the discussion of the occupational structure has yielded more evidence than that on the relative capacities of agents, and this can be seen if we take broad occupational groupings one at a time.

Industrial workers
Starting with industrial manual workers, the stagnation which is becoming increasingly evident in the proportion of auxiliary workers suggests that manual workers have very little capacity to influence even the technical division of labour, since it would clearly be in their interests to move into skilled manual occupations, thereby increasing their wages. Some manual workers manage to do this illicitly, since some of the movement into skilled grades or occupations is purely nominal, being a disguised form of wage increase. The gloomy evidence on technical 'rationalisation' and innovation in Soviet industry corroborates this inability to influence the technical division of labour. Many of these auxiliary workers are women, and the chances of them obtaining further training while working are substantially reduced by their current domestic responsibilities. This picture of poor control by manual workers of the technical division of labour is corroborated by the evidence on relations within the enterprise discussed in Chapter 3 or supplied by Lane and O'Dell[88] or Ruble.[89] It is certainly the case that trade unions are fairly good at safeguarding wages, job security and working conditions. For example, Ruble argues that it is usually lack of resources rather than negligence which is responsible for management non-compliance with health and safety regulations. However, it is clear that factory trade unions and party committees do not actively intervene in co-ordinating the technical division of labour (that is, in managing the enterprise). There may be a high rate of participation in factory trade-union meetings, but the available evidence suggests that a large proportion of Soviet industrial workers do not believe that their opinions matter.[90] Similarly with party supervision of management, Lane and O'Dell agree with Andrle's conclusion that in practice the party secretary's power is limited.[91]

This lack of control of the technical division of labour (the manner in which labour is combined with the means of production) could well be offset by manual workers, if they were able to affect substantially the division of social production or the social division of labour in a way which favoured themselves. However, it is clear that the division of social production must be determined at the level of the central state and party agencies. The same phenomenon (an inability by manual industrial workers to determine the division of social production) should be evident from the discussion of housing in Chapter 5. In the case of the social division of labour, there is some evidence of possible indirect influence by the manual workers, mediated by the All-Union Central Committee of Trade Unions and the State Committee on Labour and Social Questions. Thus the growth in the proportion of the population engaged in education and health, and in trade, could be considered as indicating a capacity by the manual workers to influence the distribution of real income in their favour. However, this would have to be set against the reliance on trade-union volunteers to administer social security, a form of participation which does not seem to enable them to have much influence on policy. Overall, then, one would have to conclude that the capacity of the manual industrial occupations to co-ordinate actively any of the three main aspects of the division of labour is not very great. National and local trade unions and local party bodies seem to act largely in a defensive capacity, if they pursue at all what might be considered as specifically manual industrial occupations' objectives.

This is perhaps not surprising, given the continued existence of a kind of labour market, and of extensive attempts at the political socialisation of the labour force. The political socialisation practices do seem to help secure support for the status quo, but the extent of this support, while substantial, does have its limits.[92] The knowledge in the central state and party agencies that these limits exist does enable manual workers to have some impact on major national economic decisions, such as wage levels. However, it is clear that manual industrial occupations do not predominate in co-ordinating the division of labour, thereby largely securing their own conditions of existence in a manner which makes other occupational groups' existence dependent on them and determining the distribution of income in their own favour. In other words, they are not a predominant class in the Soviet Union.

Collective farm workers

Yet if the economic capacities of the manual industrial occupations are limited, which is hardly surprising, it is still less surprising to find that the capacities of *kolkhozniki* are even more limited. The juridical independence of the *kolkhozy* has not precluded state intervention in various aspects of their affairs. While some of this intervention has in recent years been quite beneficial in certain respects (for example, improved wages and social security provisions, the development of agro–industrial complexes), it has also enabled the state to continue to subordinate collective farms by integrating their product-mix into the overall national economic plan for agriculture, and by imposing a certain technical division of labour on them. It is clear that their juridical independence from the state has reduced their capacity (and that of their members) to influence the division of social production and the social division of labour. Thus, while the situation of *kolkhozniki* has definitely improved considerably since the early 1960s, their access to the means of production is clearly only on terms set for them by various state agencies. Consequently, despite their internal occupational differentiation, *kolkhozniki* must be considered to be in a separate, and worse, class position from that of all those employed by the state, with the possible exception of *kolkhoz* chairmen, who are *de facto* state appointees. Until the juridical and other conditions of the differences between *kolkhozy* and *sovkhozy* are eliminated, this element of class relations will remain a feature of the Soviet social formation. The effects (in terms of the distribution of income) of their restricted access to the means of production have already been made clear earlier in this chapter.

Non-manual occupations

While it is quite evident that many non-manual occupations do not have significantly different access to the means of production from manual occupations, it is nevertheless the case that some non-manual occupations are particularly involved with the co-ordination of the division of labour. This is the case with regard to enterprise directors and other members of the 'technical intelligentsia' (the engineering and technical personnel, the ITRs), who are concerned with the technical division of labour. It is also the case with senior Ministry officials, senior party officials and members of the central planning agencies who are concerned with the division of social production and/or the social division of labour.

The enterprise director clearly predominates in co-ordinating the technical division of labour, despite the various institutional constraints on him in the form of the local trade unions, the factory party committee, the different organisations of rationalisers and innovators, labour law, the district party secretary, and so on. However, the position of an agent such as the enterprise director is not static, and could be changed by the spread of brigade autonomy or by the eventual success of the production association reform. Furthermore, even if these two changes do not extend throughout the economy, the capacity of enterprise directors to co-ordinate the technical division of labour is seriously constrained by the various central planning agencies concerned with plan implementation such as Gosstroi, Gossnab and Gosbank. These agencies, as well as the Ministries themselves, establish the conditions under which enterprise directors have access to the means of production necessary to fulfil the plan. While the enterprise directors do have a certain autonomy in this respect, the supervision by these superior agencies effectively keeps this autonomy within certain limits. This state of affairs would almost certainly continue to hold in the event of the successful spread of autonomous production brigades within enterprises, or of production associations which combine enterprises. Enterprise directors could only become a capitalist class if they could extend their access to the means of production well beyond the co-ordination of the technical division of labour to the point where their autonomous decisions affected the division of social production and the social division of labour. As it is, the capacity to determine the division of social production does reside to some extent in individual Ministries (hence the high proportion of consumer durables coming from enterprises whose Ministries are in the 'heavy-industry' sector). Yet this is only true to the extent that they are able to evade the supervision of (or get the agreement of) the central planning agencies, and it certainly is not true to any degree in the case of individual enterprises. Thus the capacities of enterprise directors, or of other ITRs working within enterprises, are effectively delimited to the co-ordination of the technical division of labour. They clearly do not predominate in determining their own conditions of existence, and could not do so unless they had greater access to the means of production, and hence a capacity to co-ordinate the division of social production. Were this to happen, it could then lead to a limited capacity to co-ordinate the social division of labour, at least to the extent that such agents could then largely secure their own conditions of existence, but at the moment changes in the social division of labour are frequently an unintended effect of changes in the other main aspects of the division of labour, or else of changes in state policy or the structure of the state itself.

The comparatively limited capacities of enterprise directors and other ITRs in production enterprises highlight the preconditions for the personnel in the central state and party agencies to constitute a 'ruling class'. For this to be the case, then the political interdiction of other agents' access to the means of production would have to be supplemented by an ability to enhance substantially their own capacity for action in a manner which rendered other agents dependent on the central state and party agencies, while leaving the latter comparatively independent of other agencies. This would imply either that one or two agencies would have to be supreme (a sovereign body), or that collectively these various agencies (which are themselves each a collective agent) would have to be capable of using their access to the means of production to co-ordinate all aspects of the division of labour (restricting the capacity of other agents to do so), thereby securing their own conditions of existence. Furthermore, since these collective agents are not themselves agents of consumption, the class relations between these agents and other economic agents would have to be utilised by the personnel who staff those agencies to alter substantially the distribution of income in their own favour. Otherwise it would be comparatively easy for these personnel to subvert the policies of these collective agents.

The concept of one or two agencies being capable of acting as a sovereign has already been rejected in the discussion of total-itarianism and elite theory in Chapter 4.[93] If these central agencies are to be included as 'collective possessors' of the means of production, then it has to be demonstrated that these central agencies were capable of exerting sufficient control not merely to establish overall co-ordination of the division of labour (preventing sub-agents from usurping such decisions as are necessary for effective national planning), but also to subordinate sub-agents to the point where they had little capacity of their own to affect the division of labour, and thus could not prevent the means of production from being used in a way which substantially altered the distribution of income in favour of the central agencies and their constituent personnel.

It is by no means clear that this is the case. For example, despite all the restrictions on the capacities of enterprise directors, they are still the main agents capable of co-ordinating the technical division of labour. Similarly, the *participation* of the Ministries in the activities of Gossnab indicates that Ministries still have a considerable impact on the division of social production, because of their capacity to secure supplies by a process of mutual accommodation with one another and with Gossnab. Because Gosplan cannot issue orders to Gossnab, there is little that it can do about this state of affairs, since it is quite likely that the Council of Ministers will reflect any mutual accommodations reached between Ministries in the process of Gossnab's decisions on material-technical supplies. The effects of this, such as the location of consumer-durables production in 'heavy-industry' Ministries, have already been indicated. The 'inordinate' size of the Ministry of Machine Building and Metal Working is surely a result of similar processes. The failure of the Kosygin reform and the repeated attempts to push through the production association reform both demonstrate that the capacity of the central state and party agencies to co-ordinate the division of social production is seriously limited by the non-compliance of sub-agents, particularly Ministries. Similarly, with regard to decisions which directly affect the social division of labour, there have been no attempts to cut back on health and education personnel to increase the central agencies' room for manoeuvre either to create other kinds of occupations or to alter the distribution of income in favour of the personnel of the central agencies. The use of voluntary workers in trade unions to administer social security might be considered as an example of an attempt to alter the social division of labour in a way which 'releases' real income for use by the central agencies, but the recent pension increases imply that this money has simply been spent on the general population rather than on professional administrators.

Consequently it is extremely difficult to argue that the undoubted predominance of the central state and party agencies in co-ordinating the overall division of labour in the social formation is sufficiently exclusive to restrict seriously the access of other state agencies to the means of production. In other words, the effect of the process of plan construction and implementation seems to be that a variety of agents (and sub-agents) do have overlapping forms of access to the means of production, so that the relations between the various agents in the state sector establish conditions in which no one agent can substantially enhance its own capacity for action at the expense of other agents, and no one agent can substantially alter the distribution of income in its own favour.

This perhaps places in a new light the 'incrementalism' in policy formation, remarked on by Hough and others. It may well be that the caution with which policy changes are introduced is an indication of successful struggle by sub-agents such as Ministries within the state sector, and that this capacity to struggle successfully is partly an effect of the 'multiple access' to the means of production which was outlined in Chapter 1 as an indication that class relations are weak or non-existent. However, there is a danger here of implying that classless societies are incapable of effective reform, or are doomed to paralysis and stagnation. Much of the 'incrementalism' in the Soviet Union seems to be simply due to a poor process of policy formulation.

In itself, the argument that sub-agents have access to the means of production which is sufficient to prevent too great a restriction on their capacity for action does not finally settle the issue of class relations within the state sector in the Soviet Union. It was argued in Chapter 1 that non-class societies would have a very egalitarian policy on the distribution of income and this policy would have to be fairly effectively pursued. This issue must now be dealt with.

The Distribution of Wages and Income Levels

All recent analyses of wage differentials and inequalities in the distribution of actual earnings concur in the view that since the mid-1950s there has been a substantial reduction in both. McAuley, in reviewing the distribution of earnings from 1956 to 1972, and the growth of earnings from 1950 to 1974, is very clear on these effects.[94] Wiles presents a similar picture from 1946 to 1970.[95] Similarly, Chapman, who concentrates on the industrial wage structure, argues that earnings differentials have narrowed since the mid-1950s, while average industrial money earnings have more than doubled.[96]

In terms of earnings, non-manual occupations cannot be considered as a homogeneous group. Office workers clearly earn between 15 and 20 per cent less than the average (including industrial manual workers), while managerial and technical personnel earn over 20 per cent more than average. Managerial and technical personnel are now much closer to average earnings than formerly. The higher-paid have had slower relative wage increases, and low-paid workers have had relatively large increases. This shows the effects of the substantial rise in the minimum wage, and the freezing of the upper-level salary rates.[97]

Chapman points out that Soviet earnings differentials are much narrower than in the USA, even ignoring US income from profits and dividends. It will be recalled that Wiles[98] gave a figure of 5.5:1 for the ratio of top to average incomes in the USSR. This is much higher than Chapman's 1.7:1 for the Soviet Union in 1970. The difference is largely explained by the fact that Chapman is referring to earnings from wages only, whereas Wiles is accepting Matthews's estimates of the real income addition of fringe benefits when added to the very top wages and salaries. Chapman is more sceptical than Matthews, it seems, on the income differentials generated by fringe benefits, for she points out that ordinary jobs also provide access to scarce goods and other sources of extra income.[99] Chapman's evidence on the USA shows that in terms of earnings (ignoring fringe benefits and profits) it too was more unequal than the USSR. Thus it is quite clear that, although the USSR has lower real earnings levels and wider earnings differentials than other countries in Eastern Europe, it also has much narrower earnings differentials than the USA and Britain.

However, earnings are only part of the real income of the population. The other major components of the real income of the Soviet population are of course comprised of housing, transport and basic food subsidies, as well as expenditures under the heading of the social consumption funds. If one is attempting to examine whether differentials in the distribution of income have declined, the impact of these measures must be assessed in some way. At the end of Chapter 5 I attempted a rough assessment of the overall effects of such non-wage forms of income and concluded that arguments that such forms of state expenditure were regressive were not substantiated. McAuley is convinced that the authorities adopted a new approach to questions of economic welfare in the mid-1950s,[100] and that while neither wage and salary policy nor expenditures on social consumption have been administered as consistently or effectively as Soviet accounts would have us believe, there has been substantial achievement.[101]

McAuley's analysis is particularly useful for a discussion of the distribution of income. Thus, for example, he points out that, whatever measure is used, the gap between *kolkhozniki* and state employees closed between 1960 and 1970, so that by the end of the decade, total or per *capita* personal income for *kolkhozniki* for the USSR as a whole was some 78 to 85 per cent of that of state employees. He rightly argues that this 'gives a better indication of the relative living standards of the two classes than money income, which suggests that peasants received about two-thirds as much as the rest of the population'.[102] He also argues that the available evidence indicates that there was a marked reduction in inequality among the non-agricultural population between 1958 and 1967.[103] Not surprisingly, this is related to the reform of social security, the reorganisation of the wage and salary system, and the increased expenditure on pensions and other transfers.

Yet his claim that the momentum in this respect which was evident up to 1970 may not have been maintained, that the drive to equality may have slackened or even been reversed, is perhaps open to question, though it is difficult to refute without as careful an appraisal of the evidence for the 1970s as he has conducted for the pre-1970 period.

Some of McAuley's work is complemented by the work of Vinokur and Ofer,[104] though their analysis is primarily restricted to industrial workers. They confirm that the rise in real *per capita* income continued until 1975, being around 73 per cent higher than in 1965 if the Soviet retail price index is used, or 50 per cent higher if the Schroeder–Severin index is taken.[105] They also confirm that the gap in real incomes between *kolkhozniki* and state employees continued to narrow after 1970, from about 36 per cent in 1965 to 32 per cent in 1975: 'This is reasonable since incomes of *kolkhozniki* and low-paid urban workers, as well as of pensioners, rose more rapidly than incomes of better-paid industrial workers.'[106] However, on the basis of survey evidence, they suggest that the predominance of industrial workers in terms of wages (in comparison with office staff and with manual workers in agriculture and services) is offset by lower supplementary income from social consumption funds.[107] This latter phenomenon would not affect the overall distribution of income very much.

Overall, the distribution of income (not simply wages) has been considerably equalised from about 1955 to 1975. While the evidence is not available to form judgements about developments since then, and while it is clear that further equalisation of incomes may be fraught with difficulty and is perhaps only recently a process which has been monitored with any sophistication,[108] it is very clear that the combined effect of various policies has been to raise general living standards and to equalise incomes. Whatever the reasons for these developments, increases in the wages of the lowest paid and improvements in welfare are not the sort of outcome which one would expect of the central state and party agencies, in a situation where their room for manoeuvre in running the economy has been declining. The available evidence on the trends in the distribution of real income is thus quite compatible with the argument in the preceding section (on the occupational structure and class relations) that no category of agents seems to be capable of establishing privileged access to the means of production.

Conclusion: The Presence of Class Relations in the Soviet Union

It is clear from the fact that substantial changes in the occupational structure have taken place since the late 1920s that the central state and party agencies are capable of co-ordinating the division of labour in a manner which broadly speaking enables them to fulfil their objectives. This has continued to be the case despite the slow-down in the rate of economic growth since the mid-1960s. However, it is equally clear that there are limits on the capacity of the central agencies to co-ordinate the division of labour. Some of these limits on their capacity derive from their form of calculation and on the organisational resources at their immediate disposal. However, the main limits on their capacity derive from the capacities of other economic agents such as Ministries, and from their sub-agents such as production associations, state enterprises (and in future even perhaps autonomous brigades within enterprises). While the access of each of these economic agents to the means of production is different, and hence their capacities are each somewhat different, the available evidence strongly suggests that within the state sector such differential access does not give rise to class relations.

This conclusion seems to hold not just for relations between collective agents but for those between individual agents: the examination of the occupational structure suggested that the most systematic enhancement and restriction of individuals' capacity for action derived from gender attribution rather than class relations. The effect of this on the occupational distribution of men and women and on the consequent distribution of income between these two categories was quite clear. Apart from this, while there are certainly differences in individual capacities deriving from occupational location, and associated differences in income level, it is clear that within the state sector these derive largely from membership of state agencies rather than being an attribute of the occupation itself, for example the educational level required to enter that occupation.

Thus the failure to find any class relations between occupations is related to the lack of class relations between state agencies. The predominance of such collective agents is of course an effect of the nationalisation of the means of production, which means that the only legal access which an individual has to the means of production is in the capacity of a member of a party or state agency. Hence the importance of analysing the relative capacities of the various state economic agents, as was attempted in Chapter 3. The complex relations between these agents, with 'dual subordination', and a multiplicity of arenas in which the decisions of superior agents can be challenged, and a degree of autonomy at the level of sub-agents due partly to the sheer burden of information at the centre, these complex relations have important effects. First, because the capacities of various state agencies cannot be strictly delimited (there are great difficulties of even achieving a legal codification of these various capacities), the processes of plan formulation and plan implementation are inevitably politicised. Second, these relations are such that, while there is adequate delimitation of sub-agents to enable an overall national co-ordination of the division of labour to be achieved, this delimitation is not sufficient to render the sub-agents incapable of having any serious impact on the division of labour. In other words, while the central agencies are capable of formulating and effectively implementing a national plan (which means they are capable of preventing sub-agents from taking over the means of production), the various agencies of plan implementation are nevertheless capable of exerting considerable control over that part of the total means of production which is at their disposal. This means they are also in a position to resist or even block certain kinds of economic policies, and to press for others. While this state of affairs continues, it will be difficult for the central agencies or the Ministries or other sub-agents to gain sufficient control of the means of production to be able to decide their own investment and income-distribution policies. Consequently the various forms of access of different agents, even those with a more restricted capacity for action such as enterprises, do seem to be such that within the state sector there is 'multiple access' to, or 'social ownership' of, the means of production. This is not to say that the present forms of 'social ownership' in the Soviet Union are the most politically desirable or economically effective.

The conclusion that the relations of production within the state sector do not give rise to class relations within it does not mean that there are no class relations in the Soviet Union. The *kolkhozy* are not simply juridically distinct, they are a category of collective agents whose access to the means of production is clearly restricted to the terms set by state agencies. While the incomes of their members are evidently approaching those of employees of state agencies, that income depends more on the economic performance of each collective farm (and on the personal plots) than is the case in state agencies, where individual incomes are much more dependent on state policy. However, it is not the dependence of their members' incomes on their economic performance which places collective farm members in a different class position from state employees. The connection between individual wage and economic perfor- mance could be strengthened in the state sector if the autonomous brigade reforms go through. Rather, it is their effective subordination to various state agencies, which, by their investment, pricing and delivery policies, determine the farms' access to the means of production and consequently the disposition of their product. These state policies operate in a way that enables the state agencies to predominate completely in determining the farms' conditions of existence, and even their 'choice' of chairmen and internal organisational form. Yet they are (or have been in the past) denied the Ministerial backing which would enable them to lobby for investment. These relations between state agencies and collective farms are of course the legacy of forced collectivisation. Fortunately conditions on collective farms are steadily improving. Yet the massive investment in agriculture is much less effective than it could be, as indicated in Chapter 3. This is because collective farms do not appear to have the autonomy to co-ordinate their own technical division of labour, and hence to decide on the most appropriate kinds of on-farm investment. Agricultural investment off the farm (that is, infrastructural work on roads and *kolkhoz* markets, etc.) is controlled by the state, which further enables the state to determine the conditions of existence of the *kolkhozy*. In the absence of rapid improvements in agricultural performance, it will be difficult for the state to speed up the transformation of *kolkhozy* into *sovkhozy*. However, it would seem that in current Soviet conditions this is the only feasible way to eliminate these class relations.

Finally, there is the possibility that class relations operate in the 'informal sector' of the Soviet economy, the so-called 'parallel market' which is sometimes divided into various different kinds of market. While it is possible that capitalist relations operate here, and in aggregate the 'informal sector' must be economically significant, it appears that most of the economic activity in this sector takes the form of self-employed 'moonlighting'. Consequently, such class relations as exist here are not of major importance at the moment, and would only become so if the 'informal sector' seriously disrupted the national planning process, which would imply a fairly serious social upheaval on the scale of, say, recent events in Poland connected with the rise of Solidarity.

One can sum up by saying that there are class relations in the Soviet Union which operate by means of mechanisms of state control of the *kolkhozy*. While other class relations may operate in the 'informal sector', they are much less important, and their exact extent is unknown. The class relations between state agencies and the *kolkhozy,* which put their respective members in different class positions, are being steadily if slowly eroded, by measures to transform *kolkhozy* and by opening up the access of *kolkhozy* to the means of production (by organisational devices such as inter-*kolkhoz* associations). In this sense the official Soviet theory of the class structure, which treats the form of property (or collective agent) as important for defining the class position of individuals and which argues that class differences are diminishing, is defensible. However, the basis of this theory is not very clear and it is weakened by the insistence on attempting to find grounds for defining the 'intelligentsia' as a separate stratum.

Notes

1. See, for example, the identification by both Goldthorpe and Halsey (in their famous Oxford mobility study publications) of the 'class structure' of occupational positions with the 'class structure' of family units, which

is criticised by B. Hindess, 'The Politics of Social Mobility', *Economy and Society*, vol. 10, no. 2, May 1981.

2. It is probably clear that the word 'disproportionate' is being used loosely here. It does not imply the possibility of establishing what a proportionate share in the distribution of income would be, as in 'to each according to his work'. It simply implies a sufficiently large share of the total available real income to sustain the predominant capacity to co-ordinate the division of labour, thereby being in a position to affect substantially one's own conditions of existence.

3. D. Lane, *The End of Inequality?*, Penguin, Harmondsworth, 1971, p.38.

4. Ibid, p.38.

5. D. Lane and F. O'Dell, *The Soviet Industrial Worker: Social Class, Education and Control*, Martin Robertson, London, 1978, p.3.

6. Ibid, pp. 4–5.

7. D. Lane, *Politics and Society in the USSR*, 2nd edn, Martin Robertson, London, 1978, p.418.

8. This is at least true of the base–superstructure metaphor. For a criticism of the 'problematic of the productive forces', see Charles Bettelheim, *Class Struggles in the USSR: Second Period 1923–1930*, Harvester Press, Brighton, 1978, 'Foreword'.

9. Lane, *Politics and Society in the USSR*, p.389.

10. Lane and O'Dell, *The Soviet Industrial Worker*, p.6.

11. Amvrosov, *Sotsial'naya Struktura Sovetskogo Obshchestva*, Politizdat, Moscow, 1975.

12. Lane and O'Dell, *The Soviet Industrial Worker*, p.9. They also provide figures on population growth and movement from country to town before making this statement.

13. Ibid, p.10.

14. J.F. Hough, 'Policy-making and the Worker', in A. Kahan and B. Ruble (eds), *Industrial Labor in the USSR*, Permagon, New York, 1979, pp. 367–96.

15. Ibid, p.383.

16. For a discussion of these issues, see B.Q. Madison, 'Trade Unions and Social Welfare', in Kahan and Ruble (eds), *Industrial Labor in the USSR*, pp.85–115, esp. p. 108, where he points out that 'unpaid activists cannot be held to an acceptable standard of performance'.

17. Lane and O'Dell, *The Soviet Industrial Worker*, p.16.

18. Ibid, p.15.

19. Ibid, p.14.

20. Ibid, p.14.

21. Ibid, p.16.

22. Ibid, p.17.

23. Ibid, p.17. Similar remarks are made in other sources with regard to medical doctors (see Chapter 5).

24. R.W. Lee, 'The Factory Trade Union Committee and Technological Innovation', in Kahan and Ruble (eds), *Industrial Labor in the USSR*, pp.116–34.

25. Lane and O'Dell, *The Soviet Industrial Worker*, p.18.
26. Ibid, p.18. For a discussion of socialisation (in the sense of cultural acquisition rather than of, say, the 'socialisation of the productive forces') see N. Swafford, 'The Socialisation and Training of the Soviet Industrial Labor Force', in Kahan and Ruble (eds), *Industrial Labor in the USSR*, pp.19–41.
27. M. Feshbach, 'The Structure and Composition of the Industrial Labor Force', in Kahan and Ruble (eds), *Industrial Labor in the USSR*, pp.3–18.
28. Ibid, p.16.
29. Ibid, p.7. The figure for 1950 was 15.3 million persons, so that it more than doubled in twenty-five years. Increasing the industrial labour force as a source of increased output is virtually impossible in the next decade or so.
30. Such mechanisms of allocation could include those distributing women to particular occupations, or the use of educational qualifications as entrance criteria for occupational selection. These will be discussed later, but mechanisms of allocation also include a conscious state policy of occupational placement. This has certainly been and remains a matter of state policy: see P. Grossman, 'The Soviet Government's Role in Allocating Industrial Labor', in Kahan and Ruble (eds), *Industrial Labor in the USSR*, pp.42–55. Grossman argues that the decline in compulsion in allocating the labour force has been accompanied by an increase in the government's participation in the process of allocation. It concentrates on serving new entrants and job changers, thus minimising unemployment, or at least its duration.
31. Feshbach, 'The Structure and Composition of the Industrial Labor Force', p.10. He points out that, in 1973, 54.9 per cent of female industrial wage-workers had completed at least general secondary school studies, compared with 47 per cent of men.
32. G. Lapidus, 'The Female Industrial Labor Force: Dilemmas, Reassessments and Options', in Kahan and Ruble (eds), *Industrial Labor in the USSR*, pp.232–79. She points out (on p.244) that 'the educational attainment of much of the female labour force actually exceeds that of males'.
33. Lane and O'Dell, *The Soviet Industrial Worker*, pp.117, 118, where the tables show that women now comprise over half the students in secondary specialised educational institutions, and exactly half the students in higher educational institutions.
34. Lapidus, 'The Female Industrial Labor Force', p.236.
35. Ibid, p.239.
36. Ibid, p.239. Lapidus points out that women comprise 80 per cent of food and textile workers, and 90 per cent of garment workers, but less than 30 per cent of workers in coal, lumber, electric power and mineral extraction.
37. Ibid, p.239. This is certainly similar to the situation in capitalist countries: see, for example, M. Guilbert, *Les Fonctions des Femmes dans l'Industrie*, Mouton, Paris, 1966. However, such similarities

in the treatment of women can hardly be explained by similar levels of technology.

38. Lee, 'The Factory Trade Union Committee and Technological Innovation', p.131. Lapidus, 'The Female Industrial Labor Force', p.242, points out that their occupational mobility is limited by their lower enrolment rate in programmes to raise professional qualifications. This is due to family responsibilities.

39. Lapidus, 'The Female Industrial Labor Force', p.242.

40. Ibid, p.242.

41. Ibid, p.244. Lapidus reports that Soviet economists treat the wage of the 'secondary' earner as being roughly two-thirds that of the 'primary' earner, for planning purposes.

42. Ibid, p.246; Lane and O'Dell, *The Soviet Industrial Worker*; A. Heitlinger, *Women and State Socialism: Sex Inequality in the Soviet Union and Czechoslovakia,* Macmillan, London, 1979.

43. Lapidus, 'The Female Industrial Labor Force', p.233.

44. Ibid, p.248.

45. Ibid, p.261.

46. Ibid, p.262.

47. Ibid, pp.264–8.

48. The internal organisation of the State Committee on Labour and Social Questions is discussed in Hough, 'Policy-making and the Worker', p.381.

49. Lapidus, 'The Female Industrial Labor Force', p.267, cites one labour economist who recalls the post-revolutionary Women's Department (*Zhenotdel*) of the Central Committee and explicitly regrets its premature abolition. For a brief history of *Zhenotdel,* see Heitlinger, *Women and State Socialism,* ch. 6.

50. Lane and O'Dell, *The Soviet Industrial Worker,* p.4.

51. See Amvrosov, *Sotsial'naya Struktura Sovetskogo Obshchestva,* pp.92–5, 99–103. These are also discussed in Chapter 3 of this book.

52. Lane and O'Dell, *The Soviet Industrial Worker,* pp.9, 10.

53. Lane, *Politics and Society in the USSR,* p.393, where he says that engineering/technical and administrative personnel in the 1960s made up 6–9 per cent of collective farmers.

54. See Z. Medvedev, 'Russia Learns to Live without American Grain', *New Scientist,* 8 January 1981, pp.58–61. This article gives a good indication of the increasingly sophisticated use of machinery, though it also shows continuing shortcomings in the use of machinery, transport and storage facilities. For another source indicating the extent of technical innovation in Soviet agriculture (without, however, throwing any light on the situation in collective farms), see G.B. Carter, 'Is Biotechnology Feeding the Russians?', *New Scientist,* 23 April 1981, pp. 216–18.

55. Amvrosov, *Sotsial'naya Struktura Sovetskogo Obshchestva,* p.49.

56. A. McAuley, *Economic Welfare in the Soviet Union,* Allen & Unwin, London, 1979.

57. This decree recommends local authorities and agricultural units to place at the disposal of citizens land which is not used or is little used

by the *kolkhozy* or *sovkhozy*, and raises the limits on the number of livestock which citizens can keep. In the light of the analysis by Wädekin of personal plots (discussed in Chapter 3), this seems to be a reasonable change, a view which is apparently shared by Medvedev, 'Russia Learns to Live without American Grain', p.61, who was already aware before the decree of 'the clear encouragement of privately owned land and livestock'.

58. L. Rzhanitsyna, *Soviet Family Budgets*, Progress Publishers, Moscow, 1977, pp.162–72. This confirms the impression given by McAuley, *Economic Welfare in the Soviet Union*.

59. McAuley, *Economic Welfare in the Soviet Union*, p.34.

60. L.G. Churchward, *The Soviet Intelligentsia: An Essay on the Social Structure and Roles of Soviet Intellectuals during the 1960s*, Routledge & Kegan Paul, London, 1973, p.6.

61. N. Lampert, *The Technical Intelligentsia and the Soviet State: A Study of Soviet Managers and Technicians 1928–1935*, Macmillan, London, 1979, p.7. Lampert is concerned with the technical intelligentsia, i.e. the ITRs, and is careful to point out that the conclusions from his study do not necessarily apply to the contemporary Soviet Union (p.10).

62. M. Hirszowicz, *The Bureaucratic Leviathan: A Study in the Sociology of Communism*, Martin Robertson, London, 1980, ch. 5 'Intelligentsia versus Bureaucracy – The Revival of a Myth'.

63. Ibid, p.179.

64. Ibid, pp.198–9.

65. This approach appears to accept a Weberian conception of bureaucracy, as well as the concept of a totalitarian order, both of which are rejected by other authors, such as Lampert, *The Technical Intelligentsia*, pp.6–7.

66. For some reason, Churchward, *The Soviet Intelligentsia*, p.6, regards his definition as 'an objective definition in the Marxist tradition', but it seems to me that this simply indicates that pre-Revolutionary Marxists often shared the nineteenth-century approach to the intelligentsia. It is true that contemporary Soviet theorists such as Amvrosov, *Sotsial'naya Struktura Sovetskogo Obshchestva*, also define the intelligentsia in educational terms, but Churchward's concept is apparently an attempt to resolve the problems of 'the Soviet definition'.

67. Hirszowicz, *The Bureaucratic Leviathan*, p.180, makes it clear that she is aware of this.

68. Churchward, *The Soviet Intelligentsia*, p.9. Lane, *Politics and Society in the USSR*, p.390, also argues that the Soviet intelligentsia cannot be considered a homogeneous group.

69. For example, M. Kaser, *Health Care in the Soviet Union*, Croom Helm, London, 1976, on the health service, as well as V. George and N. Manning, *Socialism, Social Welfare and the Soviet Union*, Routledge & Kegan Paul, London, 1980, discussed in Chapter 5, or Hirszowicz, *The Bureaucratic Leviathan*, ch. 4 'The Limitations of Rationality in a Planning Society'.

70. See Churchward, *The Soviet Intelligentsia*, pp.79–81.

71. M. Matthews, 'Top Incomes in the USSR', in *Economic Aspects of Life*

in the USSR, NATO Directorate of Economic Affairs, Brussels, 1975, pp. 131–4.

72. P. Wiles, 'Note on Dr Matthews' Calculations', in *Economic Aspects of Life in the USSR*, pp.155–8.

73. See D.K. Simes, 'The Soviet Parallel Market', in *Economic Aspects of Life in the USSR*, pp. 91–100. However, this article does not attempt to assess the income-distribution effects of the parallel market, which would be very difficult to do.

74. They are not a distinct class because, with the possible exception of senior party and state personnel, their occupational position cannot be said to give them significantly different access to the means of production from the manual working class. In both cases, their incomes are largely determined by state policy, which, as in the case of women, often holds down relative incomes of many non-manual occupations to a level comparable with manual incomes.

75. See note 30 with respect to the work of Grossman, 'The Soviet Government's Role in Allocating Industrial Labor'; the difficulties of manpower planning in the 1950s and 1960s are discussed in G. Littlejohn, 'Education and Social Mobility in the USSR', unpublished dissertation, 1968. The main difficulties discussed were those of forecasting changes in the occupational structure five years ahead (in the case of entrants to tertiary education) and of successfully placing specialised secondary and tertiary graduates in 'appropriate' jobs.

76. For critiques of such views, see A. Hussain, 'The Economy and the Educational System in Capitalist Societies', *Economy and Society*, vol. 5, no. 4. November 1976; also J. Demaine, *Contemporary Theories in the Sociology of Education*, Macmillan, London, 1981; as well as R.J.V. Waton, 'A Sociological Study of Education in Sweden and Britain', unpublished M.Phil. thesis, University of Bradford, 1980.

77. E. Hopper (ed.), *Readings in the Theory of Educational Systems*, Heinemann, London, 1971.

78. R.H. Turner, 'Modes of Social Ascent through Education: Sponsored and Contest Mobility', in A.H. Halsey *et al.* (eds), *Education, Economy and Society*, Free Press, New York, 1961. B.R. Clarke's article on 'The Cooling Out Function in Higher Education' also appears in this volume. this volume.

79. Lane and O'Dell, *The Soviet Industrial Worker*, p.51.

80. Ibid, p.77.

81. Ibid, pp.86–7.

82. Ibid, p.91. They treat the 1977 decree to improve labour training in schools as an indication of this.

83. Ibid, p.93.

84. Ibid, p.106.

85. Ibid, p.122.

86. Ibid, p.105.

87. See, for example, Amvrosov, *Sotsial'naya Struktura Sovetskogo Obshchestva*.

88. Lane and O'Dell, *The Soviet Industrial Worker*, ch. 2 'The Worker in the Industrial Enterprise'.

89. B.A. Ruble, 'Factory Unions and Workers' Rights', in Kahan and Ruble (eds), *Industrial Labor in the USSR,* pp.59–84.

90. Ibid, p.73.

91. Lane and O'Dell, *The Soviet Industrial Worker,* p.25.

92. See ibid, ch. 3. Lane and O'Dell argue that Soviet workers are incorporated rather than alienated. They thus explicitly disagree with H. Ticktin, 'The Contradictions of Soviet Society and Professor Bettelheim', *Critique,* no. 6, Spring 1976, and with M. Holubenko, 'The Soviet Working Class', *Critique,* no. 4, Spring 1975. On Lane and O'Dell's own account the participation of manual workers or of agencies claiming to represent them within the factory is rather limited. Lane and O'Dell are quite willing to accept that discontent does exist, but they argue that the political context of the factory and the political socialisation of the work-force mean that it is less 'atomised' and discontented than Ticktin or Holubenko would claim. For a different attempt to gauge the extent of manual workers' discontent, see A. Pravda, 'Spontaneous Workers' Activities in the Soviet Union', in Kahan and Ruble (eds), *Industrial Labor in the USSR,* pp.333–66.

93. The possibility that Ministries might operate like capitalist multi-enterprise companies was briefly considered and rejected in Chapter 3.

94. McAuley, *Economic Welfare in the Soviet Union,* chs. 9, 10. There seems little point here in giving an extensive account of McAuley's detailed analysis.

95. P. Wiles, 'Recent Data on Soviet Income Distribution', in *Economic Aspects of Life in the USSR,* pp.113–29.

96. J.G. Chapman, 'Recent Trends in the Soviet Industrial Wage Structure', in Kahan and Ruble (eds), *Industrial Labor in the USSR,* pp.151–83. In 1980 the average wage was 168.5 roubles, as against 96.5 roubles in 1965.

97. Ibid, p.172. Chapman also points out that at least one 'perk' of high-level officials has been ended: in 1973, a reduction in the number of official cars was begun, and officials of all but the highest rank were warned that they had three years to learn how to drive themselves. This may simply have been a political gesture, but it does indicate a sensitivity to conspicuous differences in real income. Although Chapman does not mention it in her discussion of minimum wages, McAuley *(Economic Welfare in the Soviet Union,* p.34) pointed out that the minimum wage was increased to 70 roubles in 1975, and this corroborates Chapman's analysis. McAuley relates the increase in the minimum wage to attempts to encourage female participation in the labour force (p.177). McAuley also considers that some of the changes in wages are the result of the workings of the labour market (ch. 12).

98. Wiles, 'Note on Dr Matthews' Calculations'.

99. Chapman, 'Recent Trends', p.175.

100. McAuley, *Economic Welfare in the Soviet Union,* p.304.

101. Ibid, p.306.

102. Ibid, p.306. Since social consumption funds payments do not seem to offset wage differentials between state employees and *kolkhozniki,* the

income from personal plots must have been largely responsible for closing the gap in terms of real income during the 1960s.

103. Ibid, p.307.
104. A. Vinokur and G. Ofer, 'Family Income Levels for Soviet Industrial Workers', in Kahan and Ruble (eds), *Industrial Labor in the USSR*, pp.184–208.
105. Ibid, p.187.
106. Ibid, p.187.
107. Ibid, pp.200–5.
108. See McAuley's remarks on the instruments for income equalisation at the government's disposal: *Economic Welfare in the Soviet Union*, ch. 12 *passim*. It *could* be the case that the policy of income equalisation is being partly undermined by growing wage inequalities due to the payment of bonuses: see A. McAuley, 'Wage Differentials in the USSR: Policy and Performance', paper presented to the Second World Congress of Soviet and East European Studies, Garmisch, 1980.

Glossary

Artel'	A collective farm in which part of the land and implements were still held by individual families.
Desiatina	A measure of area, equal to 1.09 hectares or 2.7 acres.
Gosbank	The State Bank, which has the constitutional status of a State Committee, attached to the Council of Ministers.
Gosplan	State Planning Committee.
Gossnab	State Committee on Material Technical Supply.
Gosstroi	State Construction Committee.
Gubernia	Province, i.e. an administrative region under the Tsarist state and in the 1920s.
Khozraschet	A form of 'economic accounting' which gives the agent using it a certain degree of financial autonomy, and is consequently regarded by some commentators as being a concession to 'the market' in a predominantly 'command economy'.
Khutor	A capitalist farm, not subject to periodic redivision of land among the village commune (see *Mir*).
Kolkhoz	A collective farm (plural *kolkhozy*).
Kolkhoznik	A collective farm member (plural *Kolkhozniki*).
Kombedy	Committee of the Poor, predominant in the Central Provinces of European Russia from mid-1918 to late 1918, but persisting in some areas to the 1920s.
Kommuna	A collective farm in which all land and property was held in common; the most communal form of *kolkhoz*.

Mir   Repartitional village 'commune', where strips of land were periodically redivided among the members of the 'commune'. Because a three-field crop-rotational system was frequently used, a period of nine years between repartitions was sometimes officially encouraged; also frequently referred to as the *obshchina*.

Oblast'   An administrative region within one of the constituent Republics of the USSR.

Politburo   The 'executive committee' of the Central Committee of the Communist Party of the Soviet Union.

Raiispolkom   *Raion* executive committee of the Communist Party of the Soviet Union.

Raion   A district, a sub-unit of an *Oblast'*.

Sel'khoztekhnika   'Agricultural Technique', an agency responsible for the supply of means of production to *kolkhozy* and *sovkhozy*.

Sel'sovet   Rural soviet, intended to be the Soviet replacement of the *Mir*, but which was effectively dominated by the latter during most of the 1920s.

Sovkhoz   A state farm (plural *sovkhozy*).

Tolkach'   A 'pusher', an agent who uses informal connections to secure supplies, usually for a state enterprise.

Toz   An association for the common cultivation of land; the least socialised form of *kolkhoz*, where there was simply joint use of certain means of production on jointly cultivated land at certain times of the year.

Trudoden'   A 'labour day unit', which was (prior to 1966) the main method of payment of *kolkhozniki*. The value of each 'labour day unit', calculated on a points system depending on the type of work contributed to the collective farm by an individual, was not known until the value of the harvest *net of state planned procurements* was known. This meant that the income of *kolkhozniki* was subject to considerable variations due to annual variations in the harvest.

Volost'   An administrative district within a *Gubernia* under the Tsarist state and in the 1920s (plural *volosti*).

Chronology

7 November 1917	October Revolution
8 November 1917	Decree on Land (Nationalisation)
April 1918	Treaty of Brest-Litovsk (peace with Germany)
Mid–1918 } early–1920 }	Civil War
May–October 1920	Polish invasion (aftermath of Civil War)
March 1921	Tenth Party Congress (ban on factions within Bolshevik Party, introduction of New Economic Policy – NEP)
Autumn 1921	Famine
July 1922	Currency reform: coexistence of paper rouble and chervonets until February 1924
1923	Scissors crisis
1924	Death of Lenin
1928–9	Crisis of NEP
1929	Adoption of First Five Year Plan, expulsion of Bukharin from Politburo, decision to force collectivisation of agriculture, end of NEP
1932–3	Famine
1934	'Congress of Victors', assassination of Kirov, beginning of terror
1936	Constitution
1937	Great Purge
1941–5	Great Patriotic War
1945	Fourth Five Year Plan
1953	Death of Stalin
1957	Sovnarkhoz Reform, revival of Comecon
1958	Education reform
October 1964	Removal of Khrushchev
1965	Kosygin enterprise reform
1973	Beginning of production association reform
July 1979	Planning reform
November 1982	Death of Brezhnev

Bibliography

A. A. Amvrosov (1975) *Sotsial'naya Struktura Sovetskogo Obshchestva*, Politizdat, Moscow.

V. Andrle (1976) *Managerial Power in the Soviet Union*, Saxon House/Lexington Books, D.C. Heath Ltd, Westmead and Lexington.

D. G. Atkinson (1971) 'The Russian Land Commune and the Revolution', Ph.D. thesis, unpublished, Stanford University.

R. Bendix and S. M. Lipset (1967) *Class, Status and Power*, 2nd edn, Routledge & Kegan Paul, London.

C. Bettelheim (1976) *Economic Calculation and Forms of Property*, Routledge & Kegan Paul, London.

C. Bettelheim (1978) *Class Struggles in the USSR: Second Period 1923–1930*, Harvester Press, Brighton.

P. Bew and C. Roulston (1982) 'Land and the European Left', *Economy and Society*, vol. 11, no. 1, February 1982.

A. H. Brown (1974) *Soviet Politics and Political Science*, Macmillan, London.

A. Brown and J. Gray (eds) (1979) *Political Culture and Political Change in Communist States*, 2nd edn, Macmillan, London.

A. Brown and M. Kaser (eds) (1975) *The Soviet Union since the Fall of Khrushchev*, Macmillan, London.

W. Butler (1978) *The Soviet Legal System: Selected Contemporary Legislation and Documents*, Parker School of Foreign and Comparative Law, Columbia University, New York.

P. Carlen and M. Collinson (eds) (1980) *Radical Issues in Criminology*, Martin Robertson, London.

G. B. Carter (1981) 'Is Biotechnology Feeding the Russians?', *New Scientist*, 23 April 1981, pp. 216–18.

L. G. Churchward (1973) *The Soviet Intelligentsia: An Essay on the Social Structure and Roles of Soviet Intellectuals during the 1960s*, Routledge & Kegan Paul, London.

A. Cutler, B. Hindess, P. Hirst and A. Hussain (1977, 1978) *Marx's 'Capital' and Capitalism Today*, vols 1 and 2, Routledge & Kegan Paul, London.

A. Cutler, B. Hindess, P. Hirst and A. Hussain (1979) 'An Imaginary Orthodoxy – A Reply to Laurence Harris', *Economy and Society*, vol. 8, no. 3, August 1979.

C. Darch (n.d.) 'Saddle Rugs for Shrouds', unpublished.

J. Demaine (1981) *Contemporary Theories in the Sociology of Education*, Macmillan, London.

M. Dobb (1928) *Russian Economic Development Since The Revolution*, London.

M. Dobb (1966) *Soviet Economic Development Since 1917*, Routledge & Kegan Paul, London.

M. Drach (1980) 'La brigade sous contrat dans l'industrie soviétique et la réforme de juillet 1979', paper read on 24 October 1980 to the Groupe de Récherche sur la Théorie de l'Economie Socialiste, Centre d'Economie Internationale des Pays Socialistes, Université de Paris, Panthéon–Sorbonne.

B. Edelman (1979) *Ownership of the Image: Elements for a Marxist Theory of Law*, Routledge & Kegan Paul, London.

A. Etzioni (1964) *Modern Organizations*, Prentice-Hall, Englewood Cliffs, New Jersey.

C. J. Friedrich and Z. K. Brzezinski (1965) *Totalitarian Dictatorship and Autocracy*, Harvard and Oxford University Presses, Oxford.

V. George and N. Manning (1980) *Socialism, Social Welfare and the Soviet Union*, Routledge & Kegan Paul, London.

S. Grosskopf (1976) *L'Alliance Ouvrière et Paysanne en URSS (1921–1928): le Probleme du Blé*, Maspero, Paris.

M. Guilbert (1966) *Les Fonctions des Femmes dans l'Industrie*, Mouton, Paris.

A. H. Halsey, J. Floud and C. A. Anderson (eds) (1961) *Education, Economy and Society*, Fress Press, New York.

L. Harris (1978) 'The Science of the Economy', *Economy and Society*, vol. 7, no. 3, August 1978.

L. Harris (1979) 'The Theory of Value and the Value of Theory – a reply to Cutler *et al.*', *Economy and Society*, vol. 8, no. 3, August 1979.

M. Harrison (1978) 'The Soviet Economy in the 1920s and 1930s', *Capital and Class*, no. 5, 1978.

J. Hazard, W. Butler and P. Maggs (1977) *The Soviet Legal System*, 3rd edn, Parker School of Foreign and Comparative Law, Columbia University, New York.

A. Heitlinger (1979) *Women and State Socialism: Sex Inequality in the Soviet Union and Czechoslovakia*, Macmillan, London.

B. Hindess (1973) *The Use of Official Statistics in Sociology*, Macmillan, London.

B. Hindess (1976) 'On Three-Dimensional Power', *Political Studies*, vol. 24, no. 3, 1976.

B. Hindess (ed.) (1977) *Sociological Theories of the Economy*. Macmillan, London.

B. Hindess (1980) 'Democratisation and the Limits to Parliamentary Democracy', *Politics and Power 1*, Routledge & Kegan Paul, London.

B. Hindess (1981) 'The Politics of Social Mobility', *Economy and Society*, vol. 10, no. 2, May 1981.

P. Hirst (1976) *Social Evolution and Sociological Categories*, Allen & Unwin, London.

P. Hirst (1979) *On Law and Ideology*, Macmillan, London.

M. Hirszowicz (1980) *The Bureaucratic Leviathan: A Study in the Sociology of Communism*, Martin Robertson, London.

M. Holubenko (1975) 'The Soviet Working Class', *Critique*, no. 4, Spring 1975.

E. Hopper (ed.) (1971) *Readings in the Theory of Educational Systems*, Heinemann, London.

J. F. Hough (1977) *The Soviet Union and Social Science Theory*, Harvard University Press, Cambridge.

J. F. Hough and M. Fainsod (1979) *How the Soviet Union is Governed*, Harvard University Press, Cambridge.

A. Hunt (ed.) (1978) *Class and Class Structure*, Lawrence & Wishart, London.

A. Hunt (ed.) (1981) *Marxism and Democracy*, Lawrence & Wishart, London.

A. Hussain (1976) 'The Economy and the Educational System in Capitalist Societies', *Economy and Society*, vol. 5, no. 4, November 1976.

A. Hussain and K. Tribe (1981) *Marxism and the Agrarian Question*, vols 1 and 2, Macmillan, London.

G. Hyde (1974) *The Soviet Health Service: A Historical and Comparative Study*, Lawrence & Wishart, London.

A. Inkeles and R. A. Bauer (1959) *The Soviet Citizen*, Oxford University Press.

N. Jasny (1949) *The Socialised Agriculture of the USSR: Plans and Performance*, Stanford University Press.

N. Jasny (1972) *Soviet Economists of the Twenties: Names to be Remembered*, Cambridge University Press.

A. Kahan and B. Ruble (eds) (1979) *Industrial Labor in the USSR*, Pergamon, New York.

M. Kaser (1976) *Health Care in the Soviet Union and Eastern*

Europe, Croom Helm, London.

A. Katsenelinboigen (1977) 'Coloured Markets in the Soviet Union', *Soviet Studies*, vol. XXIX, no. 1, January 1977.

L. Kritsman (1929) *Proletarskaya Revolyutsia i Derevnya*, State Publication, Moscow–Leningrad.

L. Kritsman (1982) 'Class Stratification of the Soviet Countryside', *Journal of Peasant Studies*, vol. 11, no. 2, January 1984.

N. Lampert (1979) *The Technical Intelligentsia and the Soviet State: A Study of Soviet Managers and Technicians 1928–1935*, Macmillan, London.

D. Lane (1971) *The End of Inequality?*, Penguin, Harmondsworth.

D. Lane (1978) *Politics and Society in the USSR*, 2nd edn, Martin Robertson, London.

D. Lane and F. O'Dell (1978) *The Soviet Industrial Worker: Social Class, Education and Control*, Martin Robertson, London.

M. Lavigne (1974) *The Socialist Economies of the Soviet Union and Europe*, Martin Robertson, London.

M. Lavigne (1978) 'The Creation of Money by the State Bank in the USSR', *Economy and Society*, vol. 7, no. 1, February 1978.

M. Lavigne (1978) 'Advanced Socialist Society', *Economy and Society*, vol. 7, no. 4, November 1978.

M. Lavigne (ed.) (1978) *Economie politique de la planification en système socialiste*, Economica, Paris.

M. Lavigne (1979) *Les Economies Socialistes: Soviétique et Européennes*, Armand Colin, Paris.

P. Lavigne and M. Lavigne (1979) *Regards sur la Constitution Soviétique de 1977*, Economica, Paris.

V. I. Lenin (1965) 'A Great Beginning', *Collected Works*, vol. 29, Lawrence & Wishart, London.

M. Lewin (1968) *Russian Peasants and Soviet Power: A Study of Collectivisation*, Allen & Unwin, London.

G. Littlejohn (1968) 'Education and Social Mobility in the USSR', unpublished dissertation.

G. Littlejohn, B. Smart, J. Wakeford and N. Yuval-Davis (eds) (1978) *Power and the State*, Croom Helm, London.

G. Littlejohn (1979) 'State, Plan and Market in the Transition to Socialism: The Legacy of Bukharin', *Economy and Society*, vol. 8, no. 2, May 1979.

G. Littlejohn (1980) 'The Soviet Constitution', *Economy and Society*, vol. 9, no. 3, August 1980.

G. Littlejohn (1980) 'Economic Calculation in the Soviet Union', *Economy and Society*, vol. 9, no. 4, November 1980.

G. Littlejohn (1981) 'Class Structure and Production Relations in the USSR', Ph.D. thesis, unpublished, University of Glasgow.

G. Littlejohn (1982) 'The Agrarian Marxist Research in its Political Context: The Soviet Rural Class Structure in the 1920s', *Journal of Peasant Studies*, vol. 11, no. 2, January 1984.

S. Lukes (1974) *Power: A Radical View*, Macmillan, London.

K. Marx (1970) *Capital*, vol. 1, Lawrence & Wishart, London.

K. Marx (1967) *Capital*, vol. 2, Lawrence & Wishart, London.

K. Marx (1972) *Capital*, vol. 3, Lawrence & Wishart, London.

M. Matthews (1972) *Class and Society in Soviet Russia*, Allen Lane, London.

A. McAuley (1979) *Economic Welfare in the Soviet Union*, Allen & Unwin, London.

A. McAuley (1980) 'Wage Differentials in the USSR: Policy and Performance', paper presented to the Second World Congress of Soviet and East European Studies, Garmisch.

R. Medvedev and Z. Medvedev (1981) 'Soviet Prices Theory is Upset by Inflation', *The Observer*, 6 September 1981.

Z. Medvedev (1981) 'Russia Learns to Live Without American Grain', *New Scientist*, 8 January 1981, pp. 58–61.

R. Miliband (1969) *The State in Capitalist Society*, Weidenfeld & Nicolson, London.

S. M. Miller (1960) 'Comparative Social Mobility', *Current Sociology*, 1960.

O. Narkiewicz (1970) *The Making of the Soviet State Apparatus*, University of Manchester Press.

NATO (1975) *Economic Aspects of Life in the USSR*, Directorate of Economic Affairs, Brussels.

A. Nove (1969) *An Economic History of the USSR*, Allen Lane, London.

A. Nove (1977) *The Soviet Economic System*, Allen & Unwin, London.

A. Nove (1980) 'Soviet Economics and Soviet Economists: Some Random Observations', paper given to the Panel on the Theory of Economic Planning and Regulation in the Socialist System, Second World Congress for Soviet and East European Studies, Garmisch.

G. Parry (1969) *Political Elites*, Allen & Unwin, London.

E. B. Pashukanis (1978) *Law and Marxism: A General Theory*, Ink Links, London.

G. A. Popov (1971) *Principles of Health Planning in the USSR*, World Health Organisation, Geneva.

N. Rose (1980) 'Socialism and Social Policy: the Problems of Inequality', *Politics and Power 2*, Routledge & Kegan Paul, London.

L. Rzhanitsyna (1977) *Soviet Family Budgets*, Progress Publishers, Moscow.

A. Sahay (ed.) (1971) *Max Weber and Modern Sociology*, Routledge & Kegan Paul, London.

F. Seurot (1980) 'Salaires et productivité en URSS: la reforme de 1979', Récherche sur la Théorie de l'Economie Socialiste, Centre d'Economie Internationale des Pays Socialistes, Université de Paris, Panthéon–Sorbonne.

S. M. Shipley (1979) 'The Sociology of the Peasantry, Populism and the Russian Peasant Commune', M. Phil. thesis, unpublished, University of Lancaster.

G. B. Smith (ed.) (1980) *Public Policy and Administration in the Soviet Union*, Praeger, New York.

K. Smith (1979) 'Introduction to Bukharin: Economic Theory and the Closure of the Soviet Industrialisation Debate', *Economy and Society*, vol. 8, no. 4, November 1979.

S. G. Solomon (1975) 'Controversy in Social Science: Soviet Rural Studies in the 1920s', *Minerva*, vol. XIII, no. 4.

I. Steedman (1977) *Marx after Sraffa*, New Left Books, London.

R. C. Stuart (1972) *The Collective Farm in Soviet Agriculture*, Lexington Books, D.C. Heath & Co., Lexington, Mass.

R. Tartarin (1981) 'Planification et régulation dans les économies socialistes: pour une Théorie de la valeur comptable', *Revue d'Etudes Comparative Est-Ouest*.

P. Thoenes (1966) *The Elite in the Welfare State*, Faber, London.

H. Ticktin (1976) 'The Contradictions of Soviet Society and Professor Bettelheim', *Critique*, no. 6, Spring 1976.

K. E. Wädekin (1973) *The Private Sector in Soviet Agriculture*, University of California Press.

R. J. V. Waton (1980) 'A Sociological Study of Education in Sweden and Britain', M.Phil. thesis, unpublished, University of Bradford.

M. Weber (1964) *The Theory of Social and Economic Organization*, Free Press, New York.

A. Weights (1978) 'Weber and "Legitimate Domination" ', *Economy and Society*, vol. 7, no. 1, February 1978.

S. White (1979) *Political Culture and Soviet Politics*, Macmillan, London.

Index